BOOK OF MORMON
Authors
Their Words and Messages

RELIGIOUS STUDIES CENTER PUBLICATIONS

BOOK OF MORMON SYMPOSIUM SERIES

The Book of Mormon: The Keystone Scripture
The Book of Mormon: First Nephi, the Doctrinal Foundation
The Book of Mormon: Second Nephi, the Doctrinal Structure
The Book of Mormon: Jacob Through Words of Mormon, To Learn with Joy
The Book of Mormon: Mosiah, Salvation Only Through Christ
The Book of Mormon: Alma, The Testimony of the Word
The Book of Mormon: Helaman Through 3 Nephi 8, According to Thy Word
The Book of Mormon: 3 Nephi 9–30, This Is My Gospel
The Book of Mormon: Fourth Nephi Through Moroni, From Zion to Destruction

MONOGRAPH SERIES

Nibley on the Timely and the Timeless
Deity and Death
The Glory of God Is Intelligence
Reflections on Mormonism
Literature of Belief
The Words of Joseph Smith
Book of Mormon Authorship
Mormons and Muslims
The Temple in Antiquity
Isaiah and the Prophets
Scriptures for the Modern World
The Joseph Smith Translation: The Restoration of Plain and Precious Things
Apocryphal Writings and the Latter-day Saints
The Pearl of Great Price: Revelations From God
The Lectures on Faith in Historical Perspective
Mormon Redress Petitions: Documents of the 1833–1838 Missouri Conflict
Joseph Smith: The Prophet, the Man

SPECIALIZED MONOGRAPH SERIES

Supporting Saints: Life Stories of Nineteenth-Century Mormons
The Call of Zion: The Story of the First Welsh Mormon Emigration
The Religion and Family Connection: Social Science Perspectives
Welsh Mormon Writings from 1844 to 1862: A Historical Bibliography
Peter and the Popes
John Lyon: The Life of a Pioneer Poet
Latter-day Prophets and the United States Constitution
View of the Hebrews: 1825 2nd Edition
Book of Mormon Authors: Their Words and Messages

OCCASIONAL PAPERS SERIES

Excavations at Seila, Egypt

OTHER

Christopher Columbus: A Latter-day Saint Perspective
Church History in Black and White: George Edward Anderson's Photographic Mission to Latter-day Saint Historical Sites
California Saints: A 150-Year Legacy in the Golden State

BOOK OF MORMON
Authors
Their Words and Messages

Roger R. Keller

Volume Nine
in the Religious Studies Center
Specialized Monograph Series

Religious Studies Center
Brigham Young University
Provo, Utah

Copyright © 1996 by
Religious Studies Center
Brigham Young University

All rights reserved

Library of Congress Catalog Card Number: 96-92452
ISBN 1-57008-276-6

First Printing, 1996

Distributed by
BOOKCRAFT, INC.
Salt Lake City, Utah

Printed in the United States of America

To Flo Beth

CONTENTS

Acknowledgments ix

Introduction xi

Chapter 1: Prophets and Theologies: The Beginnings
             of an Approach 1

Chapter 2: Laws and Commandments 21

Chapter 3: Church and Churches 41

Chapter 4: Earth 59

Chapter 5: Israel 83

Chapter 6: Land and Lands 103

Chapter 7: Summary Tests of a Method 151

Appendix 199

Index 209

ACKNOWLEDGMENTS

Several people have encouraged me to carry out and complete this research. The first of these was Robert J. Matthews. Shortly after I came to BYU, he, then dean of Religious Education, encouraged me to find an area of research within the Book of Mormon. As I made tentative steps in developing the methodology explained and developed in this book, his was a voice of continuing encouragement. Professor Matthews also read a draft of the book and made very helpful suggestions in several areas. Dean Robert L. Millet and Associate Dean Donald Q. Cannon pressed me to continue my research and encouraged me to publish the findings. To both of them I am grateful.

Others assisted in the technical area. John L. Hilton helped provide a vision of what might be done with the use of computers and statistics. Without him, none of what has been done here would have been achieved. Alvin C. Rencher was another who read the entire work and made numerous helpful suggestions. His insights, from a background in statistics and wordprint, were particularly cogent.

Finally, special appreciation goes to Kent P. Jackson for his assistance in bringing the manuscript to publication. Without his careful work and suggestions, and the untiring efforts of his staff, this book would not have seen the light of day.

In the end, however, the major thanks must go to my wife, Flo Beth, for encouraging me in those moments when it seemed that the creative well had run dry. She pressed me to write the chapters which demonstrate what was only in the realm of theory in the chapter on methodology. To her I owe an unrepayable debt.

Despite the assistance and suggestions of others, any errors or oversights that may appear are my responsibility.

INTRODUCTION

The purpose of this study is threefold: (1) to identify differences and/or similarities in meaning among select content words (words which are theologically, historically, or culturally significant) used by the Book of Mormon authors;[1] (2) to delineate among the different Book of Mormon authors based on their word usage; and (3) to suggest methodologies that may be used by others to research author individuality within the Book of Mormon. Most often the Book of Mormon is read, as are the Bible and other scriptures, to discover the eternal truths which the Lord has preserved within its pages. These truths may relate to the Atonement, the coming of Christ, the Fall, and many other topics. People of faith rejoice in these truths as they read and reread them. Such an approach is spiritually uplifting and gives great strength. However, in such an approach it is not especially important which prophet conveys what truths, since the reader basically seeks truth as he or she is guided by the Holy Ghost. Yet those who learned and conveyed the truths of and about God were persons whom the Lord commanded to speak to the people of their day. To know these prophets as individuals can only deepen our appreciation and respect for them, as well as strengthen the impact of their messages upon us.

Fundamental to this research has been the fact that prophets are persons, and that they are therefore different from one another. Many Latter-day Saints could probably distinguish between the writings of Ezra Taft Benson, Spencer W. Kimball, David O. McKay, Brigham Young, and Joseph Smith, since each prophet had characteristics and themes unique to himself. The Lord called these very unique persons, instructed them, trained them, and then summoned them to speak his message to the people of their day. Often, the issues needing to be addressed differed from period to period, and thus the messages

---

[1] Throughout this study, the term "author" will be applied to both writers and speakers within the Book of Mormon. Thus, not only are Nephi 1, Jacob, and Mormon "authors," but so are the Lord, Jesus, and the Father.

differed. If this is the case with latter-day prophets, it was probably true of ancient prophets. Since the Book of Mormon is believed by Latter-day Saints to be a compilation of writings from numerous ancient authors, then one should be able to discern the unique content words used by the authors whose messages are preserved within its pages. It should also be possible to ascertain any differences in the meanings attached to those words.

The research in this volume first separates the words of the various Book of Mormon authors from one another and then attempts to determine which of the select content words the different authors used and how they used them. If the Book of Mormon is, as it claims, an edited compilation of writings spanning a period of approximately one thousand years, then one could expect each author to exhibit some unique linguistic fingerprints. The word cluster studies of chapter 1 will test this basic hypothesis. The subsequent chapters will examine narrow word groups to determine whether the inferences of chapter 1 are supportable.

It is recognized that a significant amount of work has been done by Wayne A. Larsen, Alvin C. Rencher,[2] John L. Hilton, and Kenneth D. Jenkins[3] on what are called "wordprints." Their fundamental supposition is that one can differentiate between authors, given a sample of a few thousand words, by examining the use of the small, function words, i.e., *the, and, but, of,* etc. While wordprint studies help us recognize that different authors did indeed write the various strands within the Book of Mormon, they tell us little about what the various authors' unique subjects may have been as found in their recorded words. By contrast, this study focuses on the content words, i.e., those that are theologically, culturally, and historically signifi-

---

[2] Wayne A. Larsen and Alvin C. Rencher, "Who Wrote the Book of Mormon? An Analysis of Wordprints," In *Book of Mormon Authorship: New Light on Ancient Origins,* ed. Noel B. Reynolds, Religious Monograph Series 7 (Provo, Ut.: Religious Studies Center, Brigham Young University, 1982), 157–88. See also John L. Hilton, "On Verifying Book of Mormon Wordprint Studies: Book of Mormon Authorship," *BYU Studies* 30:89–108.

[3] John L. Hilton and Kenneth D. Jenkins, "On Maximizing Author Identification by Measuring 5000 Word Texts" (unpublished paper, 14 September 1987, available through F.A.R.M.S.) and John L. Hilton, "Introduction and a Few Book of Mormon 'Wordprint' Measurements Using 'Wrap-Around' Block Counting" (unpublished paper, September 1987, available through F.A.R.M.S.).

cant. If, on the basis of the content words, we can demonstrate differences in word use among authors—some of whom through wordprints have clearly been shown to be independent writers—then we can say the two studies reinforce one another. In addition, we also learn something about important words and how they are used by the authors.

We pursue the above objectives in two ways. First, we attempt to distinguish the general areas of expressed interest among the various authors by using word *groups* related to diverse themes, e.g., Agriculture, Christology, Church, Creation, etc. As the study will show, these word groups indicate some clear differences in usage among the Book of Mormon authors. Second, a series of word studies, focusing on *individual* words relating to Law/Commandment, Church/Churches, Earth, Israel, and Land/Lands will support and sharpen the differences among the authors suggested in chapter 1. It should be noted that at the end of each of the word studies is a section entitled "Theological Implications." This section in each chapter attempts to discover the ramifications of the given word study for daily life in the modern world.

Readers will notice that the various word studies are developed in different ways. This is all a product of exploring various ways to organize the material. Hence, there are several models that others may wish to use to perfect or to expand interpretation.

The end result is that there are clear and recognizable differences in the content words used and the meanings attached to them by the authors within the Book of Mormon. It is not, however, the intent of this study to explore the synonyms that a given author may have used in place of the particular word or words under consideration. Such a study would be interesting and instructive, but such an expanded enterprise must be left for others.

1

Prophets and Theologies: The Beginnings of an Approach

Initially, the foundation text for this research was the 1981 edition of the Book of Mormon. The text was marked to segregate the various authors. From this, computer texts of the authors' sermons, narratives, and editorial work were created, thereby separating the material by both author and genre.[1] However, as a foundation for more rigorous work, it was decided that the 1829 printer's manuscript should become the text upon which this and other studies would be based,[2] because it is the oldest complete manuscript of the Book of Mormon available. This manuscript has been used by various scholars interested in extracting statistical data relevant to the Book of Mormon. Several scholars have divided the text into its constituent genres

---

[1] This book never could have been written without the assistance of John L. Hilton. He provided the computer and statistical expertise that I do not have. Thus, chapter 1 is the product of full cooperation between the two of us in terms of both the research and the writing. Each of us brought our different skills to the process. I provided the idea for and content of the word clusters, as well as the content analysis by author. John provided on computer disks the texts of the various authors' words, a program that could search each author for the words of the clusters, and the skills to interpret, from a statistical standpoint, the results of the research. He also wrote another program that allowed me to search the various authors' texts for the words found in the later chapters of this book.

[2] This text was taken from the original handwriting of the copyists of the printer's manuscript with corrections for words which varied from existing sections of the dictation manuscript. Note that some of the spellings may vary from those in use today (e.g., baptizm).

and authors, and there is now general agreement among such scholars on those divisions.[3] Thus, we begin from this base.

Choosing the Authors

To determine word usage within the writing of an individual author, a text sample must have sufficient words to lead one to reasonable conclusions about the most important words used. Thus, no author with fewer than one thousand words of text is treated in this study. Throughout this book, the term *author* will refer to the originator of the words in question.[4] Authors identified by Rencher and others who are included in the pool for this study, along with the designations used for some of them throughout the book, are listed in figure 1:

Abinadi	Father Lehi (Lehi)	Mosiah
Alma, son of Alma (Alma 2)	Helaman, son of Alma (Helaman)	Nephi, son of Lehi (Nephi 1)
Ammon	Isaiah	Nephi, son of Helaman (Nephi 2)
Amulek	Jacob	
Angel who spoke to Nephi 1 (Angel)	Jesus	Samuel
	Lord in Isaiah (Lord-Isa)	The Father (Father)
Benjamin	Mormon	The Lord (Lord)
Capt. Moroni (Moroni 1)	Moroni, son of Mormon (Moroni 2)	Zeniff
Enos		Zenos

Figure 1

The words of these twenty-four individual authors account for 93 percent of the Book of Mormon. The remaining 7 percent comes

---

[3] Alvin Rencher and Wayne Larsen of the BYU Department of Statistics, in conjunction with their work on wordprints, suggested initial author assignments. Others have reviewed and revised these suggestions and made some modifications. Further corrections were made during the preparation of the Book of Mormon Critical Text, and all of the above were finally reworked by Alvin Rencher. Based on this collaborative work, researchers in Book of Mormon studies have a generally accepted tool which is useful to all for author designations.

[4] John L. Hilton, "Listing of the (Salt Lake) Book of Mormon References for Passages of Major Authors and their Literary Forms, Plus Word Counts from the Text of the Printer's Manuscript." Unpublished paper, 23 September 1982, 1.

from persons whose contributions are too small to consider.[5] Two of the twenty-four author texts are marginal in length, since Enos has only 997 words and the Father only 944. Most of the material from the authors in figure 1 is found in the form of sermons or didactic material. However, three of the authors write so extensively that it was possible to separate their words by genre. Therefore, Mormon's writings are separated into *third-person narrative* (Mormon:N3) in which he tells a story about others, *first-person narrative* (Mormon:N1) wherein he tells a story in which he has been personally involved, and *sermonic material* (Mormon:S). Similarly, Nephi 1 is separated into *first-person narrative* (Nephi1:N1) and *sermonic material* (Nephi1:S); and Moroni 2, the son of Mormon, is divided into *third-person narrative* (Moroni2:N3) and *sermonic material* (Moroni2:S).[6]

It is also important to realize that the texts from some of the above persons are not found in one continuous passage in the Book of Mormon but are drawn from various parts of it. For example, Mormon's *sermonic material* (Mormon:S) may be found in several places: Words of Mormon, Mosiah, Alma, Helaman, 3 Nephi, 4 Nephi, Mormon, and Moroni. Likewise, Nephi's *sermonic material* (Nephi1:S) is interspersed among the words of Lehi, the Angel, the Lord, Jacob, and Isaiah. Thus, any consistencies in word usage that appear within an author's writings do not exist simply because we are dealing with a connected text. In reality, we see authors like Nephi (Nephi 1), Mormon, and Moroni (Moroni 2) interjecting their thoughts at various points into the narratives they are editing. Normally, one would expect this patchwork-quilt effect to diminish individual uniqueness. However, when unique word-usage surfaces consistently, it supports the argument that there are indeed unique individuals at work and that their personalities have not been eliminated through either the editing or translation processes of the Book of Mormon.

---

[5] Besides the 24 major authors, there are 106 other persons whose words are quoted less frequently.

[6] Hilton, "Summary of Word Counts from the Printer's Manuscript of the Book of Mormon by Author and Literary Form." Unpublished paper, 9 October 1982, Preface.

Word Clusters

As we began to look at the theologically, culturally, and historically significant words in the various strands of the Book of Mormon text, it was evident that many of these words appeared less than the minimal five times normally desired by convention for statistical accuracy.[7] Consequently, something needed to be done to increase our ability to measure the importance of the various concepts that interested us. Thus, *word clusters* were created to increase the number of events available for comparing stated author interests. The thirty-four clusters in figure 2 were therefore created for this study:[8]

Agriculture	Editing	God	Revelation
Ancient Near East	Emotion (negative)	Government	Riches
Animals	Emotion (positive)	Judicial	Sacramental
Body	Eschatology	Military	Slavery
Christology	Ethics	Money	Society
Church	Evil	Nomadic	Spirituality
Contention	Extras	Numbers	Troubles
Creation	Family	Poor	
Directions	Gathering	Prophecy	

Figure 2

Once the major word-cluster categories were established, related words were gathered under them. For example, words like *Amos, Cain, Jeremiah, Moses, Syria,* etc., were collected under the category of Ancient Near East. There were 109 such Ancient Near East words, and they were used 1,179 times in the Book of Mormon. Under the category of Agriculture, words such as *Crops, Fields, Grain, Root, Sow, Barley,* etc., were collected, and these 60 words were used 578 times in the Book of Mormon. Under Christology, words such as *Atone, Christ, Jesus, Redeem, Savior, Messiah,* etc., were collected; we identified 58 Christology words with a total of 1,671 occurrences. This process was carried out for each of the clusters, thereby provid-

---

[7] When one is using the *Xi*-square statistic, it is not recommended that occurrences of less than five be used. This is the source of the above guideline.

[8] The words associated with each of the clusters, along with the number of times each word appears in the Book of Mormon, may be found in the Appendix. The words in the Extras cluster were words that seemed important, but at the moment we did not feel they fit into any of the established categories.

ing word pools from which to work as word use was compared from author to author.

Author Uniqueness

Example of Methodology

Two initial steps were taken to determine whether differences could be detected between the various authors based on the word clusters. First, each word in each cluster was counted within each author. Thus we know, for example, that in the Ancient Near East cluster, Mormon, in his 6,233 sermonic words (Mormon:S), uses the word *Abraham* once, while Nephi 1, son of Lehi, in his 17,982 sermonic words (Nephi1:S), uses it five times. Second, all the occurrences of words within a given cluster were totaled by author, and each cluster's occurrences per thousand words of *author text* were determined. This latter figure was then divided by the cluster's occurrences per thousand words of the full *Book of Mormon text,* giving a normalized number[9] which could be used for comparison between authors. A normalized number of 1.0 would represent a use rate for the cluster at exactly the average rate that words from that cluster are used throughout the complete Book of Mormon.

Figure 3 shows the results of the assessment of the Ancient Near East word cluster. In order of appearance are (1) the author, (2) the length of the text attributed to the individual,[10] (3) the number of times words from the cluster appear in an author, (4) the occurrences per

---

[9] This number provides a ratio between the number of times the words of a cluster appear per one thousand words of author text and the number of times the words of a cluster appear per one thousand words of Book of Mormon text. Thus, one can see the relative importance of the various word clusters in the whole of the Book of Mormon. Significant deviation from these normalized numbers delineates a greater or lesser interest on the part of an author in a particular cluster. For example, the occurrences per one thousand words of Book of Mormon text for the Ancient Near East cluster is 4.38. By contrast, this number for Animals is 0.87, for Christology is 6.0, for Church is 7.5, for Creation is 5.1, for Positive Emotions is 2.3, for Ethics is 1.9, etc. Clearly, animals are mentioned in passing, while Christology and Church are central issues in the Book of Mormon.

[10] Hilton, "Summary of Word Counts," Preface. The "Length" listing in figure 3 includes word counts only for the *principal* genres used by the major authors, i.e., Mormon, Moroni 2, and Nephi 1. Therefore, there are more words in their total texts than represented here when the words in their principal genres are totaled.

thousand words of *author text,* (5) the occurrences per thousand words of *Book of Mormon text,* and (6) the normalized number.

Author	Length	Number	Per 1000, Author Text	Per 1000, BofM Text	Normalized Number
Abinadi	2,806	19	6.77	4.38	1.55
Alma 2	20,227	37	1.83	4.38	0.42
Ammon	2,727	2	.733	4.38	0.17
Amulek	3,182	6	1.89	4.38	0.43
Angel	2,252	40	17.8	4.38	4.06
Benjamin	4,221	4	.948	4.38	0.22
Enos	997	0	0.00	4.38	0.00
Father	944	21	22.2	4.38	5.07
Helaman	5,600	5	.893	4.38	0.20
Isaiah	7,951	128	16.1	4.38	3.68
Jacob	8,491	73	8.60	4.38	1.96
Jesus	10,213	67	6.56	4.38	1.50
Lehi	4,689	34	7.25	4.38	1.66
Lord	11,507	99	8.60	4.38	1.96
Lord-Isa	4,193	80	19.1	4.38	4.36
Mormon:N1	4,613	5	1.08	4.38	0.25
Mormon:N3	86,669	82	.946	4.38	0.22
Mormon:S	6,233	45	7.22	4.38	1.65
Moroni 1	3,074	4	1.30	4.38	0.30
Moroni2:N3	11,542	12	1.04	4.38	0.24
Moroni2:S	6,736	37	5.49	4.38	1.25
Mosiah	1,180	0	0.00	4.38	0.00
Nephi1:N1	10,238	51	4.98	4.38	1.14
Nephi1:S	17,982	195	10.8	4.38	2.47
Nephi 2	2,228	17	7.63	4.38	1.74
Other	18,296	63	3.44	4.38	0.79
Samuel	3,078	2	.650	4.38	0.15
Zeniff	1,824	3	1.64	4.38	0.37
Zenos	4,261	14	3.29	4.38	0.75

Figure 3: Ancient Near East Cluster

To illustrate the value of the categories for providing distinction between authors, note that Lehi used words from the Ancient Near East cluster thirty-four times. The number of times per thousand that these words occurred in Lehi's text of 4,689 words was 7.25. To normalize this number to the average overall Book of Mormon use rate, this 7.25 was divided by 4.38, the number of times per thousand that the Ancient Near East cluster words occurred in the 269,309 words in the Book of Mormon.[11] This equation resulted in a normalized ratio of 1.66 for Ancient Near East words in Lehi's text.

In contrast, the Angel of the Lord who spoke to Nephi, Lehi's son, used Ancient Near East words 40 times, with a ratio per thousand of 17.8. When normalized through dividing 17.8 by 4.38, the resulting ratio is 4.06. Thus, while Lehi uses words related to the Ancient Near East cluster half again above the average use in the whole Book of Mormon (1.66 versus 1.00), the Angel of the Lord uses them in excess of four times the average (4.06 versus 1.00). Clearly, there is a substantial difference between the two authors in the frequency with which they use words from the Ancient Near East cluster.

On the other end of the spectrum, of the 109 possible words in the Ancient Near East cluster, neither Mosiah nor Enos, in their cumulative total of 2,177 words, use any. Benjamin, on the other hand, does use some of the terms a total of four times, giving a 0.948 use rate per thousand words of his text. His normalized use rate becomes 0.22, or approximately one-fifth of the average Book of Mormon use rate. Thus, while one can determine who most emphasizes a given cluster, one can also ascertain which authors have the least emphasis on it. Clearly, Benjamin and Mosiah—father and son—do not use the Ancient Near East words. They are removed from that culture by approximately 500 years. Even Enos, who is only 150 to 200 years distant from the Ancient Near East environment, displays no emphasis on this cluster, although his small text sample reduces the likelihood of a clear conclusion about his usage. However, we can suggest that the language of these three authors no longer utilized

---

[11] A theoretical example of the way the various columns in figure 3 relate to one another may be helpful to the reader. Suppose that an author has a text length of ten thousand words and uses words from the Ancient Near East word cluster 50 times. Since there are ten thousand-word groups (10,000 divided by 1,000 equals 10), his use per thousand words of text is 5.00 (50 uses of the cluster divided by *ten* 1,000s). The Ancient Near East word cluster has a use rate of 4.38 per thousand words of Book of Mormon text (1,179 uses of Ancient Near East cluster words divided by 269.309 thousands of Book of Mormon words, since there are 269,309 words in the Book of Mormon, gives a 4.38 ratio for the Ancient Near East word cluster). When the 5.00 uses per thousand words of author text are divided by the 4.38 uses of the Ancient Near East cluster per Book of Mormon text, the normalized number of 1.14 is obtained, indicating that our theoretical author uses words from the group occasionally, but not at a particularly high level.

Ancient Near East terms, in contrast to Lehi and Nephi's Angel, by whom the terminology was utilized.

If one examines the Ancient Near East cluster, there are generally no surprises concerning who uses the cluster words. The authors who are most distant in time from the Ancient Near East context use the words of this group the least, while those nearest in time use them the most. However, there are two exceptions. The first of these is Nephi, son of Helaman (Nephi 2), who has a normalized use ratio of 1.74, even higher than that of Lehi. His words from this cluster, followed by the number of times they appear in his text, are *Abraham* (5), *Egyptians* (1), *Isaiah* (1), *Israelites* (1), *Jeremiah* (3), *Messiah* (1), *Moses* (3), and *Zedekiah* (2). The other exception is Mormon in his sermonic material (Mormon:S), with a use rate of 1.65. His cluster words are *Abraham* (1), *Adam* (1), *Amen* (5), *Gentiles* (10), *Israel* (8), *Jacob* (9), *Jews* (5), *Joseph* (4), and *Moses* (2). Clearly, these two writers chose different words to use from within the cluster.[12] The probable explanation for Nephi 2's and Mormon's interest in the Ancient Near East cluster is that both looked back over history and tied Nephite history to God's dealings with the ancient Israelites. Thus, this preliminary examination accentuates the fact that a study which begins with numerical comparisons must be augmented by a literary and contextual examination to determine why authors' word uses vary. The following chapters will do precisely that.

The comparative process just described for the Ancient Near East cluster has been carried out on all authors and across all clusters. Clear differences have been observed, some of which will be identified later in this chapter.

Measurements of Cluster Variations

The following material will explain, in rather technical language, how the clusters were compared numerically. For those not versed in some of the statistical language, it is important to note that the statistical work simply demonstrates, in numerical terms, that signifi-

---

[12] The significance of the word choice differences within a cluster by various authors could be an area for future exploration.

cant differences exist in the way various authors used the word clusters which have been examined in this research.

A set of preliminary statistical calculations shows measurable differences in cluster use between some of the longer Book of Mormon author/genre texts. The differences between these texts are larger than would be expected, if only random or normal statistical variation were the sole variant being observed. Thus the question being investigated is: Can these differences be explained without concluding that there are *author-specific shifts* in the word-cluster use rate?

When the authors who wrote more than twelve thousand words were examined by dividing their writings into two-thousand-word segments, it was concluded that each of the authors' word clusters were used essentially uniformly across the six or more two-thousand-word subgroups.[13] This shows reasonable stability within each author. By contrast, when the writings of one author/genre were compared against another, comparatively larger differences were measured.

Measurements were made between author/genre groups by counting the number of *t*-test null-hypothesis rejections[14] (alpha = 0.05)[15] that occurred as each pair of author/genre texts were compared for thirty of the studied word clusters.[16] For example, as shown in figure 4a, when each of the thirty clusters of Mormon:N3 is compared to the corresponding clusters of Alma2:S, there are eight rejections

---

[13] The exceptions to this will be discussed briefly below, particularly as they relate to Mormon's editorial work. However, this is an area that will require further work and study, and only preliminary observations can be made in this study.

[14] The null-hypothesis is a common statistical procedure which presumes that there is no meaningful difference between the clusters in any two texts which are compared in the present study. If this statistical study shows that the difference between two compared texts is larger than we would normally expect in nineteen out of twenty trials, then the hypothesis fails because we measured a difference larger than would normally be expected, if the texts had actually been the same.

[15] That is, the probability of the two distributions being different is likely over 95 percent, if the distributions are approximately "normal." As used here the hypothesis tests are more aptly employed as a descriptive comparison of "among author" variation to "within author" variation, rather than an inferential evidence of absolute difference.

[16] Word clusters Military, Societal, Christology, and Governmental were removed from the original thirty-four categories for this particular test, since in their present form they do not consistently discriminate across author/texts.

of the thirty comparisons. Similarly, when the thirty clusters of Moroni2:N3 are compared with the clusters of Jacob:S, there are two rejections. Hence, figure 4a lists the number of hypothesis rejections for each of the author/genre tests for the nine authors who wrote at least six thousand words. From the comparisons reported in figure 4a, the number of rejections varies from zero to ten, and zero, one, two, or three seem sufficiently low that the two compared author/genres in each case may not be meaningfully different from each other. Thus, four or more rejections would increasingly demonstrate a greater likelihood that the distributions actually are different.

Some comparisons of the number of null-hypothesis rejections measured by comparing the different author and genre texts for thirty word clusters (figures 4a and 4b).

	Mormon:N3	Alma2:S	Nephi1:S	Moroni2:N3	Nephi1:N1	Isaiah:S	Jacob:S	Mormon:S	Moroni2:S
Mormon:N3	-	8	10	3	7	9	5	4	4
Alma2:S	-	-	4	7	5	6	0	0	0
Nephi1:S	-	-	-	2	3	4	2	0	0
Moroni2:N3	-	-	-	-	2	1	2	1	2
Nephi1:N1	-	-	-	-	-	5	3	1	2
Isaiah:S	-	-	-	-	-	-	3	1	3
Jacob:S	-	-	-	-	-	-	-	0	0
Mormon:S	-	-	-	-	-	-	-	-	0
Moroni2:S	-	-	-	-	-	-	-	-	-

Figure 4a

	Benjamin:S	Helaman:N1	Lehi:S	Mormon:N1	Zenos:S	Abinadi:S	Amulek:S	Angel:S	Moroni1:S	Nephi2:S	Samuel:S
Mormon:N3	4	0	4	2	3	6	6	6	0	3	4
Alma2:S	2	3	2	4	5	6	4	5	2	4	5
Nephi1:S	3	1	2	2	4	0	3	5	3	1	3
Moroni2:N3	4	2	6	2	3	5	6	4	4	3	4
Nephi1:N1	6	2	5	8	4	6	6	7	4	3	4

Figure 4b

As can be seen from the word-cluster tests using the vertical column headed Isaiah:S in figure 4a as an example, four or more rejections likely indicate a meaningful difference between Isaiah and several of the larger Book of Mormon author/genre texts. In figure 4b, eleven of the smaller Book of Mormon author/genre texts show four, five, six, seven, and eight rejections when compared against the largest author/genre texts, also likely indicating that meaningful differences exist between the word clusters used.[17]

In figures 4a and 4b the most striking separations occur when genres are different and when the comparative calculational uncertainty is reduced due to the larger text lengths. Nevertheless, when Mormon:N1 is compared to Nephi1:N1, there is produced a sum of eight rejections (figure 4b), clearly a large difference in word-cluster word use between these two Book of Mormon authors, even when written in the same genre. Other rejection numbers are very large, some being across genres or in texts which have a smaller number of words. For example, when Alma2:S is compared to Mormon:N3, a sum of ten rejections is measured, indicating an immense difference in the rate of word-cluster use rates. Likewise, a sum of seven rejections between Nephi1:N1 and Mormon:N3 indicates a clear difference.

In summary, even though there is yet much refinement necessary in the tools being used, clear differences are seen between individual author uses of the thirty measured word clusters, indicating important differences in word use.

Authors and Word Clusters
Nephi 1 and Alma 2

Through use of wordprint, John L. Hilton has objectively confirmed that the texts of Nephi1:S and Alma 2 have clearly measured

---

[17] It appears that our measurement techniques are not yet sensitive enough to provide a good separation between texts of the same genre, except for the two largest texts which provide improved comparative discrimination. Figures 4a and 4b show that many of the low rejection numbers occur when similar genres are compared between authors. For example, Jacob:S compared to Alma2:S does not separate clearly on the basis of rejections above the 95 percent probability, even though it is possible to identify significant word-use differences. So it is also with Mormon:S and Moroni2:S when compared to Alma2:S.

patterns which are indicative of different authors.[18] Thus, the sermonic works of these two authors seem to be good places to explore, initially, the differences among the word clusters used by Book of Mormon authors. The question to be asked is: Do two authors who have been shown to be different by wordprint also show differences in the word clusters which they use? On the basis of word clusters, figure 5 shows the priorities found under each author. The number represents the normalized comparative value described under "Author Uniqueness" above.

From figure 5, one can see that there are clear differences in word-cluster priorities in each writer. Note the almost complete inversion of priorities between the two authors. Nephi 1, for example, is a product of the Ancient Near East; not surprisingly, he uses Near East terminology in his sermons and teachings as a frame of reference through which to express his thoughts. Alma the Younger, on the other hand, is five hundred years removed from the land of Israel and its culture; consequently, he does not use such terms extensively.[19]

Nephi 1:S		Alma 2	
2.9	Ancient Near East	2.5	Eschatology
2.2	Gathering	1.8	Spiritual
1.8	Prophecy	1.7	Slavery
1.6	Editing	1.7	Ethics
1.5	Xology	1.6	Xology
1.4	God	1.6	Trouble
1.4	Creation	1.5	Evil
1.2	Spiritual	1.4	God
1.1	Eschatology	0.8	Prophecy
1.1	Evil	0.6	Creation
0.9	Ethics	0.4	Gathering
0.8	Slavery	0.4	Ancient Near East
0.7	Trouble	0.3	Editing

Figure 5

---

[18] Hilton, "On Verifying Wordprint Studies: Book of Mormon Authorship," *BYU Studies* 30.3 (summer 1990): 89–108.

[19] The "Xology" abbreviation in figure 5 is not meant to be disrespectful. The "X" represents the Greek letter *chi* (X), the first letter in the Greek word "Christos," Christ. Therefore, "Xology" is simply shorthand for "Christology."

It is interesting that the Gathering cluster appears in Nephi 1. He uses eight[20] of the twelve words in the cluster with emphasis on both scattering and gathering. Since Nephi 1 is one who is a participant in the scattering of Israel, it should not be surprising to see him concerned with these concepts.

It is also clear that Nephi 1 is concerned with the language of prophecy, using such words as *Prophecies* (10), *Prophecy* (4), *Prophesied* (6), *Prophet* (22), and *Prophets* (22). Further, he uses *Account* (18), *Book* (28), *Books* (2), *Record* (23), *Records* (10), *Write* (22), and *Written* (41) from the words composing the Editing cluster. Similarly, Christological issues seem important to him because he uses such words as *Christ* (51), *Jesus* (9), *Lamb* (22), *Redeemer* (13), *Salvation* (4), and *Spirit* (50). Similarly, the clusters God and Creation are particularly important to him.

Thus one might profile Nephi 1, when he preaches, as one who is looking forward to the coming of Christ. He talks of prophets and of the need to prepare a record of the acts of God. He conveys this using the language of the Ancient Near East. While this broad characterization will not surprise anyone familiar with the Book of Mormon, the words which Nephi uses under each of the major categories are uniquely his.

In contrast, Alma 2 uses different language. The stated concern which is held in common with Nephi 1 is that of Christology, but the words Alma 2 used to express his Christological concerns are different, in many instances, from those used by Nephi. For example, Alma's Christological language uses *Atone* (2), *Mercy* (27), *Redemption* (17), *Resurrection* (34), *Sanctified* (3), and *Washed* (3), in addition to *Christ* (33) and *Jesus* (10). Thus the work of the Savior is characterized differently, linguistically, by each author, even though they both speak generally of the same events.

Alma 2 seems most concerned with concepts included in the Eschatology cluster. This arises from his use of words like *Endless* (5), *Eternal* (12), *Everlasting* (15), *Forever* (15), *Last* (17), and *Restored* (16). It is clear from context that these words do not all

---

[20] *Gather* (2), *Gathered* (12), *Gathereth* (1), *Remnant* (9), *Remnants* (1), *Restoration* (3), *Scattered* (18), *Scattering* (1).

necessarily imply "last things."[21] However, they serve to segregate concepts, and future studies could involve the examination of the differences in word choices between authors in the various clusters. Undoubtedly we will see differences in other clusters similar to those differences observed between Alma 2 and Nephi 1 in their Christological language.

Alma 2 appears to be deeply concerned with spiritual things (normalized number of 1.8), and only one author—Mormon:S (normalized number of 2.4)—seems to be more concerned. Of the sixty-five words in the Spirituality word cluster, Alma 2 uses thirty-nine of them, while Mormon uses twenty-eight. Thus, while Alma 2 places stress on the words *Believe* (21), *Faith* (41), *Humble* (19), *Repent* (26), *Repentance* (25), *Righteous* (11), *Soul* (39), *Souls* (21), and *Worship* (7), embellishing them with a variety of other words related to spirituality, Mormon's Spirituality cluster includes *Believe* (49), *Faith* (62), *Repent* (35), and *Repentance* (39), but with a stronger stress on *Charity* (10), a word Alma 2 uses only once.

Alma 2 uses concepts related to the Slavery cluster through the use of *Bondage* (9), *Bonds* (4), *Captivity* (11), and *Chains* (7). In like manner he focuses, in the Ethics cluster, on the words *Commandments* (29) and *Justice* (21), with additional words used one or two times to round out the theme. In the Evil cluster, Alma 2 uses *Abominations* (8), *Devil* (14), *Evil* (26), *Iniquities* (9), *Iniquity* (13), *Sins* (30), *Wicked* (8), and *Wickedness* (13). Beyond these, he uses fifty other words from the 137 words in the cluster. One also observes that the principal words which Alma 2 uses from the Evil cluster are relatively general words.[22]

From what has been said above, it is appropriate to suggest that Alma 2 and Nephi 1 are two very different individuals with unique word usage. Even in those areas where they use the same cluster at a similar normalized rate, such as Christology, their word use reflects their differences and thus their uniqueness.

---

[21] One of the areas to be refined will be the word clusters themselves.

[22] Future work might be enhanced by separating this cluster into two clusters, i.e., one which contains general terms about evil and another which deals with evil acts.

Mormon and Moroni 2

Mormon is especially interesting because his fingerprints are found throughout most of the Book of Mormon, and also because he is the only author who writes extensively in three separate genres. Thus, it is possible to examine Mormon not only against other authors, but also against himself. In addition, it is interesting to examine Moroni 2 in his sermonic mode to see how his word use either coincides with or differs from that of his father. Figure 6 outlines the four strands which will concern us in this section.

Moroni2:S		Mormon:S		Mormon:N1		Mormon:N3	
3.2	Xology	3.2	Xology	3.5	Numbers	1.8	Money
2.0	Sacramental	2.8	Gathering	2.3	Editing	1.8	Directions
1.8	Spiritual	2.4	Spiritual	2.2	Directions	1.8	Contention
1.8	God	2.1	Eschatology	2.0	Military	1.6	Military
1.8	Eschatology	2.0	Sacramental	1.5	Neg. emotions	1.6	Government
						1.5	Numbers

Figure 6

Moroni2:S reflects Moroni 2's personal word use, and a comparison with Mormon will be instructive concerning the similarities and differences between father and son. In contrast to a comparison between two persons, the differences represented between Mormon's genres are also striking. Mormon:S is Mormon's didactic or sermonic material and thus reflects things nearest to his heart. Mormon:N1 is material in which Mormon speaks about those things of which he has firsthand knowledge, while Mormon:N3 reflects Mormon as he edits material and is therefore dependent upon a source for his information. From these strands, we can learn not only what word clusters were most often reflected in Mormon, but we may gain a glimpse of the way in which sources influenced Mormon's use of language.

In Mormon:S, Christological words are dominant. Of the fifty-eight Christological words he uses sixteen,[23] with the dominant ones by far being *Christ* (57) and *Jesus* (23). Moroni2:S also has Chris-

---

[23] *Ascended* (1), *Ascension* (1), *Atonement* (2), *Christ* (57), *Grace* (3), *Jesus* (23), *Mercies* (3), *Merciful* (1), *Mercy* (4), *Redeemer* (2), *Redemption* (4), *Remission* (3), *Resurrection* (2), *Salvation* (2), *Savior* (4), *Spirit* (7).

tological language at the top of his word usage, and *Christ* (48) and *Jesus* (21) are the pivotal words, although *Christ* is used with less relative frequency than in Mormon:S.[24] By contrast, of the fifty-eight words, Moroni2:S uses seventeen,[25] but there are fourteen differences between Mormon2:S and Moroni2:S in the words used from this cluster. This suggests that the central emphasis on *Jesus* and *Christ* is imparted from father to son, but the son had his own style and expressed himself through his own choice of additional words.

Mormon:S also has a high use of terms related to the Gathering cluster, higher, in fact, than any other author in the Book of Mormon. The pivotal word is *Remnant* (12), in contrast to the scattering/gathering language of Nephi1:S discussed above. Interestingly, *Remnant* is of no significance in Moroni 2's writings. However, there are many similarities between father and son when it comes to the Spirituality cluster. Both Mormon:S and Moroni2:S use approximately one-third of the possible sixty-five words in the Spirituality cluster, with Mormon:S using twenty-eight[26] and Moroni2:S using twenty-two.[27] The dominant word for both is *Faith*, but Moroni 2 uses it more frequently than does Mormon. Mormon adds emphasis with the words *Believe, Charity, Repent,* and *Repentance*. Moroni 2 also uses *Charity,*[28] but less frequently than does Mormon. Moroni 2 stresses no additional words. Both Mormon and Moroni 2, by use of multiple words relating to *Prayer,* seem to express concern for this aspect of spiritual life.

---

[24] The normalized numbers for the use of *Christ* by the two authors are 9.1 for Mormon:S and 7.1 for Moroni2:S.

[25] *Christ* (48), *Forgiven* (2), *Forgiveness* (1), *Grace* (7), *Jesus* (21), *Lamb* (5), *Merciful* (3), *Merits* (1), *Redeemed* (2), *Redemption* (3), *Remission* (1), *Resurrection* (1), *Salvation* (1), *Sanctified* (1), *Spirit* (9), *Transfigured* (1), *Washed* (1).

[26] *Believe* (10), *Believeth* (1), *Charity* (10), *Faith* (26), *Faithful* (1), *Humble* (2), *Lowliness* (2), *Lowly* (3), *Meek* (3), *Meekness* (3), *Praise* (1), *Praises* (1), *Pray* (4), *Prayer* (2), *Prayers* (3), *Prayeth* (1), *Praying* (1), *Repent* (12), *Repentance* (8), *Repented* (3), *Righteous* (4), *Righteous'* (1), *Righteousness* (1), *Soul* (4), *Souls* (2), *Thanksgiving* (1), *Unbelief* (2), *Unbelieving* (1).

[27] *Believe* (4), *Believed* (1), *Believeth* (2), *Believing* (1), *Charity* (6), *Faith* (43), *Humility* (1), *Praise* (1), *Pray* (2), *Prayed* (1), *Prayer* (1), *Prayers* (4), *Repent* (2), *Repentance* (1), *Repented* (3), *Righteous* (3), *Righteousness* (1), *Souls* (5), *Spiritual* (1), *Thanks* (1), *Unbelief* (5), *Unbelieving* (1).

[28] Normalized numbers for *Charity* are Mormon:S (1.6) and Moroni2:S (0.89).

The Eschatology cluster appears important in both authors. Here the language is basically similar. Mormon:S uses ten[29] of the possible eighteen words and Moroni2:S uses only six,[30] but the most important words for each seem to be *Eternal, Last,* and *Forever.* Finally, both Mormon and Moroni 2 use words from the Sacramental word group. Mormon clearly peaks on the word *Baptism,* while Moroni 2 uses more words but shows no particular favorite.

In contrast to the above, in both Mormon:N1 and Mormon:N3 we see the historian at work. In Mormon:N1, Mormon seems to be concerned that his readers understand the historical context. He sets the stage by telling how many people were involved in events, where things happened, what the military situation was, and why he wrote the things that he did. In Mormon:N3, Mormon appears to be influenced by the material he is editing, yet he still seems to have had a concern that people know where things occurred (directions), what was happening with the government, and how much time had passed. Clearly, he reflects the periods of contention and military activity. His high use of monetary terms is in contrast to other authors. He is the only author who uses such terms to any significant degree. Mormon:N1 and Mormon:N3 reflect no significant theological language use. Thus, Mormon:S stands in sharp contrast to these two.

In summary, Mormon clearly uses different word groups when he writes or speaks for himself than when he is narrating or editing. When his editorial work is divided into twelve-thousand-word blocks, it becomes clear that the material he is editing causes his normal language use to fluctuate significantly at times.[31] It is also evident that there are similarities between Mormon and Moroni 2, yet it is possible to identify the sorts of differences that one would expect to find in the

---

[29] *Endless* (2), *Eternal* (4), *Eternally* (1), *Eternity* (2), *Everlasting* (4), *Forever* (3), *Immortality* (1), *Incorruptible* (1), *Last* (3), *Visitation* (1).

[30] *Endless* (2), *Eternal* (5), *Everlasting* (1), *Forever* (6), *Last* (6), *Visitation* (1).

[31] These differences measured statistically by the student 't' are often "highly significant" (alpha 0.01). For example, when one compares Mormon:N3 measured between Alma 16:14 and Alma 30:43 against Mormon:N3 measured between Alma 50:32 and Helaman 3:9, "highly significant" differences are shown for the word clusters God, Military, Church, Spirituality, Societal, Christology, and Riches. One may additionally add those which demonstrate "significant" (alpha 0.05) differences, i.e., Numbers, Negative Emotions, and perhaps Nomadic/Wilderness.

language use of two different individuals, no matter how close their relationship might be.

Similar analyses could be done for all the authors used in this study, but what has been shown so far is sufficient to suggest the possibilities of the methodology. It might, however, be interesting to see the dominant word categories of authors not considered above. Figure 7, below, lists those clusters by author which show a normalized use value at least half again as great as the normal use in the Book of Mormon, i.e., 1.5 or greater.

An examination of the authors in figure 7 and the clusters which are prominent under each author clearly demonstrates that there are differences among the writers in their word use. There is still much to be done in defining what those differences are. The abbreviation ANE stands for Ancient Near East.

Conclusions

In this chapter, I have shown that the methodology described above permits the separation of Book of Mormon authors on the basis of their unique word use. These are preliminary suggestions. The study only tells us what word clusters, and what words within those clusters, are used by the various authors, but it tells us nothing about *how* they are used. Thus, the next logical step would be to study select words in the literary contexts in which the authors used them. It is on this issue that the following chapters will focus. Those chapters will more sharply delineate the differences between the authors.

Abinadi

3.7 Xology
3.7 Prophecy
2.8 Eschatology
2.0 Evil
1.9 Slavery
1.8 Ethics
1.7 Body
1.6 God
1.5 ANE

Ammon

3.7 Eschatology
2.5 Agriculture

2.4 Sacramental
2.0 Gathering
1.9 Church

Amulek

3.8 Eschatology
2.6 Trouble
2.6 Revelation
2.4 Sacramental
2.1 Judicial
1.6 Spiritual
1.6 Evil

Angel

4.6 Editing

4.4 ANE
3.4 Slavery
3.2 Xology
3.0 Church
2.8 Eschatology
2.0 Riches
1.8 Numbers
1.8 Evil
1.5 God
1.5 Body

Benjamin

5.2 Poor
3.8 Ethics
1.5 Riches

Enos
- 7.0 Animals
- 2.9 Nomadic
- 2.6 Pos. emotions
- 2.4 Agriculture
- 2.1 Editing
- 1.9 Neg. emotions
- 1.5 God

Father
- 4.4 ANE
- 2.0 Societal
- 2.0 Sacramental
- 1.9 Evil
- 1.8 Church
- 1.6 Spiritual

Helaman
- 4.1 Military
- 2.1 Numbers
- 1.9 Societal
- 1.6 Nomadic

Isaiah
- 4.3 Animals
- 4.1 ANE
- 3.1 Agriculture
- 2.7 Poor
- 2.7 Creation
- 2.0 Neg. emotions
- 1.6 Societal
- 1.6 God
- 1.5 Slavery
- 1.5 Gathering

Jacob
- 3.2 Trouble
- 2.8 Eschatology
- 1.9 ANE
- 1.8 Ethics
- 1.7 Revelation
- 1.7 Prophecy
- 1.7 Evil
- 1.6 Xology
- 1.6 God
- 1.5 Pos. emotions

Jesus
- 2.9 Sacramental
- 2.8 Animals
- 2.3 Poor
- 2.3 Family
- 2.2 Gathering
- 1.7 Ethics
- 1.6 ANE

Lehi
- 3.8 Eschatology
- 2.6 Slavery
- 2.5 Sacramental
- 1.7 Ethics
- 1.6 Trouble
- 1.6 ANE

Lord
- 2.1 Sacramental
- 2.1 Animals
- 2.0 ANE
- 1.6 Spiritual
- 1.6 Creation
- 1.5 Body

Lord-Isa
- 4.2 Poor
- 3.9 ANE
- 3.6 Animals
- 2.8 Body
- 2.5 Trouble
- 2.3 Neg. emotions
- 2.1 Creation
- 1.7 Slavery
- 1.6 Societal
- 1.5 Riches

Moroni 1
- 3.8 Slavery
- 2.5 Military
- 1.6 Govern
- 1.6 Pos. emotions
- 1.5 Gathering
- 1.5 Ethics

Moroni2:N3
- 3.2 Animals
- 2.0 Sacramental
- 1.8 Spiritual
- 1.8 Eschatology

Mosiah
- 8.8 Judicial
- 4.5 Contention
- 3.3 Government
- 2.7 Evil
- 2.2 Ethics
- 1.8 Pos. emotions

Nephi1:N1
- 4.8 Nomadic
- 3.0 Editing
- 1.9 Family
- 1.8 Prophecy
- 1.7 ANE

Nephi 2
- 2.3 Prophecy
- 2.3 Judicial
- 2.1 Neg. emotions
- 1.9 ANE
- 1.8 Evil

Samuel
- 4.1 Revelation
- 2.9 Prophecy
- 1.8 Spiritual
- 1.8 Riches
- 1.5 Evil
- 1.5 Creation

Zeniff
- 5.2 Agriculture
- 3.3 Nomadic
- 3.2 Military
- 1.7 Ethics
- 1.6 Riches
- 1.6 Numbers

Zenos
- 23.0 Agriculture
- 3.9 Creation
- 2.4 Nomadic
- 2.1 Eschatology
- 1.5 Neg. emotions

Figure 7

2

Laws and Commandments

In chapter 1, a methodology using word clusters was developed which suggested that unique word usage could be identified among the various Book of Mormon authors. This chapter and those that follow are designed to test that suggestion.

When Latter-day Saints think of the Lord's commandments, they frequently think of paying tithing, living the law of chastity, attending meetings, performing temple ordinances, following the Brethren, and magnifying callings. This would hardly be an exhaustive list of "commandments," however, and the list varies from person to person, depending on circumstances. Why do we have commandments anyway? What is the Lord's purpose in giving them to us? This chapter will attempt to answer these questions by examining the authors within the Book of Mormon and their use of the words related to Law/Command.

This chapter will extend the research explained in chapter 1. Here a comparative methodology has been applied to a very specific and narrow set of words. While the previous chapter dealt with large groups of words centered around specific themes, here we deal with a small group of eleven words related to Law/Command. They are *Command, Commanded, Commandest, Commandeth, Commanding, Commandment, Commandments, Commands, Law, Law of Moses,* and *Laws.* While the previous chapter simply identified significant groups of words by author and noted the differences between authors, this chapter and the following ones will not only determine the differences in word use but will also show, through contextual analysis, the often different meanings attached to the words by the various authors. Only those authors who use enough words from the Law/Command word group for reasonable comparison will be addressed in this study.[1]

Two things will be seen as a result of this study: (1) there are significant differences in the ways the words are used by the various authors; and (2) according to Jesus, all laws and commandments given by God lead to only one commandment—"Come unto Christ."[2]

Significant Use of the Law/Command Word Group

Figure 1 shows how the use of this word group is distributed across the various authors. Listed are simply the number of occurrences of the various words. Their use ratios will be noted in the text or in footnotes.

Even a cursory glance at figure 1 makes it clear that there are variations between the authors in their choice of words. *Command, Commanded, Commandment,* and *Commandments* are most generally used, but there are clear differences in who chooses to use what.

---

[1] If there are not at least five occurrences of words from the word group in an author's text sample, no conclusions are drawn. Similarly, if the use per thousand words of text for the entire word group does not exceed 1.00, that author will be viewed as making a limited contribution to this study, except to say that for him, the material under consideration is of limited importance.

The use-per-thousand figure is determined by taking the number of words in an author's text (e.g., twenty thousand), dividing it by one thousand to determine the number of "thousands" of words in the text (e.g., twenty), and then dividing the number of occurrences by the number of "thousands" (e.g., forty occurrences divided by twenty thousands, giving a use ratio per thousand of 2.00). If the number of occurrences had been ten, then the ratio would have been 0.50 (ten occurrences divided by twenty thousands). A use ratio of less than 1.00 will not generally be considered of major significance in an author. However, if an author has a long text, such as Mormon, a use ratio of less than 1.00 need not be a barrier in considering the way he uses the words under consideration.

Given these criteria, the following authors will not be considered in chapter 2 because the available sample is too small: Ammon, Nephi 1's angel, Enos, the Father, Helaman, Isaiah, the Lord in Isaiah, Captain Moroni, Nephi 2, Samuel, Zeniff, and Zenos.

[2] See the section entitled "Jesus' Theological Key" later in this chapter.

	Abinadi	Alma 2	Ammon	Amulek	Angel	Benjamin	Enos	Father	Helaman	Isaiah	Jacob	Jesus	Lehi	Lord	Lord-Isa	Mormon	Moroni 1	Moroni 2	Mosiah	Nephi 1	Nephi 2	Samuel	Zeniff	Zenos
Command	-	11	-	1	-	-	-	-	1	1	2	2	-	6	1	20	3	-	2	2	-	-	-	-
Commanded	5	7	-	-	-	7	-	-	1	-	1	16	2	2	1	78	-	16	-	33	-	3	3	1
Commandest	-	-	-	-	-	-	-	-	-	-	-	-	-	-	-	-	-	-	-	-	-	-	-	-
Commandeth	-	2	-	-	-	-	-	-	-	-	1	2	-	-	-	1	-	2	-	5	-	-	-	-
Commanding	-	-	-	-	-	-	-	-	-	-	-	-	1	-	-	1	-	-	-	-	-	-	-	-
Commandment	-	-	-	-	-	-	-	-	-	-	8	11	2	2	-	7	-	4	-	7	-	-	-	-
Commandments	7	29	-	-	-	16	-	-	2	-	3	9	-	21	1	53	-	1	4	26	1	1	1	3
Commands	-	-	-	-	-	-	-	-	-	-	4	-	-	-	-	5	-	-	-	-	-	-	-	-
Law	17	13	1	8	-	1	-	-	-	5	7	14	10	3	1	64	-	4	4	23	-	-	-	-
Law of Moses	9	-	-	-	-	-	-	-	-	-	1	-	-	1	-	16	-	1	-	4	-	1	-	-
Laws	-	-	-	-	-	1	-	-	-	-	-	-	-	-	-	17	1	1	6	-	-	-	-	-
Come Unto	-	9	-	-	1	-	1	3	-	-	8	15	4	16	1	16	5	11	-	7	5	1	-	-

Figure 1

Similarly, many of the authors speak of *Law,* but not all refer explicitly to the *Law of Moses.* Finally, a number of the authors use the phrase *Come Unto,* and we will explore what each means by the special use of that phrase. We will divide the following material into three categories which deal with various meanings and contexts for these words, i.e., ethical and secular, theological, and editorial. Finally, we will turn to Jesus' theological key which unlocks the ultimate meaning of this complex of words.

A Predominantly Secular or Ethical Meaning

The Law/Command complex is often used in relation to secular laws and rules for governing the state. It may also be used to delineate how a person should behave in everyday life. Even though these commands or laws may come from God, they deal predominantly with person-to-person relationships, as opposed to theological uses which are essentially concerned with the relationship between God and human beings. The following material will examine those authors whose word usage is predominantly concerned with these person-to-person relationships.

Alma 2

For Alma 2, the Law/Command word group is comparatively important, with a use ratio of 3.03 per thousand words. *Commandments* has a use ratio of 1.44, while *Command*[3] and *Law*[4] are the other words primarily used.

The word *Law* focuses most clearly on the secular/ethical aspects of life, since it refers either to the secular law of Mosiah (Alma 1:14; 30:34) or to the Law of Moses (Alma 42:17–24) with its ethical content. The words related to *Command,* however, straddle the line between secular/ethical and theological meanings. As can be seen, *Commandments* seems to have a strong ethical content, although it is often cast in a context which stresses the goodness and graciousness of God. For example, the first time Alma 2 uses the word is in Alma 5:18, which states the following: "Can ye imagine yourselves brought before the tribunal of God with your souls filled with guilt and remorse, having a remembrance of all your guilt, yea, a perfect remembrance of all your wickedness, yea, a remembrance that ye have set at defiance the commandments of God?"

This occurrence immediately follows Alma 2's question to the people of Zarahemla asking whether they have been spiritually born of God. He then asks them about their faith in God and if they are prepared to be judged against the deeds they have done while in their mortal bodies—i.e., judged against their ethical behavior. Would they be invited to come to God because of their righteousness, or would they be filled with remorse and guilt because they violated God's commandments (Alma 5:14–18)?

For Alma 2, a person's spiritual relationship with God (Alma 5:14) was clearly a precursor to all that followed ethically, yet ethics—living by God's commandments—did matter (Alma 5:16, 18). Other texts show a similar spiritual/ethical relationship.[5] However, no mere ethical norm was meaningful unless it was fulfilled in

---

[3] Eleven times with a 0.55 use ratio.

[4] Twelve times with a 0.60 use ratio.

[5] Alma 7:15–16, 23; 9:8, 13; 12:30–32, 37; 13:1, 6; 36:1, 13, 30; 37:13–16, 20, 35; 38:1–2, 39.

relationship to Christ's atoning work. Thus the Father states, "Therefore, whosoever repenteth, and hardeneth not his heart, he shall have claim on mercy through mine Only Begotten Son, unto a remission of his sins; and these shall enter into my rest" (Alma 12:34).

The word which reinforces the above relationship between spirituality and ethics is *Command*. On the one hand, *Command* has the rather mundane meaning of ordering or directing someone to keep the records (Alma 37:1–2) or not to impart certain knowledge (Alma 12:9, 14; 37:1–2, 16, 20, 27; 39:10, 12). On the other hand, *Command* appears in Alma 5:60–62 as the culmination of a magnificent chapter on the work of Christ. Clearly the ethical element is present, but of even greater importance is the emphasis on coming to Christ, repenting, and being baptized.

Amulek

Amulek makes almost no use of the Law/Command word group with the exception of the word *Law,* which has a use ratio of 2.52. Interestingly, the word carries a variety of meanings. It may mean the law of Ammonihah (Alma 10:26), Mosiah's law (Alma 34:11–12), or the Law of Moses, which points to Christ (Alma 34:13–14, 16).

Benjamin

The Law/Command word group is of major significance in Benjamin with a use ratio of 5.92. The two dominant words used by king Benjamin are *Commandments*[6] and *Commanded.*[7] *Law* and *Laws* are each used only once.

Commandments carries a strong ethical context (Mosiah 1:3–4; 2:13, 21–22), but there is the added dimension of being commanded to know the history of God's dealings with his people, thereby placing ethics within God's promises of redemption (Mosiah 1:5–7, 11; 2:41; 4:6, 30). Even the king's commandments are the commandments of God (Mosiah 2:31).

---

[6] 3.79 use ratio.

[7] 1.66 use ratio.

Benjamin's use of *Commanded* sharpens the picture, for he makes it clear that service to one's fellow human beings is the essence of God's commands (Mosiah 2:13, 17, 23, 27). In addition, Benjamin is commanded to reveal the mysteries of God to his people (Mosiah 2:2–10), the essence of which seems to be "that ye are eternally indebted to your heavenly Father, to render to him all that you have and are" (Mosiah 2:34). Such knowledge came from the records, the holy prophets, and the fathers (Mosiah 2:34–35).

Mosiah

Proportionately, the Law/Command word group is of immense importance to Mosiah, with a use ratio of 14.41. In stating this, however, it must be recognized that we have only 1,108 words from Mosiah, certainly not a full representation of his thought. The words he uses from the word group are *Command, Commandments, Law,* and *Laws*. In virtually every instance where *Law* or *Laws* is used, the reference is to secular issues (Mosiah 29:11, 15, 22–23, 25–27). *Commandments* seems to be Mosiah's word for the commandments of God which are the basis of secular law (Mosiah 29:11, 13–14, 22).

Nephi 1

Nephi 1's use of the Law/Command word group produces a use ratio of 2.92. Most of the time his concerns are with commands from the Lord which relate to events of his life, such as leaving Jerusalem (1 Nephi 2:3–4), returning to Jerusalem (1 Nephi 2:14; 3:7, 15, 18; 7:1–2), building the ship (1 Nephi 17:49), Laman and Lemuel not touching him (1 Nephi 17:48), and making plates (1 Nephi 9:2; 19:1).

Almost universally in Nephi 1's writings, the word *Commandments* means *instructions,* a meaning that is unique to Nephi 1. Of the twenty-eight occurrences of the word, twenty bear the meaning of instructions,[8] while of the remaining eight occurrences, three others may mean this in part (1 Nephi 22:30–31; 2 Nephi 31:7).

The word *Law* always means the Law of Moses (e.g., 1 Nephi 4:15; 2 Nephi 25:25–30), and where *Law of Moses* is used explicitly,

---

[8] E.g., 1 Nephi 3:7, 15; 4:11; 16:8; 2 Nephi 5:19, 31.

Nephi 1 tells us that it points toward Christ (2 Nephi 11:4) or is to be kept until Christ comes (2 Nephi 25:24).

Summary

Among those authors who use the Law/Command word group in a predominantly ethical or secular vein or both, there are clear differences in the ways the words are utilized. For example, Alma 2 and Amulek, missionary companions, do not use the same vocabulary. Amulek uses the word *Law* to mean a variety of things. Alma 2 uses *Law* predominantly to designate the Law of Moses. Benjamin stresses service and that the king's commands are God's commands, while his son Mosiah stresses secular law. By contrast, Nephi 1 speaks of God's commands to him as addressing a variety of life's problems. He uses the word *Commandments* uniquely to mean instructions.

From these examples, one observes precisely what one would expect to see among different authors whose works had been edited and recorded in a single volume—diversity in language and diversity in the meanings attached to a single word. Figure 2 is a summary table of the above results.

SECULAR/ETHICAL	
Alma 2 (3.03)	
Commandments	Ethical and lead to righteousness
	Living by God's directions
	Fulfilled in relation to Christ
Law	Secular or Law of Moses
Amulek (2.52)	
Law	Secular
Benjamin (5.92)	
Commandments	Ethics or know the history of God
Commanded	Service
Mosiah (14.41)	
Commandments	God's commands the basis of secular law
Laws	Secular laws
Nephi 1 (2.92)	
Commandments	Instructions on daily issues
Law	Law of Moses

Figure 2

A Predominantly Theological Meaning

In this section, the Law/Command word group will be examined within an overtly theological context. Here the words are less concerned with person-to-person relationships but are instead predominantly concerned with the divine/human encounter.

Abinadi

For Abinadi, the Law/Command word group is quite important, with a use ratio of 10.39. As with Mosiah, the length of text is small (2,792 words), thus limiting our ability to decide how important these words might have been within a broader range of Abinadi's thought. However, given the fact that Abinadi's sermon contains his final words before death, we can surmise that we are reading what he believed to be of greatest importance.

When Abinadi uses *Commanded,* it is almost always in the context of God commanding persons, through Abinadi's preaching, to repent (Mosiah 11:20–21, 25; 12:1; 13:3; 16:12) and, in the broader context, to come to Christ and his atonement. The people's repentance must focus on their violation of the Ten Commandments, which clearly state God's will for them (Mosiah 12:33; 13:4, 11, 25; 15:22, 26). The priests of Noah claim that salvation comes through the Law of Moses, but Abinadi gives an interesting twist to that argument. He says he knows that if they keep the commandments of God, they will be saved. He then quotes the beginning of the Ten Commandments: "I am the Lord thy God, who hath brought thee out of the land of Egypt. . . . Thou shalt have no other God before me" (Mosiah 12:34–36). Abinadi's basic charge is that the priests of Noah have not kept God foremost in their lives, thereby giving rise to all their other sins (Mosiah 12:37). Thus, the Law of God is central, but specifically the law which places the *person* of God and one's relationship with him above all other things. When the Law of Moses is rightly understood, it is a type of him who is to come (Mosiah 13:31–32; 16:14). Until such time, the ordinances are given to keep the remembrance of God constantly before the people (Mosiah 13:29–30).

Jacob

Jacob uses most of the Law/Command words, but he does not seem to have a favorite. Thus, while the word group is important in his writing, with a use ratio of 3.05, there is a variety of meanings attached to the words. The natural world may be commanded (Jacob 4:6, 9), God (or Nephi 1) commands that precious things be written down (Jacob 1:1–2, 8; 7:27), and the Lord commands that persons be baptized in the name of the Holy One of Israel (2 Nephi 9:23). Monogamy is commanded (Jacob 3:5–6), and the Nephites are no longer to revile the Lamanites, but rather to contemplate their own sins (Jacob 3:8). Further, the commandments come from God (2 Nephi 9:27; Jacob 2:10, 16; 4:5), and to keep them is to glorify the Lord (Jacob 2:21).

Jacob's use of the word *Law* appears, in part, to mean the Law of Moses. But it goes beyond this to a sense that is equivalent to the plan of salvation, for it seems to encompass the work of Christ and God's overall purposes (2 Nephi 9:17, 24–27, 46). Finally, the Law of Moses points souls to Christ (Jacob 4:5). Hence, Jacob's use of the word group is different from that of other authors in that there is not a dominant theme attached to the word group.

Moroni 2

The Law/Command word group is not of great interest to Moroni 2, whose use ratio is 1.46. Moroni 2's use of these words is almost wholly in an editorial context, and they consistently refer to commands of the Lord. Only once are any of the words used in the Book of Moroni, and there Christ's commandments concerning the sacrament are referenced (Moroni 4:1). All other occurrences are in Mormon 8–9 or Ether. The Lord commanded individuals to do various things,[9] and Moroni 2's father commanded Moroni 2 to write about the end of the Nephite people (Mormon 8:1). Moroni 2's use of *Law* or *Laws* is less than the average of all other writers.

---

[9] E.g., Ether 2:5; 4:1; 9:20; 12:22, etc.

Lehi

The use ratio of the Law/Command word group is 2.70 for Lehi, and he uses these words differently than do other writers. Lehi speaks in the first person and then refers to the Lord's commanding of individuals to do certain things, almost in the format of the Old Testament messenger formula. For example, Lehi tells Nephi that "the Lord hath commanded me that thou and thy brethren shall return to Jerusalem" (1 Nephi 3:2). Other occurrences have this same format (1 Nephi 3:4–5; 2 Nephi 1:27; 2:21). The most used word in the group is *Law*. It consistently refers to the Law of Moses, but we cannot draw too much from this since the occurrences are all in one passage (2 Nephi 2:4–26).

Summary

Among those authors who stress the predominantly theological sense of the Law/Command word group, there is once again a divergence in the way the various terms are used. Abinadi focuses on the people's need to repent because they have violated the Ten Commandments, which, when rightly understood, point to Christ. No single term stands out for Jacob, and thus his use is varied. Moroni 2 uses the words almost solely in his work as an editor, but in most instances it is the Lord who gives commands. Finally, Lehi's use is slightly unique—he speaks in the first person and refers to the Lord's commanding. Figure 3 is a summary chart of the above analysis.

	THEOLOGICAL
Abinadi (10.39)	
Commanded	God commands repentance
Commandments	No other God—relational
Law	Law of Moses points to Christ
Jacob (3.05)	
Commandments	No favorite meaning
Law	Law of Moses
Moroni 2 (1.46)	
Command	Lord or his father commands
Lehi (2.70)	
Command	Messenger formula—Lord commands
Law	Law of Moses

Figure 3

Predominantly Editorial in Nature

This section is reserved for Mormon, who, although he might have been placed with those whose word use was primarily secular, must be analyzed separately to see the uniqueness that he brings to his work. As is generally accepted, Mormon's words begin with the Words of Mormon, are interspersed as he edits the books of Mosiah through 4 Nephi, appear in Mormon 1–7, and are present once again in Moroni 7–9. Given the immense amount of material which Mormon edits and the numerous and separate places where his personal words and thoughts appear, it is important to note that he maintains, across the spectrum of his writings, several unique meanings for words within the Law/Command word group.

Words from this word group appear 245 times with a moderate use ratio of 2.50. The word group clearly has importance to Mormon. However, because of the size of Mormon's writings (97,912 words), no single word in the group reaches a use ratio of 1.00, even when it appears seventy-eight times as does *Commanded* (0.80) or fifty-three times as does *Commandments* (0.54). Even so, the Law/Command group is clearly important, and if a specific word appears throughout Mormon's writings and bears a meaning significantly different from the surrounding material, it is worth examining. This is certainly the case for several of Mormon's words.

Command is one such word. In Alma 2, for example, the word appears nine times as a verb[10] and twice as a noun meaning "an order" (Alma 5:62; 12:9). In Jesus' words it occurs twice as a verb (3 Nephi 15:16; 16:4), and in the Lord's words four times as a verb (2 Nephi 3:8; 29:11; Jacob 2:30; Helaman 10:11) and twice in the phrase "at my command" (Ether 4:9). Mormon's use is very different. *Command* appears seventeen times as a noun[11] and three times as a verb (Alma 52:4; 3 Nephi 3:17; Mormon 7:4). The dominant meaning as a noun is that of military or social "leadership," a definition no other writer gives to the word.

---

[10] Alma 5:61; 12:14; 37:1–2, 16, 20, 27; 39:10, 12.

[11] Mosiah 27:3; Alma 43:16–17; 47:3, 5, 13; 52:15; 53:2; 59:7; 62:3, 43; Helaman 12:8; 3 Nephi 4:23, 26; Mormon 5:1, 23; Moroni 7:30.

Commanded also displays unique characteristics when used by Mormon, being dominated by kings, prophets, or military leaders who command. Thus, Benjamin, Limhi, Ammon, Noah, Alma 1, Amulon, Alma 2, and Gidgiddoni all command their followers to do a variety of secular things.[12] In almost all instances the meaning is essentially nontheological. When Mormon is not editing material, however, it is the Lord who commands (Mormon 3:16; 6:6; 7:10; Moroni 8:21).

The secular motif within the word group continues with the words *Law* and *Laws*. In virtually every instance *Law* means secular law[13] or, more specifically, the Law of Mosiah (e.g., Mosiah 29:39; Alma 1:17; 11:1). Only in Mormon's sermonic material does the secular motif vanish with the meaning being either the Law of Moses or, perhaps, shorthand for the plan of salvation (Moroni 7:28; 8:22, 24). *Laws* is also secular in meaning, i.e., Mosiah's law (e.g., Alma 1:1; Helaman 4:21) or tribal law (3 Nephi 7:11, 14).

Mormon is not, however, without interest in things theological. This is manifest in his use of the word *Commandments,* signifying things which come from God and which seem to convey the idea of "the Christian life." The term is extremely broad in scope, and no single definition such as Abinadi's Ten Commandments, Mosiah's judicial commandments, or Alma the Younger's ethical commandments is sufficient. Thus, "Christian Life" seems to be the best equivalent for Mormon's use.[14] Even in his sermonic material, this broad meaning still seems to be operative (Moroni 8:11, 25).

Finally, when Mormon refers specifically to the Law of Moses, it bears theological meaning only in relation to Christ, for it is a type, it points to Christ (e.g., Alma 25:15–16), and it passes away at his coming (3 Nephi 1:24; 15:2).

In summary, Mormon used the terms of the Law/Command word group in his own unique ways, despite the manner in which these same words may have been used in the surrounding material which he was editing. The major emphasis is secular, but it is theologically bal-

---

[12] E.g., Mosiah 1:17; 7:8; 17:1; 18:21; Helaman 4:22; 3 Nephi 4:13, etc.

[13] E.g., Alma 1:32; 10:14; 30:9; Helaman 2:10; 3 Nephi 5:5; 6:30.

[14] See Mosiah 6:1; 17:20; Alma 1:25; 31:9; 48:25; Helaman 3:20, 37; 3 Nephi 5:22.

anced, in part, by the terms *Commandments* and *Law of Moses*. Figure 4 is a synopsis of Mormon's word usage.

Mormon (2.50)	Editorial	Sermonic
Command	Noun: "Leadership"	
Commanded	Royal secular commands	The Lord commands
Law	Secular (Mosiah's)	Law of Moses
Laws	Mosiah's or tribal	
Commandments	Christian Life	
Law of Moses	Type of Christ	

Figure 4

Jesus' Theological Key

In this book, "Lord" refers to the Lord who speaks from the heavens. In actuality, this is Jesus, either before his mortal birth or as the resurrected Lord when he speaks from the heavens. Until now neither the words of the resurrected Jesus nor those of the Lord speaking from the heavens have been considered. Yet for each, the Law/Command word group is highly significant. For Jesus the word-use count is 5.50, and for the Lord the count is 2.97. If we are ever to understand the true significance of the laws and commands that we are to obey as members of The Church of Jesus Christ of Latter-day Saints, it will be because we hear from the Lord himself what the laws and commands are to be and to mean in our individual lives.

The Lord

The Lord's use of the Law/Command word group, as he speaks to his servants, leaves little doubt that he is in charge of all things. It is at his order that his work is done (2 Nephi 3:8), that scriptures are written (2 Nephi 29:11), that seed may be raised up for him (Jacob 2:30), that messages are conveyed (1 Nephi 2:1; Helaman 10:11), and that the heavens are opened or shut (Ether 4:8–9). The most important word is *Commandments,* which covers all things the Lord asks his servants to do. The unique element is that there is almost always a promise or curse attached to the word. For example, in 1 Nephi 2:20 we read, "And inasmuch as ye shall keep my commandments, ye shall prosper, and shall be led to a land of promise."¹⁵ In contrast, however, we also read in 2 Nephi 1:20, "Inasmuch as ye will not keep my commandments ye shall be cut off from my presence."¹⁶ The word *Law* is used only twice meaning the Law of Moses (2 Nephi 3:17; Moroni 8:8), and the one time the Law of Moses is referred to directly, it is said to point to the Lord himself (Alma 9:17–18).

The Resurrected Jesus

As we turn to the resurrected Jesus and his use of the Law/Command word group in 3 Nephi, with a use ratio of 5.50, we finally come to understand the reason why all the Lord's commands and laws were and are given: they point us to Christ. Apart from Christ and his atoning work, laws and commandments are meaningless.

As we study the words Jesus uses, the first thing to note is his consciousness that even he does nothing that the Father does not direct him to do. For example, because his Father has so directed, he does not tell his disciples in the Old World about the Nephites (3 Nephi 15:13–15), yet he goes to other scattered peoples at his Father's command (3 Nephi 16:3). Further, he completes the work which his Father has commanded him to do, i.e., the gathering of Israel (3 Nephi 20:10).

The heart of the issue, however, is to be found in 3 Nephi 12:17–20. Here Jesus makes clear both his and his Father's will for members of the Church. Jesus tells us what *his* command is for those persons who seek to do God's will:

> Think not that I am come to destroy the law or the prophets. I am not come to destroy but to fulfil; For verily I say unto you, one jot nor one tittle hath not passed away from the law, but in me it hath all been fulfilled. And behold, *I have given you the law and the commandments of my Father, that ye shall believe in me, and that ye shall repent of your sins, and come unto me with a broken heart and a contrite spirit.* Behold, ye have the commandments before you, and the law is fulfilled. Therefore come unto me and be ye saved; for verily I say unto you, that except ye shall keep my commandments, which

---

¹⁵ See also 1 Nephi 2:22; 4:14; 15:11; 17:13; 2 Nephi 1:20; 4:4; Enos 1:10; Jarom 1:9; Mosiah 13:14; Alma 9:13; 50:20; Helaman 10:5.

¹⁶ See also 2 Nephi 4:4; Jacob 2:29; Enos 1:10; Omni 1:6; Alma 9:13; 50:20.

> I have commanded you at this time, ye shall in no case enter into the kingdom of heaven (emphasis added).

These verses appear in the midst of Jesus' sermon at the temple in Bountiful and give focus to all else that is said in the sermon. What Jesus is instructing the people to do is entirely possible, unless they seek to separate their lives from a relationship with him. Perfection of life—our lives—is to be found in Christ, for he fulfills perfectly the essence of the law (3 Nephi 12:18–19, 46; 15:4–5, 8–10).

The emphasized text above states the relationship between the laws and commandments of God and Jesus as our Savior. The text may be interpreted in at least two ways, neither of which necessarily precludes the other. It could mean that Jesus has given *in the past,* through the Law of Moses and other commands, the directions of his Father, all of which should lead persons to believe in him as the Christ, repent of their sins, and come to him with a broken heart and a contrite spirit.

It could also mean that Jesus was *at that moment* conveying the Father's fundamental commands to his children, which are that they shall believe in Christ, repent of their sins, and come to Christ with a broken heart and a contrite spirit. This would mean that obedience to all other commands, particularly those contained in the sermon at the temple, grows out of a person's relationship with Christ, as well as pointing him or her toward that relationship. This interpretation is supported by Jesus' next statement: "Except ye shall keep my commandments, which I have commanded you *at this time,* ye shall in no case enter into the kingdom of heaven" (emphasis added). This seems to suggest that it is not past commandments with which the Lord is concerned, but rather the fundamental commandment to come to him which he wants us to hear. From that relationship comes a "mighty change of heart" which then enables those who have become true Saints to keep the other articulated commands of God—to live the life which the children of God should live—meaning that they possess the mind of God or are Godlike.

Jesus' use of the other words in the Law/Command word group supports this relational view of his commandments. The people are to do what Christ commands them, i.e., they are to be baptized unto his death and resurrection and are to take the sacrament which is a remembrance of their relationship to Christ, a relationship made possible by his sacrificial atonement (3 Nephi 18:10–12). The Father commands all persons to repent and believe in Christ (3 Nephi 11:32). Whoever breaks the command to come to Christ is in danger of being led into temptation (3 Nephi 18:25), and this danger is forcefully emphasized once again in Jesus' culminating commandment: "Repent, all ye ends of the earth, and *come unto me* and be baptized in my name, that ye may be sanctified by the reception of the Holy Ghost, that ye may stand spotless before me at the last day" (3 Nephi 27:20; emphasis added). Finally, Christ's last words in 3 Nephi are directed to the Gentiles: "Turn, all ye Gentiles, from your wicked ways . . . and *come unto me,* and be baptized in my name, that ye may receive a remission of your sins, and be filled with the Holy Ghost, that ye may be numbered with my people who are of the house of Israel" (3 Nephi 30:2; emphasis added).

The centrality of coming to Christ is never left in doubt throughout Book of Mormon history. The Lord, speaking from the heavens, constantly directed the people to turn to him.[17] Nephi also called his people to come to the God of Abraham (1 Nephi 6:4), to God (1 Nephi 10:18; 2 Nephi 26:33), to the Redeemer, and to the fold of God (1 Nephi 15:14–15). Similarly, Jacob summons all to come to the Lord (2 Nephi 9:41), to God (2 Nephi 9:45), to the Holy One of Israel (2 Nephi 9:51), and to Christ (Jacob 1:7). Finally, Moroni 2 bears his witness of the need to come to the Lord (Mormon 9:27), to the Father in the name of Jesus (Ether 5:5), to the fountain of righteousness (Ether 8:26), and to Christ (Moroni 10:30, 32). In addition, as seen in the earlier sections of this chapter, Alma 2, Amulek, Nephi 1, Abinadi, Jacob, and Mormon all use certain of their words from the Law/Command group to point to Christ. Thus, in Christ alone can we find the power to live as God would have us live.

---

[17] 2 Nephi 26:25; 28:32; Alma 5:34; 3 Nephi 9:14, 22; Ether 3:22; 4:13–14, 18; 12:27; Moroni 7:34.

Conclusions

As a result of the above discussions, two areas need to be highlighted: (1) the divergent ways in which the above authors use the words within the Law/Command word group under consideration, and (2) the theological implications of the word group for us in our daily lives.

Author Individuality

Precisely the kind of diversity that one would expect to find between authors, separated sometimes by centuries in time, has been observed as we considered the ways in which the various authors used the Law/Command word group. Some were concerned with secular meanings while others sought the theological implications of the word group. Perhaps of greatest interest is the uniqueness of Mormon who, despite the fact that he edited almost everybody else's work, has his own unique linguistic imprint which runs throughout his material.

Theological Implications

As suggested at the beginning of this chapter, we as Latter-day Saints tend to place a strong emphasis on obedience to the commands of the Lord. Generally, we have in mind ethical commands or commands which direct us to fulfill certain ordinances. In doing so, however, there is a danger that the real commandment—to come unto the Lord—may become lost in the shuffle, causing us to misunderstand the essence of our faith and substitute slavish pharisaism where there should be Christian freedom. Below are some suggestions concerning how this may have occurred and how we may once again realize the incredible freedom that exists in Latter-day Saint theology.

Much of our attention with our young people is turned toward trying to keep them safe in a terribly wicked world. We realize that teenagers do not yet have enough experience with life to see the long-range consequences of their actions. Thus adults, in their wisdom, stress to the younger generation the ethical commands of the Lord in order to keep that generation safe until they have developed the spiritual equipment to keep themselves out of trouble. No active Latter-day Saint would or could deny the validity of this approach.

We lay down the law that the young may enter adulthood clean and unsullied by the world, and our study of the Book of Mormon authors certainly validates this approach.

The question to be answered, in light of the above study, is whether we as adults have ever ceased to be spiritual teenagers. Have we gone on to the deeper meanings of the faith? In the end, the "thou shalts" and the "thou shalt nots" are only interim ethics until we have achieved spiritual adulthood in the gospel—an adulthood which means being of one mind with Christ and the Father. A key passage concerning what the Lord understands our goal to be in relation to his law is found in Jeremiah 31:31–34:

> Behold, the days come, saith the Lord, that I will make a new covenant with the house of Israel, and with the house of Judah: Not according to the covenant that I made with their fathers in the day that I took them by the hand to bring them out of the land of Egypt; which my covenant they brake, although I was an husband unto them, saith the Lord: But this shall be the covenant that I will make with the house of Israel; After those days, saith the Lord, I will put my law in their inward parts, and write it in their hearts; and will be their God, and they shall be my people. And they shall teach no more every man his neighbour, and every man his brother, saying, Know the Lord: for they shall all know me, from the least of them unto the greatest of them, saith the Lord: for I will forgive their iniquity, and I will remember their sin no more.

For all of us the day must come when we know God's will naturally, not because we have a list of things to do or not to do, but because the will of God is ingrained in our very being. In doing so we become one with the Father in the same way the Son is one with the Father, no longer needing to have external rules and laws, because our knowledge of divine things is instinctive. Granted, until such time as we become perfected through the work of the Holy Ghost, we need the laws of God as a tutor and a guide. But the day will come when we no longer need the law, for we will be perfectly one with the Father through the work of Jesus Christ.

Thus, each day that we walk with Christ toward the full realization of our existence in the presence of the Father, we should be less and less dependent on external norms and mandates and more and more dependent upon Christ in whom we will finally live and move and have our full being. The relationship with the Father through Jesus Christ should grow day by day, so that even our thoughts and desires are perfected, and all commands but the one command, "Come unto me," will fade away and will be no longer needed.[18]

---

[18] This is not meant to diminish the necessity of the ordinances of the Church. There is not a single ordinance with a purpose other than to bring us to Christ.

3

Church and Churches

The Church is central to Latter-day Saints. Normally, when we think of "church," we think of prophets, apostles, seventies, stake presidents, bishops, quorums, the Relief Society, and local congregations. In other words, our thought is often structural. Given this, it is interesting and instructive to see how Book of Mormon authors use the words *Church* and *Churches*. No author uses the words with any great frequency. In itself this is interesting, for we might expect a greater emphasis on things ecclesiastical since these are so important to us today.

However, as chapter 1 indicates, the Church word group is of minimal importance to the writers of the Book of Mormon: only the Angel, Ammon, the Father, and Jesus show any significant interest in the cluster. Interestingly, the Father never uses the words *Church* or *Churches* but uses other words of the group, such as *Appoint, Bless, Blessed,* and so forth.

On the other end of the spectrum, Alma 2, Captain Moroni, Jacob, the Lord, Mormon, Moroni 2, and Nephi 1 use words of the Church cluster very rarely. It therefore does not appear to have been very important to any of them. However, each of these authors uses the words *Church* or *Churches*. Figures 1 and 2 show how the words *Church* and *Churches* are distributed in meaning for the authors who use them.

	Alma 2	Ammon	Angel	Jacob	Jesus	Lord	Mormon	Moroni 1	Moroni 2	Nephi 1
Christ's, NW	5	1	-	-	-	-	80	1	-	-
Local	3	-	-	-	1	1	20	-	7	-
Christ's, not NW	2	-	-	-	-	-	-	-	-	-
Great and abom.	-	-	9	1	-	1	-	-	-	6
Of the Lamb	-	-	2	-	-	-	-	-	-	3
Of the devil	-	-	1	-	-	-	-	-	-	-
Universal	4	-	-	-	10	5	44	-	2	1
Not true	-	-	-	-	-	-	3	-	-	-
NW/universal	1	-	-	-	-	-	-	-	-	-
Jews	-	-	-	-	-	-	-	-	-	1

Figure 1: Church

	Angel	Mormon	Moroni 2	Nephi 1
Other churches	2	-	-	-
Two churches	1	-	-	-
Local	-	10	-	-
Local/denomin.	-	5	7	6

Figure 2: Churches

The categories may need some explanation. "NW" indicates the New World. A local church is a gathering of Christians in a particular spot, e.g., the church in Gideon, Zarahemla, or Nephi. In contrast, the universal church includes all the followers of Christ—past, present, and future—in whatever places they have been or may be found. A more complete explanation of each category will be given as the chapter progresses. It is important to note here that there are both similarities and differences already apparent between the authors, even though only a few persons speak of *Church* or *Churches*. For example, several of the authors speak of the universal church. In contrast, the Angel and Nephi 1 speak of the great and abominable church, while Mormon and Moroni 2 seem to talk of local entities.

Having laid this preliminary groundwork, we now turn to an in-depth examination of the words *Church* and *Churches* to determine how they are used by various authors who will be grouped under the most dominant theme of their texts. We will then seek the theological implications of those usages for the Church today.

The Great and Abominable Church

Nephi 1 and the Angel

For both Nephi's Angel and Nephi 1, the word *Church* is used with distinctly negative connotations. Unquestionably, the word *Church* is more important in the Angel's words than in the words of any other individual who will be considered, being used 5.78 times per thousand words of author text. In virtually every instance it refers to the great and abominable church (nine times—1 Nephi 13:5, 8, 26, 28, 32; 14:3, 9, 10, 17) or to the church of the devil (one time—1 Nephi 14:10). The great and abominable church is a church which prizes fine clothing and is lustful (1 Nephi 13:8), takes away precious parts of the Bible (1 Nephi 13:28, 32), is founded by the devil and leads people away from God (1 Nephi 14:3), stands in opposition to the church of the Lamb (1 Nephi 14:10), and is known as the mother of harlots (1 Nephi 14:17). The only positive use of the word *Church* by the Angel occurs when he refers twice to the church of the Lamb of God, which stands in opposition to the church of the devil (1 Nephi 14:10).

When the Angel uses the word *Churches* he does so once in contrasting two churches, i.e., the church of the Lamb of God and the church of the devil (1 Nephi 14:10), both of which have been referenced above. However, the two other uses of the word are also interesting and potentially instructive. In 1 Nephi 13:5, 26, the Angel refers to the great and abominable church "which is most abominable above all other churches." It would seem that there may be other organizations, known as churches, which, while perhaps not fully correct, are certainly not to be identified with the great and abominable church. The implication seems to be that they have something which is positive about them—something which cannot be said for the great and abominable church. Perhaps all earthly organizations (1 Nephi 13) contain, to a greater or lesser degree, aspects of the cosmic entities known as the church of the Lamb and the church of the devil (1 Nephi 14). Earthly entities of any time or place which are so utterly immersed in evil that they are virtually beyond redemption are identified as part of the great and abominable church; but there are other "churches" which have not sunk to such depths and may thus be open to fulfillment or completion.

Nephi 1's use of the word *Church* parallels that of the Angel. Once again, one encounters the confrontation between the church of the Lamb of God and the great and abominable church. The earthly manifestation of the abominable church is found among the Gentiles (1 Nephi 13:4), the devil is the founder of it (1 Nephi 13:6), God's wrath is poured out upon it creating wars and rumors of wars (1 Nephi 14:15), and in the end it will fall (1 Nephi 22:14; 28:17). While Nephi 1 saw that the great and abominable church would cover the earth and have great strength, he also saw the church of the Lamb, which would be small but would also be found throughout the earth (1 Nephi 14:12). It consisted of the Saints or the covenant people of God (1 Nephi 14:12, 14), bore the power of the Lamb of God, and its people were armed with righteousness (1 Nephi 14:14). Thus, the cosmic powers of Satan and Christ come into conflict on the earthly stage.

Nephi 1 uses *Church* in two other ways. The first is to refer to the Jewish religious community as a church when Nephi 1 commands Zoram to get the plates of brass so Nephi 1 can take them to his brethren. He indicates that Zoram presumed Nephi 1 spoke of "the brethren of the church," i.e., the Jews (1 Nephi 4:25). The other usage seems to indicate Christ's universal church, i.e., all those people who accept Christ as their Lord and Savior and belong to his church. Nephi 1 states the following: "And behold it shall come to pass that after the Messiah hath risen from the dead, and hath manifested himself unto his people, unto as many as will believe on his name, behold, Jerusalem shall be destroyed again; for wo unto them that fight against God and the people of his church" (2 Nephi 25:14). This church cannot in the end be defeated but will ultimately prevail, not merely in the meridian of time or in the latter days, but for all time.

Finally, all Nephi 1's uses of the word *Churches* are negative. Churches contend with other churches. It is not possible to determine whether local churches or denominational entities are here envisaged, but given Nephi 1's prophetic foresight, it is probably both. Pride, the desire for gain through the suffering of the poor (2 Nephi 26:20; 28:12), arrogant exclusiveness (2 Nephi 28:2–3), and false doctrine (2 Nephi 28:12) all give rise to "churches" which are not the Lord's.

In summary, the Angel and Nephi 1 both use *Church/Churches* in a primarily negative manner, referring to entities opposed to the church of the Lamb of God, the only true church.

The Universal Church

Jesus

Jesus' use of the word *Church* refers only to *his* church. The church is universal because Israelites and Gentiles alike may be included within it (3 Nephi 21:22). Because it is Christ's church, it must bear his name; any "church" which bears the name of another, such as Moses, is an untrue church (3 Nephi 27:7–8). Christ's one and only church is founded upon the good news of his gospel (3 Nephi 27:9–10), and its members are to pray to the Father as Christ taught them to pray, i.e., in Christ's name (3 Nephi 18:16; 27:9). Such a church will do what it has seen its Savior do (3 Nephi 27:21).

The Lord

Not surprisingly, the same themes are sounded by Jesus as the Lord when he speaks from heaven, both before and after his mortal ministry. Before Jesus is born, he, as the Lord, states that those who hear his voice (Mosiah 26:21), repent, and are baptized (Mosiah 26:22) are of his church. Nothing can overthrow the church except transgression (Mosiah 27:13), and those who will not hear his voice or repent must be excluded from the church (Mosiah 26:28). Even so, in the dark days in which Mormon lived, the hope and the grace of God were still available, if the errant people would but accept the divine offer. Once again, the church was to be based on faith in Jesus

Christ, repentance, and baptism (Mormon 3:2); the Lord's invitation to come to him was put before the people by Mormon.

In two instances, the Lord uses the word *Church* differently from that discussed above. In the first instance, he refers to the great and abominable church as that entity which has kept back part of the plain and precious truths of the gospel (1 Nephi 13:34). In the second instance, he commends Alma the Elder for establishing a church in the land of Nephi. Here the meaning of *Church* is that of a local congregation, rather than the all-encompassing idea of Christ's church as more generally used by the Lord.

Jacob

One other author, Jacob, seems to use the word *Church* with a universal meaning. He asserts that the Jews—members of the house of Israel—have been addressed by prophets from generation to generation and that eventually "they shall be restored to the true church and fold of God" (2 Nephi 9:1–2). Likewise, Gentiles who repent, who do not oppose Zion, and who do not join the great and abominable church will be saved (2 Nephi 6:12)—the implication being that they will be saved in Christ's church.

In summary, both the resurrected Jesus and Jesus as the Lord from heaven use the word *Church* predominantly to refer to the one church which is the Church of Jesus Christ, a church which is to be entered through faith, repentance, and baptism. This is also the church in which Jacob sees the Jews and Gentiles being united.

A Local Congregation

While Alma 2, Jesus, and the Lord all use *Church* to mean a local congregation, they have few such references. Their uses will be discussed in other contexts. Moroni 2, however, uses the word *Church* seven times to refer to the congregation of people in a local area when he explains how church affairs were conducted in his day. Thus, Moroni 2's understanding of the local church will be examined by itself. For example, he tells us how priests in a local church were ordained by elders (Moroni 3:1) and how the sacrament was administered, with the elders and priests kneeling with the members of a local church and praying to the Father in the name of Christ (Moroni 4:1–2). People were received for baptism only when they had demonstrated to the local church that they had repented and that they bore a broken heart and a contrite spirit (Moroni 6:2). The local congregations met often for prayer and fasting, and the meetings were conducted under the influence of the Spirit (Moroni 6:5, 9). When a person sinned, three witnesses from the local church were required as witnesses before the elders. If the person then did not repent, his name was removed from the rolls of the church (Moroni 6:7).

In two instances, Moroni 2 uses *Church* in a broader way. In Mormon 8:38 he asks persons of the latter days, whom he has been shown, why they have, by their greed and pride, polluted the church of God. Likewise, Moroni 2 tells us that once persons have been baptized and cleansed by the Holy Ghost, they are incorporated into the church of Christ (Moroni 6:4). Clearly, these uses of *Church* transcend the idea of a local unit and take on the nature of Christ's universal church. However, the majority of Moroni 2's uses reflect a local congregational situation.

The local church situation is heightened when one turns to Moroni 2's use of the word *Churches*. All uses refer to either denominational entities or to local congregations in the latter days. Clearly, the organizations are separate and distinct and are in conflict with their neighbors. Churches are defiled because they deny the power of God and are lifted up in pride and envy (Mormon 8:28, 36). Some churches will offer forgiveness of sins for money (Mormon 8:32), others are built to enhance the reputations of their members (Mormon 8:33), and still others love fine clothing and expensive church decorations more than they love the poor (Mormon 8:37). Thus, all references to *Churches* by Moroni 2 have a negative connotation. But since the churches are separated from each other, this usage supports Moroni 2's tendency to use *Church* to mean a local unit.

The Church in the New World

Captain Moroni

There is a fine line between *Church* referring to Christ's universal church and the designation referring to the church in the New World. But it seems reasonable to make such a distinction. For example, Captain Moroni says:

> And now, Zerahemnah, I command you, in the name of that all-powerful God, who has strengthened our arms that we have gained power over you, by our faith, by our religion, and by our rites of worship, and by our church, and by the sacred support which we owe to our wives and our children, by that liberty which binds us to our lands and our country (Alma 44:5).

He seems to be referring to a portion of Christ's church, a portion which is the organization present in the New World.

Ammon

Ammon, the son of Mosiah, seems to do the same thing when he refers to his attempts to destroy Christ's church with his brothers and Alma 2 (Alma 26:18). Clearly, these destructive activities were in relation to the church organization in the New World.

Alma 2

Alma the Younger's use of *Church* has elements similar to those present in Captain Moroni's and Ammon's, but it is harder to distinguish his references to the New World church from those which refer to Christ's universal church. However, there are differences which can be identified. As does Ammon, Alma 2 speaks of his attempts to destroy the church (Alma 36:6), but, as with Ammon, the destructive activities were aimed at the church community in the New World. Alma 2 also speaks of his work within the church, references which could be construed as meaning Christ's universal church, but which, upon closer examination, seem to refer once again to the gathered peoples in the New World. These people could be the only logical individuals who paid Alma 2 nothing for his work in the church (Alma 30:33–34).

Even more to the point, Alma 2 was "the high priest over the church of God *throughout the land"* (Alma 8:23, emphasis added; see also Alma 5:3). Alma 2 is not claiming to be the high priest or earthly head of Christ's whole church (wherever it may have been); rather, he was high priest over only that portion of the church found among his brethren in the New World. Finally, he addressed his "brethren of the church" (Alma 5:14) and commanded those who belonged to "the church" (Alma 5:62). These references seem to relate most directly to persons in the Western Hemisphere who were part of an organization called "the church." Thus, Alma 2 appears to use the word *Church* in several instances to refer to those who follow Christ in the New World. The importance of this distinction is heightened when one realizes that Alma 2 refers to Christ's church *outside* the New World by stating that when the Lord delivered Israel out of Egypt "God did establish his church among them" (Alma 29:11–13).

But this does not exhaust all meanings of the word *Church* for Alma 2. Some uses are clearly universal in nature. When he says, "And we were brought into this land, and here we began to establish the church of God throughout this land also" (Alma 5:5), the "church of God" refers to Christ's universal church. It was branches of this one and only church which were planted in "this land," i.e., the land of Zarahemla. Similarly, when Alma 2 speaks to those "who do not belong to the church" (Alma 5:62), this has to be a reference to the universal church, for one cannot belong to a "local church" without first being a member of Christ's one church.

Alma 2, of course, recognizes the legitimacy of the local worshipping community. He refers to his father, Alma 1, establishing a church in the land of Mormon, clearly a reference to a local community (Alma 5:3). Alma 2 also addressed the members of "this church," i.e., the one in Zarahemla (Alma 5:6), and rebuked his listeners for persecuting the humble who had been brought into "this church" (Alma 5:54)—clearly referring to local communities.

Thus, in summary, one can say that Ammon and Captain Moroni use the word *Church*[1] to mean the New World church. On the other

---

[1] Ammon and Captain Moroni each use the word only once. Therefore, we must not deduce too much about their views from such minimal evidence.

hand, Alma 2 also uses this meaning but adds dimensions of the universal church, the local church, and the church which existed outside the New World.

The Church in Mormon

Mormon is somewhat unique. First, the word *Church* appears 147 times in his writings and is distributed throughout them. It also has a use rate of 1.50 per thousand words of Mormon's text, higher than that of anyone except the Angel. Since Mormon's text is so lengthy, this means that Mormon writes more about the church than any other author in the Book of Mormon.

Second, Mormon has a clear propensity to use *Church* to mean the church in the New World (eighty times). However, as with Alma 2, it is not always easy to determine whether Mormon means the church in the New World or Christ's universal church, to which he refers clearly forty-four times. He also has twenty references to the local community and three to false churches. Since Mormon uses the word *Church* so many times, it will not be possible to examine every instance, but significant occurrences will be considered to show the variety of his meanings.

New World Church in Mormon

Some of the clearest references by Mormon to the church in the New World occur in Mosiah 26. In this chapter we learn about those who were children in king Benjamin's day and did not understand him or make the covenants that their parents did. Perhaps the central passage is Mosiah 26:9, in which we read that king Mosiah gave Alma 1 authority over "the church." This authority was over the church in the New World, and Alma 1 and others "did regulate all the affairs of the church" (Mosiah 26:37–38; see also Mosiah 29:42–43, 47; Alma 16:5). Thus, most other references to the church in this chapter refer to the New World church. The errant children deceived many in the church and led them to sin, thus requiring that the church admonish them (Mosiah 26:6). Nothing of this nature had occurred before in the church (Mosiah 26:9); therefore, Alma 1 sought the Lord's guidance. When the Lord's instructions came, Alma 1 wrote them down so he could judge the people of the church by those standards (Mosiah 26:33). Those persons who repented of their errors were counted "among the people of the church," while those who would not were excluded (Mosiah 26:35–36; see also Alma 6:3). Mormon shows us that the church of the New World possessed authority, structure, and continuous divine guidance.

Mormon's sense of a New World church continues in Mosiah 27 when he talks about the persecution endured by the church, the participation of Alma 2 and the sons of Mosiah in that activity (Mosiah 27:1, 10), and the ultimate efforts by Alma 2 and the sons of Mosiah to repair the damage they had done (Mosiah 27:33, 35).

Other chapters in which Mormon's predominant word usage reflects a New World church are Alma 1 (Nehor and priestcraft), Alma 4 (Alma gives up the judgment seat to preach), Alma 46 (Amalickiah wants to be king, and Moroni 1 raises the standard of liberty), and Helaman 3 (northward migration, many are converted, and Helaman's son Nephi becomes chief judge).

Other specific instances of New World usage which are scattered through the material Mormon edited are Alma 2:2–4 (the people of the church are alarmed by Amlici), Alma 43:30, 45 (the Nephites defend their liberties and church), Alma 45:19 (the saying went around the church that Alma 2 had been taken up as had Moses), Alma 45:21 and 62:44 (a regulation should be made throughout the church), Helaman 4:1, 23 (there were dissensions and iniquities within the church), Helaman 11:21 (Nephites and Lamanites belong to the church in the land), 3 Nephi 2:12 (Lamanites and Nephites oppose the Gadianton robbers to preserve their church), 3 Nephi 6:14 (inequality leads to the breakup of the church), and 4 Nephi 1:20 (a few people leave the church and take the name *Lamanites*).

Universal Church in Mormon

Mormon is clearly aware that the church is something that embraces more than just the Western Hemisphere. Throughout his writing, and in the midst of references to the New World church, one finds a consciousness of the all-encompassing church of Christ. For example, in Mosiah 26, which is so heavily oriented toward the New

World church, one finds two clear references to the universal church. First, those persons who were young when king Benjamin gave his sermon would not be baptized and join the church (Mosiah 26:4). Second, Alma 1 and his brethren suffered much from those who did not belong to the church of God (Mosiah 26:38). In the first instance, one cannot be baptized into the New World church; one is baptized into Christ's church (see Alma 4:4–5), a part of which may exist in the New World. In the second instance, the church of God clearly transcends any geographical barriers.

Interestingly, Mormon often designates the universal church by defining it as "the church of God" or "the church of Christ." This is true when he speaks of Alma 2 and the sons of Mosiah trying to destroy "the church of God" (Mosiah 27:9–10; see also Alma 46:10), when Nehor meets Gideon, a member of the church of God (Alma 2:7), when those outside the church of God begin to persecute those within it (Alma 1:18–19; 2:4), and when, after more than 150 years of peace, some Nephites begin to deny the true church of Christ (4 Nephi 1:26).

In a more positive vein, the people of Ammon were included in the church of God (Alma 27:27), true believers belonged to the church of God (Alma 46:14), and the church of God was reestablished through baptisms following the wars in which Captain Moroni fought so valiantly (Alma 62:46; Helaman 3:26). Further, Lamanites joined the church of God (Helaman 6:3), those baptized in the name of Jesus were called the church of Christ (3 Nephi 26:21), and all the people were converted to the church of Christ (3 Nephi 28:23).

In addition, Mormon makes a very interesting distinction between the church of God and those who *profess* to belong to the church of God. Pride enters into the hearts of those who only profess to belong to the church of God, when in reality they are members of convenience only without the humility sufficient to be members of the true church of Christ (Helaman 3:33–34; 4:11–12).

At times Mormon uses the word *Church* alone to indicate the universal church. Those baptized are added to *his* church, i.e., Christ's church (Mosiah 18:17; Alma 6:2). The order of the church is established (Alma 6:4; 8:1), and this order must refer to the transcendent order found only in Christ's universal church. The church is established throughout the land (Alma 16:15, 21; 45:22; 3 Nephi 5:12). The Zoramites would not continue in the performances of the church, i.e., prayer and supplication to God (Alma 31:10), and those who followed Amalickiah dissented from the church (Alma 46:7). Finally, in a personal letter to his son Moroni, Mormon identifies the church as the peaceable followers of Christ (Moroni 7:3) and tells those who have no faith in Christ that they are not fit to be part of Christ's church (Moroni 7:39).

False Churches in Mormon

In three instances, Mormon uses the word *Church* to designate a body in opposition to the true church. In Alma 1:6, Nehor is said to establish a church which reflected his untrue doctrines. Similarly, in 4 Nephi, churches are mentioned which either opposed the true church (4 Nephi 1:28) or actually persecuted it (4 Nephi 1:29).

Local Churches in Mormon

Mormon also uses *Church* to designate the local congregations in various regions. The church of God or the church of Christ was formed by Alma 1 at the waters of Mormon (Mosiah 18:17; see also Mosiah 23:17; 3 Nephi 5:12), its members were to assist one another with material needs (Mosiah 18:27), and Mosiah gave Alma 1 authority to ordain priests and teachers over *every* church which Alma had established (Mosiah 25:19, 21). In the land of Nephi, Limhi's people mourned for Abinadi and for the people who had formed a church under Alma 1 (Mosiah 21:30). But because there was no authority available, they did not themselves form a church, even though they desired to do so (Mosiah 21:34).

Later, Alma 2 spoke to the people of the church in Zarahemla and ordained priests and elders to watch over it (Alma 5:2; 6:1, 7), preached in the church in Gideon (Alma 6:8), established a church in the land of Sidom (Alma 15:13), left the church in Zarahemla to go on a preaching mission (Alma 31:6), and blessed the church in Zarahemla just before his departure (Alma 45:17). Similarly, Ammon established a church among the people of Lamoni who were Lamanites (Alma 19:35), and a church was established among the people of Ammon in the land of Jershon (Alma 28:1).

This sense of a local entity is enhanced when one notes that all Mormon's uses of the word *Churches* relate to local groups—ten times in Mosiah and Alma and five times in 4 Nephi. In Mosiah and Alma all references bear a positive tone. King Mosiah gave Alma 1 permission to establish churches (Mosiah 25:19), and the people were assembled in different bodies called churches (Mosiah 25:21). Although there were seven churches in the Land of Zarahemla (Mosiah 25:23), they were all one church and preached the common doctrines of repentance and faith in God (Mosiah 25:22). People who took upon themselves Christ's name joined the churches of God (Mosiah 25:23), and there were to be no persecutions or inequalities among the members of the churches (Mosiah 27:3). Similarly, in Alma, Mormon tells us that church leaders went from city to city establishing churches and ordaining local leaders (Alma 23:4; 45:22–23).

In 4 Nephi, however, when Mormon uses the word *Churches,* the connotation is always negative. Churches at that time were those entities which were corrupted or stood in opposition to the true church. People built churches to themselves (4 Nephi 1:25, 41), or members of churches professed to follow Christ while denying the central tenets of the gospel (4 Nephi 1:27). Also, priests and false prophets led the people to build churches and to commit many sins (4 Nephi 1:34).

In summary, Mormon uses the words *Church* and *Churches* in a variety of ways, all of which complement one another. His language reflects most clearly his identity with the church as it existed in the New World. But that church is only a piece of the broader universal church which manifests itself among the people in local congregations. However, there is always opposition to Christ's church, whether the church be local, regional, or universal; thus, there are also untrue churches which deny the truth taught by those of Christ's church.

Conclusions

Author Individuality

Clearly there are differences in the way the various persons considered above have used the words *Church* and *Churches* in the Book of Mormon. The Angel and Nephi 1 refer to the church in connection with the great and abominable church, and where they use the word *Churches* it appears to be groups of people in opposition to the true church, much as we find in Mormon and Moroni 2. The exceptions to this were two instances where the Angel indicates that the great and abominable church is more abominable than *all other churches,* thereby implying that there may be groups of religious people who, while not having the fullness of the gospel, may not be fully wrong.

Moroni 2 uses the word *Church* predominantly to refer to local congregations, while Mormon's favorite usage refers to the church in the New World, although he does refer to the local congregations several times. By contrast, the major emphasis in Jesus' and the Lord's words is on Christ's universal church, a meaning that is also quite important to Mormon and Alma 2. Alma 2 is also concerned with the New World church and local churches; he even uses the word *Church* in the context of the Israelites after their flight from Egypt. Ammon and Captain Moroni, who use *Church* once each in reference to the New World church, and Jacob, who once refers to the abominable church and once to the universal church, have too few usages for us to gain much sure insight into their general understanding of *Church.*

Once again we observe what one would expect of different authors, i.e., different meanings and different content when their uses of common words are examined. In this case, Mormon has the most all-inclusive use of the words under consideration.

Theological Implications

Given this analysis of the way the words *Church* and *Churches* are used in the Book of Mormon, what can we finally say that is applicable to the church in our day? To answer this question, it is necessary to revisit, from a theological perspective, 1 Nephi 13 and 14 and recognize that chapter 13 must be understood in light of chapter 14. Chapter 14 speaks of two churches—the church of the Lamb of God and the church of the devil. These two churches are the cosmic realities which signify the constant confrontation between good and evil, between God and Satan. But both entities are also present on the historical plane. Thus, the description of the great and abominable church in 1 Nephi 13:5–9 defines what characterizes the abominable church in its earthly manifestations. It is oriented toward the material and physical things of the world. As it follows those lusts, it always persecutes the Saints and tries to remove truth from the world whether in the first century (1 Nephi 13:23–29) or in the last days (1 Nephi 14:13–14).

No matter where or at what time the great and abominable church manifests itself, it will always have more adherents than will the Church of God (1 Nephi 14:12). Its ultimate end, however, is destruction—a fact, according to Nephi 1, that John the Beloved will reveal (1 Nephi 14:18–28). Consequently, when we turn to the Book of Revelation, we find the great and abominable church portrayed as the great whore, Babylon, who has fallen. Over her an angel sings a dirge in which the merchants of the earth, the recipients of her material wealth, mourn her demise (Rev. 18:1–20). Thus, the church of God will overcome the great and abominable church cosmically as well as temporally.

In summary, there is ultimately only one universal church, and that is Christ's church. It is that church which is not contaminated by pride, envy, lust, avarice, or jealousy. In opposition to it stands the great and abominable church, which is never long absent from any group of people. It leads individuals and groups away from Christ's universal church, and its footprints are everywhere in evidence, even within the Latter-day Saint community, for we too are human beings and subject to its temptations.

However, the footprints of Christ's church are also universally present, and where we find people trying to live in accord with the light that God has given—even though it may not be the fullness of light—there we see the influence of Christ to challenge the great and abominable church. The universal church meets people where they are—among Lehi's descendants in the ancient New World, but also in India, Korea, Russia, Argentina, America, Taiwan, Thailand, and Nigeria. Christ's church is found in small groups of people gathered together to worship, to learn, and to grow under the leadership of duly appointed teachers, priests, and elders. Thus, the church may gather in a building in Buenos Aires or Bangkok or Seoul, in a home in New Delhi or Moscow or inner-city Chicago, or perhaps even under a tree in Lagos.

In the end, the church is people, all trying to do the best they can while frequently falling short of God's call to them. Consequently, they all belong to the church of Christ, whose atonement transcends all human sins, frailties, inadequacies, and ultimately ushers those who are faithful into the presence of God—spotless by virtue of the blood of the Lamb.

4

Earth

The word *Earth* poses some interesting problems for a word study. It is a word which virtually all authors in the Book of Mormon use, with the exceptions of Enos, Mosiah, and Zeniff. Amulek, Captain Moroni, and Helaman each use the word only once, and therefore little can be said with any certainty about their understanding of the word. However, all the other authors use it at a rate of once or more per thousand words of their text. The Lord in the heavens uses the word *Earth* the most with a use ratio of 3.32 per thousand words of his text. Next in use frequency would be the Lord in Isaiah (3.01), Isaiah (2.94), Samuel (2.92), and the Father (2.74).

Authors with use ratios below 2.00 are Lehi (1.91), Moroni 2 (1.87), Nephi 2 (1.80), Ammon (1.75), Nephi 1 (1.73), Jesus (1.45), the Angel (1.44), Benjamin (1.42), Mormon (1.29—he also has the most numerical uses of the word), Abinadi (1.07), and Jacob (1.06). Finally, those below 1.00 but who still have a useful number of occurrences of the word *Earth* are Alma 2 (0.94) and Zenos (0.70).

As one first looks at the various ways the word *Earth* is used, no clear-cut lines seem to exist between the authors, except for Mormon, who has a different usage from everyone else. However, as one begins to read the various passages where the word appears and to group the usages into common categories, some distinctions begin to surface.

The categories that seem useful in distinguishing the ways in which the various authors used the word *Earth* are "God's acts,"

"Globe," "Inhabitants," "Ground," "Land," and "Values." The first category refers to the earth as the realm which God created or in which he acts. "Globe" denotes the place where humans dwell, and "Inhabitants" recognizes the earth as the place where humans act or are acted upon, either by God or by one another. "Ground" indicates that *Earth* may simply refer to the material upon which we walk. The last two categories are very small, with "Land" referring to a geographic region and "Values" indicating the "ways of the world." Figure 1 shows the various categories from a percentage standpoint, in the order in which I will discuss them.

	Without Mormon	With Mormon
God's acts	20.1%	16.0%
Globe	35.2%	28.2%
Inhabitants	17.2%	12.5%
Ground	22.1%	36.0%
Land	2.5%	5.1%
Values	2.9%	2.2%
	100.0%	100.0%

Figure 1

Mormon is excluded in the first column of figure 1 because his use of *Earth* is so different from the way the others use it. Inclusion of his statistics warps the use percentages of the other writers. In the second column of figure 1, one can see the dramatic shift in the percentages when Mormon's usage is included. Thus, *Earth* in the Book of Mormon will be explored under the above categories, with Mormon's uniqueness being highlighted.

God's Acts

The dominant emphasis in this category is on God as Creator. God created the earth, and having created it he also rules over it. His ruling may reflect either mercy or judgment. In figure 2 we can see the distribution by author of the various meanings of *Earth* in this category.

	Abinadi	Alma 2	Ammon	Angel	Benjamin	Father	Isaiah	Jacob	Jesus	Lehi	Lord	Lord-Isa	Mormon	Moroni 2	Nephi 1	Nephi 2	Samuel	Zenos
God comes to/in	1	-	-	-	-	-	3	-	-	-	-	-	-	-	-	-	-	-
God father of	1	-	-	-	-	-	-	-	-	-	1	-	-	-	1	-	1	-
God creates	-	-	1	-	2	-	-	3	-	3	2	3	-	2	1	-	-	-
God's mercy over	-	-	1	-	-	-	-	-	-	-	-	-	-	-	-	-	-	-
God over	-	-	-	1	1	-	-	-	-	-	-	-	-	-	-	-	-	-
God smites	-	-	-	-	-	-	1	-	-	-	-	-	-	-	1	-	-	-
God of	-	-	-	-	-	-	1	-	1	-	-	-	-	-	-	-	-	-
God commands	-	-	-	-	-	-	-	1	-	-	-	-	-	-	-	-	-	-
God has power over	-	-	-	-	-	-	-	1	-	-	-	-	-	-	-	-	-	-
God's footstool	-	-	-	-	-	-	-	-	1	-	-	-	-	-	1	-	-	-
God's will done in	-	-	-	-	-	-	-	-	1	-	-	-	-	-	-	-	-	-
God lord of	-	-	-	-	-	-	-	-	1	-	-	-	-	-	-	-	-	-
God's purposes on	-	-	-	-	-	-	-	-	-	-	-	1	-	-	-	-	-	-
God rules	-	-	-	-	-	-	-	-	-	-	1	-	-	-	-	-	-	-
God shakes	-	3	-	-	-	-	2	-	-	-	1	-	10	2	1	-	-	-

Figure 2: Earth—God's Acts

The most common emphasis among the authors in figure 2 is that God created the earth. It is worth noting, however, that two dominant authors in the Book of Mormon, Alma 2 and Mormon, have no references to God's activity in relation to the earth, except to note that God or an angel (in Alma's case) may shake the earth.

God as Creator

Lehi

Lehi speaks of God as Creator without relating this role to other attributes of God. Thus he indicates that those who fall away from the truth, having once experienced God's blessings and having a knowledge of God as Creator, will suffer God's judgments (2 Nephi 1:10). Further, if there were no God there would be no earth, for there could have been no creation (2 Nephi 2:13). Finally, Lehi affirms that God created all things in the heavens and on the earth (2 Nephi 2:14).

Moroni 2

Similarly, Moroni 2 asserts that God is Creator of the earth (Mormon 9:11, 17) as well as humankind, which is made from the dust of the earth (Mormon 9:17—*Earth* here meaning "ground"). In addition, he notes that through faith, Saints can cause the earth ("ground") to tremble by the power of God's word (Mormon 8:24).

Ammon

Some writers tie God's creative activity to his other attributes, particularly his mercy or his ruling power. Ammon, for example, asks king Lamoni whether he believes that God created the heavens and the earth (Alma 18:28); after they clarify who God is, Lamoni affirms his belief that God did in fact create the earth. Later, Ammon affirms to his brothers that the mercy of this same God is over all the earth (Alma 26:37).

Benjamin

King Benjamin states that God is Creator (Mosiah 4:9) and ties him as Creator with his divine attributes of wisdom, power, mercy, and justice, all of which are exercised both in heaven and on earth (Mosiah 4:9; 5:15).

Jacob

For Jacob, God—the Creator of the earth and humankind (Jacob 2:5; 4:8–9)—is also the God who is able to command his creation and have power within it (Jacob 4:9; 7:14).

The Lord in Isaiah

The Lord in Isaiah affirms that God is the Creator of the earth (2 Nephi 8:13, 16). Consequently, his purposes will be fulfilled on the earth (2 Nephi 24:26).

The Lord

The Lord heightens his role as Creator (Mosiah 8:13; 3 Nephi 9:15) by asserting that he is father of the earth (Ether 4:7) and thus has the right to rule over it (2 Nephi 29:7). That rule may even include the right to command the earth ("ground") to shake (Ether 4:9).

Nephi 1

Nephi 1 likewise identifies the Lord as Creator of the earth (1 Nephi 17:36) and Jesus as the father of the earth (2 Nephi 25:12) who rules over it. Thus the earth may be identified as the Lord's footstool (1 Nephi 17:39), and the earth ("ground") may shake at the sound of the Lord's voice (1 Nephi 17:45).

Samuel and Abinadi

Like Nephi 1, Samuel identifies Jesus as the father of the earth (Helaman 14:12). A similar situation appears with Abinadi, who identifies the Father and the Son as one God who is the father of heaven and earth (Mosiah 15:4). This is the same God who will come down among the earth's inhabitants (Mosiah 13:34).[1]

God as Ruler

Jesus

Jesus stresses that God rules over the earth, first making clear that he himself is the God of the whole earth (3 Nephi 11:14). However, in other places where he notes the ruling power of God, it seems to be the Father to whom he refers. When he tells his hearers not to swear by the earth, because it is God's footstool (3 Nephi 12:35), he appears to have the Father in mind as God. This is further supported when Jesus first teaches the Nephites to pray and to ask that the Father's will be done on earth as it is in heaven (3 Nephi 13:10). He also indicates that he will strengthen his people with whom the Father has covenanted, and that he, Jesus, will see that all things are consecrated to the Lord, i.e., to the Father (3 Nephi 20:19).

---

[1] The one time Amulek uses the word *Earth,* he identifies God as the father of it.

The Angel

The Angel makes one reference to God's lordship when he states that the Bible and the Book of Mormon will come together as one common witness to God, for there is only one God of the earth (1 Nephi 13:41). The implication is that although there may be two records, they will both bear witness of the same things, for they reflect the work of one God.

Isaiah

Finally, Isaiah has a strong sense of God's presence in the world. God's glory is in the world (2 Nephi 16:3). The earth will be full of the knowledge of the Lord in the millennium (2 Nephi 21:9), and God has done things which the inhabitants of the earth comprehend (2 Nephi 22:5). He is therefore God of the whole world (3 Nephi 22:5), but this means that he may in judgment smite the earth with his word (2 Nephi 21:4) and cause it to shake terribly (2 Nephi 12:19, 21).

In summary, God is the one who has created the earth and who rules over it. He rules in both mercy and justice. In his wrath, God may shake the earth to its very foundations. It should be noted in closing that Mormon has not been discussed in this section, largely because he makes no reference to God's creative activity or his rulership, except to mention that God's power can shake the earth. Mormon will be discussed as a separate category later in this chapter.

The Earth as the Globe

When Mormon is not included in the percentages, reference to the Earth as the globe is the largest category into which the use of the word *Earth* falls among the authors under consideration. Even with the inclusion of Mormon, this category still contains a significant percentage of the uses of *Earth*. Without the inclusion of Mormon, 91.3 percent of all uses of *Earth* in this category seem to refer to this planet or globe upon which people live and upon which God acts in relation to his people. Thus we see God acting upon, or people living on, the "face of the earth," people scattered to the "ends of the earth," the "four corners of the earth," the "four parts of the earth," and the "four quarters of the earth." The distribution may be seen in figure 3.

	Abinadi	Alma 2	Ammon	Angel	Benjamin	Father	Isaiah	Jacob	Jesus	Lehi	Lord	Lord-Isa	Mormon	Moroni 2	Nephi 1	Nephi 2	Samuel	Zenos
Face of (positive)	-	3	-	-	-	-	-	-	-	-	1	-	2	1	4	-	-	-
Face of (negative)	-	6	-	-	1	-	-	-	-	-	3	-	2	7	5	1	-	-
Ends of	-	1	-	-	-	-	4	-	3	-	6	2	2	3	2	-	-	-
Planet	-	1	-	-	-	-	-	-	-	-	2	3	10	2	8	-	-	-
Witnesses to God	-	1	-	-	-	-	-	-	-	-	-	-	-	-	-	1	-	-
Four corners of	-	-	-	-	-	-	1	-	-	-	-	-	-	-	-	-	-	-
At rest	-	-	-	-	-	-	1	-	-	-	-	-	-	-	-	-	-	-
Treasures of	-	-	-	-	-	-	-	-	1	-	-	-	-	-	-	-	-	-
Be joyful	-	-	-	-	-	-	-	-	-	-	-	1	-	-	-	-	-	-
Four parts of	-	-	-	-	-	-	-	-	-	-	1	-	-	-	-	-	-	-
Swear by	-	-	-	-	-	-	-	-	-	-	-	-	1	-	-	-	-	-
New	-	-	-	-	-	-	-	-	-	-	-	-	1	-	-	-	-	-
Four quarters of	-	-	-	-	-	-	-	-	-	-	1	-	2	1	1	-	-	-
World	-	-	-	-	-	-	-	-	-	-	-	-	-	-	3	-	-	1

Figure 3: Earth—Globe

From figure 3 it can be seen that there are both similarities and differences among the authors when *Earth* is considered to be the "globe." Several use the expression "the ends of the earth," while others use the phrase "the face of the earth" in either a positive or a negative context. Several authors also refer to the earth as a "planet." In addition, there is a scattering of individual expressions.

Face of the Earth

The phrase most commonly used in conjunction with *Earth* is "the face of." It is interesting that in two out of three instances there is a negative or threatening context with the phrase. Various writers, i.e., Alma 2, the Lord, Mormon, Moroni 2, Nephi 1, and Nephi 2, use the phrase.[2]

---

[2] Captain Moroni's one use of *Earth* appears with the phrase "the face of" and is in a negative context, i.e., he threatens to destroy Ammoron from off the face of the earth (Alma 54:12).

Alma 2

Alma 2 uses "face of the earth" predominantly in negative contexts. As he preaches to the people of Zarahemla, he asks whether they can imagine God inviting them to come to him because of their works of righteousness upon the face of the earth (Alma 5:16—positive context), or whether they imagine that they can lie to God about their works (Alma 5:17—negative context). While preaching in Ammonihah, Alma 2 reminds the people that if it had not been for God's patience, they would have been "cut off from the face of the earth" (Alma 9:11) long ago, and that if they do not repent now, they will be cut off (Alma 9:12, 24). It was precisely for their failure to repent that the Jaredites were destroyed (Alma 37:22). Finally, Adam and Eve were cut off from the tree of life and were thereby destined to suffer death or to "be cut off from the face of the earth" (Alma 42:6). On a more positive note, Alma 2 declares that angels have issued to all those scattered abroad a call to repentance in preparation for Christ's coming (Alma 13:22). And Alma 2 wishes that he could declare repentance and redemption to all so that there might be no more sorrow on the earth (Alma 29:2).

The Lord

When one turns to the words of the Lord, it is discovered that he promises to destroy from off the face of the earth those who do not repent among king Noah's people (Mosiah 12:8), among the Jaredites (Alma 37:25), and among the Nephites (Mormon 3:15). In a more positive vein, he promises the brother of Jared that he will raise up a great nation from him on the face of the earth (Ether 1:43).

Moroni 2

Moroni 2's use of "the face of the earth" is uniformly in negative contexts, with one exception in which he notes that rain came upon the land when the Jaredites, at one stage of their existence, finally repented (Ether 9:35). Otherwise, he states that at the time of the great tower, people were scattered on the face of the earth (Ether 1:33). Later, the Jaredites were dying because there was no rain (Ether 9:30), and there would be great destruction among them in the days of

Shiblom and Ethem if they did not change their ways (Ether 11:6–7, 12). In addition, in the days of Cohor, none of his sons or daughters on the face of the earth repented (Ether 13:17). Finally, the Book of Mormon would appear in a day when great pollutions covered the earth (Mormon 8:31).

Mormon

In two instances, Mormon notes that people were scattered on the face of the earth: the first use concerns the time of the great tower (Mosiah 28:17), the second concerns the scattered remnant of Israel (3 Nephi 5:24). In another place Mormon states that Jesus explained to the people of Bountiful the entirety of human history from its beginnings until his future return to the earth in glory (3 Nephi 26:3). Finally, Mormon tells us that the three Nephites ministered upon the face of the earth (3 Nephi 28:16).

Nephi 1

The majority of Nephi 1's uses of "face of" in negative contexts result from his concern for scattered Israel. Thus Israel is like an olive tree whose branches are scattered across the earth (1 Nephi 10:12), for the Lord promised that he would scatter it (1 Nephi 10:13). The Book of Mormon comes to Jews who are also scattered (1 Nephi 13:39). However, the power of God descends upon the scattered covenant people (1 Nephi 14:14) when they confront the great and abominable church which has adherents all over the earth (1 Nephi 14:13). More positively, in Lehi's first recorded vision the twelve who descended with the Savior traveled across the earth (1 Nephi 1:11). Later, Nephi 1 sees that though the church of the Lamb is small, its dominion still covers the earth (1 Nephi 14:12).

Nephi 2

Nephi 2 uses "face of" once in relation to the globe, when he tells the Nephites that their lands will be taken from them and that they will be destroyed from off the earth unless they repent (Helaman 7:28).

In summary, "face of the earth" is used numerous times by various authors, often in the context of people being scattered upon or removed from the earth. However, promises are given to those scattered or errant peoples which can give them hope.

Ends of the Earth

A significant number of authors use phrases other than "face of" to stress that things will happen across the earth. These phrases are "ends of," "four corners of," "four parts of," and "four quarters of."

Alma 2 wishes he were an angel so that he could proclaim the gospel to the ends of the earth (Alma 29:17). In the Isaiah passages, Jacob shall be gathered from the ends (2 Nephi 24:2) and the four corners (2 Nephi 21:12) of the earth, and the whole world shall see God's salvation (Mosiah 12:24; 3 Nephi 16:20). Jesus commands his disciples to preach the gospel to the ends of the earth (3 Nephi 11:41), quotes Isaiah as saying that the whole earth will see the Father's salvation (3 Nephi 20:35), and commands all the ends of the earth to repent (3 Nephi 27:20).

The Lord in Isaiah commands Israel to proclaim to the ends of the earth that God has redeemed Jacob (1 Nephi 20:20) and that the Messiah will be God's salvation to all the earth (1 Nephi 21:6). Similarly, the Lord commands the ends of the earth to repent (3 Nephi 9:22; Ether 4:18; Moroni 7:34) and to come to him (2 Nephi 26:25). Also, his words will go across the earth for a standard to Israel (2 Nephi 29:2), and the Lord will confirm his own words (Mormon 9:25). In addition, from the four quarters and the four parts of the earth, Israel will be gathered (1 Nephi 19:16; 2 Nephi 10:8).

Moroni 2 tells us that whatever one asks in the name of Christ will be granted, and that this is a promise given to the ends of the earth (Mormon 9:21). He states that the Lord showed the ends of the earth to the brother of Jared (Ether 3:25) and that those washed in the blood of the Lamb will be gathered from the four quarters of the earth (Ether 13:11). Moroni 2 himself speaks to the ends of the earth (Moroni 10:24). In a similar way, Mormon writes to the ends of the earth (Mormon 3:18) and desires that he could persuade all to repent (Mormon 3:22). He also has concern for scattered Israel, for it will ultimately be gathered from the four quarters of the earth (3 Nephi 5:24, 26). Nephi 1 also notes this gathering which will occur from the four quarters of the earth (1 Nephi 22:25), and summons his brethren, the Jews, the House of Israel, and the ends of the earth to accept Christ (2 Nephi 33:10, 13).

Planet Earth

Mormon

In a number of instances, it appears that the authors are referring to the earth as a planet. One of the clearest references occurs in Mormon's writing. In Helaman 12, Mormon discusses the power of God and how various things respond to His commands; God has created people (Helaman 12:6), the dust of the earth moves at his command (Helaman 12:8), hills and mountains tremble and break up, and the earth shakes at the sound of his voice (Helaman 12:9–12). Then Mormon reports the following:

> Yea, and if he say unto the earth—Move—it is moved. Yea, if he say unto the earth—Thou shalt go back, that it lengthen out the day for many hours—it is done; And thus, according to his word the earth goeth back, and it appeareth unto man that the sun standeth still; yea, and behold, this is so; for surely it is the earth that moveth and not the sun. (Helaman 12:13–15)

Clearly, Mormon is talking about the earth as a planet which moves around the sun. Other instances in his writing where the idea of a planet seems to be in view are Nehor's acknowledgment of guilt which occurred "between the heavens and the earth" (Alma 1:15), Jesus' garments becoming whiter than anything on earth (3 Nephi 19:25), the earth being wrapped up as a scroll and passing away (3 Nephi 26:3; Mormon 5:23), and the power of the Holy Ghost remaining as long as the earth stands (Moroni 7:36).

Nephi 1

Nephi 1 uses *Earth* to mean "planet" proportionately more than Mormon. God's power can cause the earth to pass away (1 Nephi 17:46). Joseph's seed will never pass away as long as the earth shall stand (2 Nephi 25:21–22). The sealed portion of the Book of Mormon will reveal everything to people down to the end of the earth (2 Nephi

27:11). Also, God will bring about a restoration of his people upon the earth (2 Nephi 30:8), nothing is sealed on the earth except it be loosed (2 Nephi 30:17), and what God's servants seal on earth shall be brought against persons at the last judgment (2 Nephi 33:15). Nephi 1 uses *Earth* with a slightly different but closely related meaning to that of "planet" when he says that the whore of all the earth had dominion over the earth (1 Nephi 14:11), that the Lord will "judge the poor, and reprove with equity for the meek of the earth" (2 Nephi 30:9), and that "the earth shall be full of the knowledge of the Lord" (2 Nephi 30:15). Clearly, the last two instances are quotations from Isaiah, but even so, in all three verses *Earth* seems to mean people, human enterprises, or values that are found on the face of the planet.

Others

When Moroni 2 refers to the earth as a planet, it is either in the context of the earth passing away (Mormon 9:2; Ether 13:8) or of a new earth coming into being (Ether 13:9). Twice the Lord refers to the earth standing in contrast to heaven (Mosiah 12:36; 13:12), and in Isaiah he refers to the earth as that which will pass away or be destroyed (2 Nephi 8:6; 23:13). Alma 2 uses *Earth* once to have this same meaning (Alma 5:16).

In this section, we have sought those uses of *Earth* which clearly refer, without other connotations, to the globe which revolves around the sun. It is this latter definition which is of interest here. And as has been seen, Mormon, Nephi 1, Moroni 2, the Lord, and the Lord in Isaiah clearly use *Earth* in this sense.

Miscellaneous

There are five miscellaneous uses of the word *Earth* meaning "globe" in a general sense. The earth witnesses to God's existence (Alma 2—Alma 30:44), is at rest (Isaiah—2 Nephi 24:7), should be joyful (Lord in Isaiah—1 Nephi 21:13), and was sworn by (Moroni—Ether 8:14). Finally, Jesus tells people not to lay up treasures upon the earth (3 Nephi 13:19).

Earth

In summary, various writers refer to the earth in a sense that can be defined as the "globe." People live and events occur on the face of it, to its ends, and in its four parts, quarters, and corners. In some instances, *Earth* may even refer to the planet earth which revolves around the sun.

Inhabitants of the Earth

Some authors clearly refer to the people who live on the earth, but the usages are quite disparate and individual, as figure 4 demonstrates.

	Abinadi	Alma 2	Ammon	Angel	Benjamin	Father	Isaiah	Jacob	Jesus	Lehi	Lord	Lord-Isa	Mormon	Moroni 2	Nephi 1	Nephi 2	Samuel	Zenos
Will see salvation	1	-	-	-	-	-	-	-	-	-	-	-	-	-	-	-	-	-
Abr's seed blesses	-	-	-	-	-	2	-	-	-	-	-	-	-	-	-	-	-	-
People of	-	-	-	-	-	1	-	-	-	-	-	1	-	-	-	-	-	-
Midst of	-	-	-	-	-	-	1	-	-	-	-	-	-	-	-	-	-	-
Trouble	-	-	-	-	-	-	1	-	-	-	-	-	-	-	-	-	-	-
Meek of	-	-	-	-	-	-	1	-	1	-	-	-	-	-	-	-	-	-
Chief ones of	-	-	-	-	-	-	1	-	-	-	-	-	-	-	-	-	-	-
People of tremble	-	-	-	-	-	-	1	-	-	-	-	-	-	-	-	-	-	-
Nation(s) of/on	-	-	-	-	-	-	-	1	-	-	2	-	-	-	-	-	-	-
Salt of	-	-	-	-	-	-	-	-	1	-	-	-	-	-	-	-	-	-
Remnant of	-	-	-	-	-	-	-	-	3	-	-	-	-	-	-	-	-	-
Gathered people of	-	-	-	-	-	-	-	-	-	-	1	1	-	-	-	-	-	-
Inhabitants of	-	-	-	-	-	-	-	-	-	2	2	-	-	1	1	-	-	-
Family of	-	-	-	-	-	-	-	-	-	1	-	-	-	-	-	-	-	-
Kindreds of	-	-	-	-	-	-	-	-	-	-	2	-	-	-	2	-	-	-
Smite the	-	-	-	-	-	-	-	-	-	-	1	-	-	-	-	-	-	-
Seal on	-	-	-	-	-	-	-	-	-	-	1	-	-	-	-	-	-	-
Loose on	-	-	-	-	-	-	-	-	-	-	1	-	-	-	-	-	-	-
Wickedness of	-	-	-	-	-	-	-	-	-	-	1	-	-	-	-	-	-	-
Land(s) of	-	-	-	-	-	-	-	-	-	-	1	-	-	-	1	-	-	-
(Die) like other people	-	-	-	-	-	-	-	-	-	1	-	-	4	1	-	-	-	-
Multitudes of	-	-	-	-	-	-	-	-	-	-	-	-	-	-	3	-	-	-

Figure 4: Earth—Inhabitants of

As can be seen, one finds few repetitions of words which identify the earth's inhabitants, even within the same author. The most used phrase is "inhabitants of the earth," but even so it is only used six times: twice by Lehi, twice by the Lord, once by Moroni 2, and once by Nephi 1. Thus we will see a blend of usages in this section.

Abinadi states that all the ends of the earth will see salvation (Mosiah 15:31). The Father says that Abraham's seed will bless the kindreds of the earth (3 Nephi 20:25, 27) and that when the Gentiles shall be lifted up in pride above all the peoples of the earth, the fullness of the gospel will be taken from them (3 Nephi 16:10). Isaiah sees trouble and anguish on the earth (2 Nephi 28:22), states that God will deal justly with the meek of the earth (2 Nephi 21:4), indicates that those "chief ones" who are dead will be raised up at the time of the restoration of Israel (2 Nephi 24:9), and mocks Lucifer who once made the people of the earth tremble (2 Nephi 24:16).

Jacob refers to the Jews as the only nation on earth that would crucify its God (2 Nephi 10:3). Jesus calls those who follow him the salt of the earth (3 Nephi 12:12–13) and promises that remnants of Israel which are scattered on the earth will be gathered (3 Nephi 16:4–5; 20:13). Likewise, the Lord in Isaiah is concerned with the gathering of scattered Israel (1 Nephi 21:8; 2 Nephi 20:14). In other places in the Book of Mormon, the Lord affirms that the kindreds of the earth shall be blessed through Abraham (1 Nephi 15:18; 22:9), that the Jews, when they believe in Jesus, will be restored in the flesh to their lands (2 Nephi 10:7), that those inhabitants of the earth who repent will not be destroyed (2 Nephi 28:17; 3 Nephi 9:2), that Nephi 2 has been given the sealing power to smite the earth with famine and pestilence (Helaman 10:6–7), and that the inhabitants of the city of Jacob were destroyed because their wickedness was greater than that of the whole earth (3 Nephi 9:9).

Lehi asserts that God's power is over all the inhabitants of the earth (1 Nephi 1:14), that the family of the earth arose from Adam and Eve (2 Nephi 2:20), and that the gospel must be proclaimed to the inhabitants of the earth (2 Nephi 2:8). He also says, "I go the way of all the earth," meaning that he must die (2 Nephi 1:14). The *only* way Mormon uses *Earth,* with reference to its inhabitants, is in this last sense in which Lehi uses it, i.e., with reference to death. Mormon uses it in this way four times (Mosiah 1:9; Alma 1:1; 62:37; Helaman

1:2). The only other person with this usage is Mormon's son, Moroni, when he tells us that Corom died (Ether 10:17). Yet whereas Mormon says that people go "the way of all the earth,"[3] Moroni 2 notes that Corom "did pass away, even like unto the rest of the earth." Moroni 2 speaks one other time of the inhabitants of the earth when he says that the Lord showed them to the brother of Jared (Ether 3:25).

Finally, Nephi 1 saw the "multitudes of the earth" who were gathered to fight against the apostles and who went into the great and spacious building (1 Nephi 11:34–35), as well as the multitudes of Nephites and Lamanites who were gathered to fight one another (1 Nephi 12:13–15). Among the kindreds of the nations, Nephi 1 saw wars and rumors of wars (1 Nephi 14:15) but noted that the kindreds could be blessed if the Lord bared his arm (1 Nephi 22:10). In a similar vein, Gentiles and Jews alike will one day be wicked upon all the lands of the earth (2 Nephi 27:1), and the day will come when the Lord will visit the inhabitants of the earth in judgment (2 Nephi 28:16).

Thus, as indicated at the beginning of this section, there are several ways in which the authors talk about the inhabitants of the earth. There seems to be no particular pattern, but there are rather highly individualistic ways of saying much the same things about the peoples of the earth. An interesting anomaly is Mormon, who is not interested in speaking of the world's inhabitants with the word *Earth,* except that he uses the phrase "the way of all the earth" to indicate the death of people.

The Earth as the "Ground"

Among the various authors, there are a few scattered references to the earth meaning the "ground," either as that to which people relate in some way,[4] i.e., they fall on it, sit on it, etc., or as that stuff of which the earth is composed and which may bear fruit, be smitten, bear seeds, etc. We see this distribution in figures 5 and 6.

---

[3] In chapter 6, which speaks of "Land" and "Lands," we will see that Mormon has a very individual trait, i.e., he uses expansive terminology, often speaking of "all" the land, just as he here speaks of "all" the earth.

[4] In Helaman's one use, he rejoices when he finds that not one of his stripling warriors had fallen to the earth in battle (Alma 56:56).

	Abinadi	Alma 2	Ammon	Angel	Benjamin	Father	Isaiah	Jacob	Jesus	Lehi	Lord	Lord-Isa	Mormon	Moroni 2	Nephi 1	Nephi 2	Samuel	Zenos
Fall to	-	3	-	-	-	-	-	2	-	-	-	-	26	2	3	-	1	-
Smite to	-	-	1	-	-	-	-	-	-	-	-	-	3	-	-	-	-	-
As dust of	-	-	-	-	3	-	-	1	-	-	-	-	3	-	-	-	-	-
Return to	-	-	-	-	-	-	-	-	-	-	-	-	-	-	-	-	-	-
Face to	-	-	-	-	-	-	-	-	-	-	-	2	-	-	-	-	-	-
Till	-	-	-	-	-	-	-	-	-	1	-	-	2	3	-	-	-	-
Man from	-	-	-	-	-	-	-	-	-	-	-	-	-	1	-	-	-	-
Prostrate on	-	-	-	-	-	-	-	-	-	-	-	-	4	-	-	-	-	-
Raise from	-	-	-	-	-	-	-	-	-	-	-	-	2	-	-	-	-	-
Bowed to	-	-	-	-	-	-	-	-	-	-	-	-	4	-	-	-	-	-
Level to (kill)	-	-	-	-	-	-	-	-	-	-	-	-	2	-	-	-	-	-
Cut down to (kill)	-	-	-	-	-	-	-	-	-	-	-	-	1	-	-	-	-	-
Kneel upon	-	-	-	-	-	-	-	-	-	-	-	-	4	-	-	-	-	-
Sit on	-	-	-	-	-	-	-	-	-	-	-	-	1	-	-	-	-	-

Figure 5: Earth—As Related to Humans

	Abinadi	Alma 2	Ammon	Angel	Benjamin	Father	Isaiah	Jacob	Jesus	Lehi	Lord	Lord-Isa	Mormon	Moroni 2	Nephi 1	Nephi 2	Samuel	Zenos
In ground	-	-	1	-	-	-	-	-	-	-	4	-	7	5	1	1	-	-
Caves of	-	-	-	-	-	-	1	-	-	-	-	-	-	-	-	-	-	-
Fruit of	-	-	-	-	-	-	1	-	-	-	-	-	-	-	-	-	-	-
Surface of	-	-	-	-	-	-	1	-	-	1	1	-	1	-	-	-	2	-
Seeds of	-	-	-	-	-	-	-	-	-	1	-	-	-	-	-	-	-	-
Dirt	-	-	-	-	-	-	-	-	-	-	-	-	9	2	3	-	-	-
Face of	-	-	-	-	-	-	-	-	-	-	-	-	3	-	-	1	-	-
Is smitten	-	-	-	-	-	-	-	-	-	-	-	-	2	-	-	-	-	-
Ground	-	-	-	-	-	-	-	-	-	-	-	-	5	-	1	-	1	1
Smite	-	-	-	-	-	-	-	-	-	-	-	-	1	-	-	-	-	-
God shakes	-	3	-	-	-	-	2	-	-	-	1	-	10	2	1	-	-	-

Figure 6: Earth—Ground as Ground

As can be seen from figures 5 and 6, the majority of authors have only marginal interest in the earth as ground, with one exception—Mormon. A total of 71.4 percent of all Mormon's uses of *Earth* refer to the ground. Therefore, we will examine the occurrences of earth meaning "ground" in all authors except Mormon, and then we will examine the way in which he uses the word.

People and the Ground

Alma 2 tells us that after his experience with the angel, whose voice shook the earth (Alma 36:7; 38:7), he fell to the earth (Alma 36:7, 10–11). He also wishes he could speak with a voice that would shake the earth (Alma 29:1). Ammon threatens to smite king Lamoni's father to the earth, i.e., kill him (Alma 20:24). Benjamin tells us that people are created from the dust of the earth, that he is about to return to the earth, and that people are less than the dust (Mosiah 2:25–26). In a like manner, Jacob tells us that if there had been no Atonement, our flesh would have simply crumbled to mother earth, never to rise again (2 Nephi 9:7). Jacob also states that when the power of God came upon Sherem, Sherem fell to the earth (Jacob 7:15); after Sherem told the people that he had lied to them and to God, the power of God fell on the people, who then also fell to the earth (Jacob 7:21). This event pleased Jacob, for he knew God was working to change the people's hearts.

In addition, the Lord in Isaiah tells Israel that in the last days kings and queens shall bow before Israel with their faces to the earth (1 Nephi 21:23; 2 Nephi 6:7). Lehi states that Adam and Eve, after being driven out of the garden, tilled the earth (2 Nephi 2:19). Nephi 1 indicates that Laban had fallen to the earth (1 Nephi 4:7), that he (Nephi) saw many cities which had tumbled to the earth (1 Nephi 12:4), and that the whore of all the earth must fall to the earth (2 Nephi 28:18). Samuel states that when the signs of Christ's birth are given, people will fall to the earth in wonder (Helaman 14:7).

Finally, Moroni 2 is the only author, apart from Mormon, who seems to have a significant interest in using the word *Earth* to mean "ground." While his interest is not as high as Mormon's, since only 44.4 percent of his uses of *Earth* refer to "ground," it is still interesting that it is father and son who differ so distinctly from all the other authors being considered in their usage of *Earth*.

Moroni 2 tells us that the brother of Jared fell to the ground after seeing the Lord's spirit body (Ether 3:7), and that Coriantumr fell to the ground after his battle with Shiz (Ether 15:32). Further, people till the earth (Ether 6:13, 18; 10:25), humans were created from the dust of the earth (Mormon 9:17), and people may have such great faith that they can cause the earth to shake and prisons to fall to the earth (Mormon 8:24).

The Ground as the Essence of the Earth

The most common way in which the authors speak of the ground is when something is said to be *in* the ground. Ammon speaks of his Lamanite converts burying their weapons in the ground (Alma 26:32). The Lord warns that those who hide treasures in the earth will not find them again (Helaman 13:18) and later reveals that the inhabitants of Moronihah, Gilgal, and other cities have been buried in the depths of the earth (3 Nephi 9:5–6, 8). In other instances he speaks of the water under the earth (Mosiah 13:12), commands the brother of Jared to collect the seeds of the earth (Ether 1:41), and states that at his word the earth will shake (Ether 4:9).

Nephi 1 warns that those who kill the prophets and Saints shall be swallowed in the depths of the earth (2 Nephi 26:5). He also refers to earth as "dirt." Nephi 1's people began to till the earth and plant seeds in the plowed earth (1 Nephi 18:24). He also states that were the Lord to command him to change water to earth, i.e., dirt, he could do so (1 Nephi 17:50). Finally, he tells his brothers that God shook the earth to get their attention (1 Nephi 17:45), and in vision he sees the earth (ground) convulsing and rending (1 Nephi 12:4). Nephi 2 reports to the Lord that the Gadianton robbers have been destroyed in the land and that their secret plans are buried in the earth (Helaman 11:10). He requests also that rain fall on the face of the earth (Helaman 11:13).

Moroni 2 refers four times to the records, on which he is working, being put in the earth or being drawn from the earth (Mormon 8:4, 16, 26; Ether 4:3). One time he speaks of ore in the earth which, in the process of its being mined, resulted in heaps of earth being thrown up (Ether 10:23). Similarly, Moroni 2 tells us that the prophets in the days of Shiblom testified that unless the people changed their ways, their bones would become like heaps of earth upon the face of the land (Ether 11:6).

Authors who speak of earth as ground, but do not refer to anything being in it, are Isaiah, Lehi, Samuel, and Zenos. Isaiah speaks of caves of the earth (2 Nephi 12:19), of the fruit of the earth

(2 Nephi 14:2), of waters which would not again cover the earth as in the days of Noah (3 Nephi 22:9), and of God shaking the earth (2 Nephi 12:19, 21). Lehi says that the great and spacious building was high above the earth (1 Nephi 8:26). Samuel prophesies that at the time of Jesus' death, the earth will shake, tremble, and split (Helaman 14:21–22); Zenos predicts the same thing (1 Nephi 19:11).

Earth in Mormon

As already indicated, 71.4 percent of all Mormon's uses of *Earth* mean ground. Of those usages, 57.8 percent refer to people in relationship to the ground, and 42.2 percent refer to the ground as the essence of the earth, thus making Mormon distinctly different from all other authors with the possible exception of his son, who may have been influenced by his father's language. We will examine Mormon under the same two categories used with the other authors.

Mormon's dominant use is to say that people or things (such as scalps, prison walls, or buildings) fall to the earth, a statement he makes twenty-six times.[5] Related uses are that people prostrate themselves on the earth (Alma 19:17–18; 22:17; 24:21), bow down on it (Alma 46:13; 3 Nephi 1:11; 19:19, 27), rise from it (Alma 22:22; 3 Nephi 17:20), kneel on it (3 Nephi 17:14; 19:6, 16–17), and sit on it (3 Nephi 18:2). In a similar vein, people or their weapons may be smitten to the earth (Alma 20:16; 44:12; 51:20), leveled to the earth (Alma 51:17–18), or cut down to the earth (Helaman 1:24). More peaceful uses include Benjamin's people tilling the earth (Mosiah 6:7) and comparing people to the dust of the earth (Mosiah 4:2). Mormon also states that people are not as obedient as the dust (Helaman 12:7–8). A number of things are said by Mormon to be in the earth. The weapons of the Anti-Nephi-Lehies are buried in the earth (Alma 24:17), bodies are in the earth (Alma 28:11), treasures may be in the earth (Helaman 12:18; Mormon 1:18), Saints are spared from burial

---

[5] *People:* Mosiah 4:1; 27:12, 18; Alma 14:27; 18:42; 19:16–17; 27:17; 47:24; Helaman 9:3–5, 7; 3 Nephi 1:16–17; 4:8; 11:12. *Things:* Alma 14:27–29; 44:12; Helaman 5:27, 31; 3 Nephi 4:28; 8:14.

in the earth (3 Nephi 10:13), and the three Nephites are thrown into pits in the earth (3 Nephi 28:20).

For Mormon, *Earth* also means "dirt." The Nephites built up great banks of earth to protect their cities (Alma 48:8; 49:4, 22; 50:1–2; 53:4). But earth may also be used to destroy cities, as we see at the time of Jesus' crucifixion (3 Nephi 8:10). We also return to the earth at death (Mormon 6:15).

In addition, the surface of the earth is referred to when it is recorded that the bones of peoples were heaped upon the earth (Lamanites—Alma 2:38; 28:11; Ammonihahites—Alma 16:11) or that it rains upon the earth (Helaman 11:17). The earth (ground) is also that which shakes and is torn apart at the time of Jesus' crucifixion (3 Nephi 8:17, 19; 10:14) or that which comes back together (3 Nephi 10:10).

God's power may be felt through natural means when he chooses to smite the earth with drought (Helaman 11:6), when others use his power to deliver themselves from the earth (3 Nephi 28:20), or when God shakes the earth to get the attention of people, either through his angel who appeared to Alma 2 and the sons of Mosiah (Mosiah 27:11, 18), or when he does it himself to open a prison (Alma 14:27; Helaman 5:27, 31–33, 42), or to demonstrate his power (Helaman 12:11).

In summary, Mormon has the richest vocabulary when *Earth* means "ground." In that he is unique.

Land

Only three writers use *Earth* to mean a "land" or "region." These authors are Samuel, Nephi 1, and Mormon. In each instance, the region referred to is the New World. Samuel speaks of the rocks on the face of *this* earth—the New World—being broken up, of cracks and fragments on the face of the whole land, and of the darkness that will cover the face of the earth (Helaman 14:21–22, 27). Nephi 1 speaks of exactly the same things because he sees them in a vision (1 Nephi 12:4–5). In addition, Samuel states that the Lamanites will be driven about on the face of the earth (Helaman 15:12). All of these passages apparently refer to the New World.

Most striking is Mormon's use of *Earth* to refer to the New World, for we have already seen that he is the author who emphasizes the Church in the New World. In the present context, Mormon talks about the Nephite people spreading over the face of the earth (Mosiah 27:6; Helaman 3:8). He tells us that Alma 2 blessed the earth for the sake of the righteous (Alma 45:15). The Nephites were hunted, murdered, plundered, and driven forth upon the face of the earth (Helaman 3:16). The righteous Lamanites sought to drive the Gadianton robbers from off the face of the earth (Helaman 6:20). The Nephites "on the face of the whole earth" were astonished by the signs of Jesus' birth (3 Nephi 1:17). Only when *Earth* means "New World" do these passages make any sense.

Finally, Mormon tells of the destruction that occurred at the time of Jesus' death. The thunder shook the whole earth (3 Nephi 8:6). The face of the land was changed because of the tempests and the great quaking of the earth (3 Nephi 8:12). The face of the whole earth was deformed (3 Nephi 8:17–18). All the inhabitants "of the earth, upon all the face of *this* land" heard a voice pronouncing woes (3 Nephi 9:1; emphasis added). The darkness dispersed from off the land and the earth ceased to tremble (3 Nephi 10:9). Once again, the region referred to must be the New World. Thus Mormon has a New World emphasis on *Earth* which supports what we have observed already under his use of *Church*.

Values

There are a few usages of the word *Earth* which occur in conjunction with words that refer to values, particularly the values of the earth as opposed to those of heaven. For example, Alma 2 tells his son Helaman that if he will do what God commands him to do, no power of earth or hell can take the sacred objects from him (Alma 37:16). Similarly, Mormon tells us that Satan could have no power over the three Nephites once a change had come upon them, that they were holy, and that the "powers of the earth could not hold them" (3 Nephi 28:39).

The three authors who were concerned about the great and abominable church (the Angel, Nephi 1, and the Lord) in the study on *Church/Churches* are also those who refer to it in relationship to *Earth*. The Angel refers to the great and abominable church as the whore of all the earth (1 Nephi 14:10) and notes that when God's wrath is poured out on this church, then the Father will be preparing the way for the fulfilling of his covenants (1 Nephi 14:17). Similarly, Nephi 1 refers three times to the "whore of all the earth" which he sees in vision and which is the great and abominable church. She has dominion over the earth (1 Nephi 14:11), causes warfare among those who have followed her (1 Nephi 22:13), and must ultimately fall (2 Nephi 28:18). Finally, the Lord states that whoever fights against Zion will perish, for they are the whore of all the earth (2 Nephi 10:16).

Conclusions

Author Individuality

The various authors use the word *Earth* in many ways. There are some commonalities in that many refer to God as the Creator of the earth, use similar phrases like "face of" or "ends of" the earth, and refer to the earth as the planet earth. But here the commonalities end and individualities begin. There are not enough repetitions of these individualities that one can say with certainty that such meanings are truly unique to the various authors. However, the diversity does seem to indicate a certain degree of individuality.

If we look back over the various charts included in the text above, we note that there are distinct differences among the authors when different categories are assigned to the meaning of *Earth*. Authors such as Alma 2, Mormon, Nephi 2, and Zenos all have meanings related to the earth as the globe, while Abinadi, Ammon, the Angel, Benjamin, the Father, Jacob, Lehi, and Samuel have no uses in this category of meaning. We see another distribution of word use when we look at the category called "Inhabitants of the Earth." There the Father uses language that others do not.

Finally, if one looks once again at figures 5 and 6, it becomes clear how different Mormon's uses of *Earth* are from those of any other author. Clearly, the writer most closely allied with Mormon is his son Moroni, but as noted above, even Moroni 2 does not use *Earth* to mean "ground" to the degree that Mormon does. From all that has been said above, it seems clear that Mormon uses the word *Earth* very differently from all other authors, including the authors he edits.

Mormon's word use breaks down as follows:

Ground	71.4%
Globe	14.3%
God's acts	0.0%
New World	10.3%
Die like others	3.2%
Powers of the world	0.8%

Figure 7

Clearly, figure 7 indicates the differences between Mormon and the other authors. As figure 1 showed, without Mormon, "Ground" was only 22.1 percent, whereas "Globe" was 35.2 percent, "God's acts" was 20.1 percent, "Land" (equivalent to New World) was 2.5 percent, "Inhabitants of the Earth" (equivalent to "Die like others") was 17.2 percent, and "Values" (equivalent to "Powers of the world") was 2.9 percent. Thus, if this study has shown nothing else, it has highlighted how individualistic Mormon is when compared to his fellow authors.

Theological Implications

It is clear that *Earth* may refer to a variety of things. Probably the least useful theological category is "Ground." The others, however, can give us some insights into God's workings on the earth. First, the earth is God's creation. He does not walk away from it but populates it with his children, with whom he constantly interacts throughout history. It is to those who live on the earth that God gives commands and extends his mercy. It is they whom he rules and ultimately destroys, if necessary, in an act of justice. Thus, this globe is no piece of space junk, aimlessly following an orbit. Rather, it is a unique creation of God designed for his children, a creation which we know he will finally bring to its full celestial glory.

5

Israel

In the study on the Ancient Near East word group in chapter 1, it was seen that only some of the Book of Mormon persons used words from that group with a normalized number in excess of 1.00. Those authors or speakers are noted in figure 1:

Author	Normalized #
Father	5.07
Lord-Isa	4.36
Angel	4.06
Isaiah	3.68
Nephi1:S	2.47
Jacob	1.96
Lord	1.96
Nephi 2	1.74
Lehi	1.66
Mormon:S	1.65
Abinadi	1.55
Jesus	1.50
Moroni2:S	1.25
Nephi1:N1	1.14

Figure 1: Use of Ancient Near East Word Cluster

Not all of the above, however, used the word *Israel*. Their tie to the Ancient Near East cluster came through the use of other words. For example, Nephi 2 uses "Abraham," "Egyptians," "Isaiah," "Israelites," "Jeremiah," "Messiah," "Moses," and "Zedekiah," thus qualifying himself for inclusion among those whose writings have

Near East words. However, he does not use *Israel* and therefore is not part of the current study. Similarly, Abinadi uses "Isaiah," "Messiah," "Moses,"[1] "Sinai," and "Zion." He uses *Israel* one time,[2] but a single use is insufficient for us to consider his usage significant for the current study. Ammon also uses it only one time,[3] but in contrast to Abinadi, Ammon's use reflects no emphasis on the Near East word group, since his normalized use rate for it is 0.22.

As noted in chapter 1, it was primarily those persons who were closest to the Near Eastern culture who used that word cluster. A similar relationship is apparent in the study of the word *Israel*. Figure 2 shows two things: (1) those who use the word *Israel* and the use rate per thousand words of their text, and (2) those who use the word and their percentage of the total uses of *Israel*.

Author	Per 1000
Father	10.95
Angel	5.30
Isaiah	4.06
Jacob	3.28
Lord	2.27
Jesus	1.97
Lord-Isa	1.51
Nephi 1	1.48
Zenos	1.41
Lehi	0.85
Ammon	0.44
Abinadi	0.36
Moroni 2	0.26
Mormon	0.15

Author	Percent
Nephi 1	19.2
Isaiah	14.8
Jacob	13.8
Lord	12.8
Jesus	9.4
Mormon	7.4
Father	5.9
Angel	4.9
Lord-Isa	3.4
Zenos	3.0
Moroni 2	2.5
Lehi	2.0
Abinadi	0.5
Ammon	0.5

Figure 2: Israel

Note that the divine figures (for whom Israel is a special people) and persons recently removed from the Near East use the word *Israel* the most per thousand words of their text. When one examines the

---

[1] Abinadi uses "Moses" eleven times.

[2] In Mosiah 13:29 Abinadi states that it was necessary that a strict law be given to Israel, because they were a people prone to do evil.

[3] In Alma 26:36 Ammon says that God has been mindful of the Nephites and Lamanites as a branch of *Israel* who are wanderers in a strange land.

percent of numerical use, it is still these same figures that appear, with some slight variations in order, because Nephi 1 and Mormon have large numbers of occurrences owing to the large size of their writings.

As interesting as the examination of those who use *Israel* may be, it is also important to note which writers and speakers do not use it. Those who never use the word are Alma 2, Amulek, Benjamin, Captain Moroni, Enos, Helaman, Mosiah, Samuel, and Zeniff. All of these individuals were removed in time from the Near Eastern culture, and the fact that they do not use *Israel* only reinforces what has already been seen in chapter 1 concerning the Ancient Near East word cluster. As we examine Mormon and Moroni 2's writings later in this chapter, we will attempt to determine why they, removed as they were from the Near East, should have been concerned with Israel.

In the materials that follow, we will examine the use of the word *Israel* in the following order: the heavenly or divine figures,[4] prophetic figures of the plates of brass, Lehi and his sons, and Mormon and Moroni 2. Each author will be examined in light of the various word phrases he uses with *Israel* and then with reference to various categories of meaning that surround *Israel*.

Words or Phrases Used in Conjunction with *Israel*

As we examine the Angel, the Father, Jesus, the Lord in Isaiah, and the Lord who speaks from the heavens, we will look first at the words and phrases that are used in conjunction with the word *Israel*. Figure 3 shows the distribution of those phrases.

Note that the principal concern of the divine figures is with the people of Israel. They all use, relatively often, the phrase "house of Israel." Interestingly, the resurrected Jesus and the Lord are the only figures of this group who speak about the "people of the house of Israel." In addition, they are the only ones of the group who speak of the "God of Israel," the "tribes of the house of Israel," and the "lost tribes of Israel." While Jesus speaks in one place of the "remnant of the house of Israel," the Lord speaks twice of the "remnant of Israel." The only real difference between Jesus and the Lord lies in the fact

---

[4] While the Angel is not technically divine, he will be included in this designation.

that the Lord speaks once of the "Holy One of Israel," and Jesus speaks once of "my people Israel." Thus, the same person speaks in the same language, whether that person speaks from the heavens as the Lord or appears among the Nephites at Bountiful as the resurrected Jesus. Given the complexity of the Book of Mormon, it seems improbable that any one person could have created these similarities, especially since the passages from which the above information was drawn are found in various places in 1 Nephi, 2 Nephi, Jacob, 3 Nephi, Mormon, and Ether.

	Angel	Father	Jesus	Lord	Lord-Isa
House of	9	12	2	8	3
Tribes, house of	-	-	1	1	-
People, house of	-	-	12	11	-
Children of	-	-	-	-	-
12 tribes of	1	-	-	-	-
People of	-	-	-	-	-
Both houses of	-	-	-	-	-
Nation of	-	-	-	-	-
Escaped of	-	-	-	-	-
Preserved of	-	-	-	-	1
King of	-	-	-	-	-
Remnant of	-	-	-	2	-
Outcasts of	-	-	-	-	-
Lost tribes of	-	-	1	2	-
Remnant, house of	-	-	1	-	-
Scattered tribes of	-	-	-	-	-
God of	-	-	1	1	-
Holy One of	-	-	-	1	-
Redeemer of	-	-	-	-	1
Mighty One of	-	-	-	-	-
My people	-	-	1	-	-
My called of	-	-	-	-	1
My servant	-	-	-	-	1

Figure 3: Israel

None of the divine figures seems especially interested in speaking about himself. There is little mention by these figures of "the God of Israel," the "Holy One of Israel," or the "Mighty One of Israel." The Lord in Isaiah does speak once of the "Redeemer of Israel."

Israel by Itself—Categories of Meaning

As we examine the categories into which *Israel* falls, we will also turn to the specific texts in which the word appears. First, however, it will be helpful to see in graphic form how the word is used. Note that the first group of categories in figure 4 deals with Israel as an earthly people, while the second group deals with Israel in relationship to God's actions upon her.

	Angel	Father	Jesus	Lord	Lord-Isa
Nation	2	1	1	2	4
Spiritual entity	3	7	4	3	2
Covenant with	5	2	5	3	-
Scattered	-	2	3	11	-
Lehites, part of	1	-	2	2	-
People of God	-	-	-	-	-
Olive tree	-	-	-	1	-
A king of	-	-	-	-	-
Judged/destroyed	-	-	2	1	-
God redeems	-	-	1	-	1
God judges	-	-	-	-	-
God is	-	-	-	-	-
Jesus is God	-	-	1	1	-
God opposed	-	-	-	1	-
Praise/rejoice in	-	-	-	1	-
Fear God	-	-	-	-	-
God will reign	-	-	-	-	-

Figure 4: Israel

It should be noted that the same emphasis on the people of Israel which is observed in figure 3 is also seen in figure 4. Clearly, Israel is seen as a people (as a political or spiritual entity), as a group in exile, as a people with whom God has covenanted, and so forth. It is not always easy, however, to draw these distinctions sharply, especially when trying to decide whether *Israel* refers to the nation as an all-encompassing group or whether it refers in a more narrow sense to a group with certain spiritual values that bind them together. Even so, we have attempted to make such distinctions as well as they can be made.

Angel

In the two instances where the Angel seems to refer to Israel as a nation, he states that the house of Israel fights against the apostles of Jesus (1 Nephi 11:35) and that writings have been sealed which are to come forth in their purity to the house of Israel (1 Nephi 14:26). In contrast, when he notes that the Gentiles may be numbered among the house of Israel and that the house of Israel will not be confounded, he seems to refer to Israel as a spiritual entity which shares common beliefs (1 Nephi 14:2). Similarly, the apostles will judge the twelve tribes of Israel (1 Nephi 12:9), and the judgment, if positive, will be based on spiritual merit and not simply on national identity.

The Angel speaks five times of God's covenants with Israel. A book (the Bible) contains the covenants that God made with Israel (1 Nephi 13:23). Nephi 1 knows the covenants of God with the house of Israel (1 Nephi 14:5) and is asked whether he remembers those covenants (1 Nephi 14:8). He is told that when the wrath of God begins to be poured out on the harlot of the earth, then God is preparing the way for the fulfilling of his covenants with Israel (1 Nephi 14:17). It seems that the covenants are both spiritual and temporal and convince persons either to come to peace and everlasting life or to go to captivity and destruction (1 Nephi 14:7). It appears that the covenants involve the two most basic themes of the Book of Mormon: (1) that people must come to Christ, and (2) that through Christ, scattered Israel will be gathered. Finally, the Angel tells Nephi 1 that the twelve apostles will judge Israel and therefore will also judge Nephi's seed, for his descendants are a scattered portion of the house of Israel (1 Nephi 12:9).

The Father

The Father speaks once about the Gentiles scattering his people (3 Nephi 20:27), a reference which seems to deal with Israel as a nation, particularly as it may still be found among the Lamanites in this hemisphere. Closely related to this, but leaning toward Israel as a spiritual entity—albeit a negative one—is the Father's assertion that because of Israel's unbelief, the truth would be given to the Gentiles (3 Nephi 16:7). Similarly, those who will not come to Christ in the last days will be cut off from the people of Israel (3 Nephi 21:20).

Israel as a spiritual gathering is further emphasized when the Father says that the Gentiles can have no power over Israel (3 Nephi 16:12), that the Gentiles may be numbered among Israel (3 Nephi 16:13), and that Israel may not tread down the Gentiles unless they are disobedient (3 Nephi 16:14–15). God's covenants with Israel involve bringing the fullness of the gospel to them after the Gentiles have rejected it (3 Nephi 16:11–12). When the Father speaks of his people being scattered, it refers to the Gentiles scattering the Lamanites in the Western Hemisphere (3 Nephi 16:8).

The Lord in Isaiah (Lord-Isa)

In Isaiah, the Lord refers three times to Israel as a nation. In typical, repetitive, Hebrew poetic form, he calls Jacob and Israel, which are, of course, the same thing, to listen to him (1 Nephi 20:12). In addition, scattered Israel will be gathered (1 Nephi 21:12). Also, God does not forget Israel, even though some claim that Israel's troubles arise from the Lord's neglect (2 Nephi 7:1–2). On the spiritual plane, God will be glorified through his servant Israel, whose role will not only be to gather scattered Israel but to be a light to all nations (1 Nephi 21:3, 6).[5] So says the Lord, the Redeemer of Israel (1 Nephi 21:7).

Jesus

Because of Israel's wickedness, which troubles Jesus as he visits the Nephites (3 Nephi 17:14), the nation of Israel has been judged and smitten by God (3 Nephi 16:9). She has been scattered (3 Nephi

---

[5] A common interpretation of this servant psalm in Isaiah sees the servant as the Messiah and is, in the fullest sense, accurate. However, to neglect the fact that Israel, as a spiritual people, has a servant role to play among the nations is to overlook an important part of its mission.

15:15), and the Nephites are a part of that dispersion (3 Nephi 20:10, 25). Yet there is hope, for Jesus is the very God who covenanted with Israel to gather her (3 Nephi 15:5; 16:5; 21:1) and to bring her to a full knowledge of her Redeemer (3 Nephi 20:12–13). This knowledge will come about when the Book of Mormon is given and will be a sign that God is beginning to fulfill his covenants with Israel (3 Nephi 21:4, 7). In the end, Jesus will establish his people (3 Nephi 20:21) who are of the House of Israel (3 Nephi 23:2), namely, those who come to Christ, including the Gentiles (3 Nephi 21:6; 30:2). Clearly, Jesus' main concern is with the gathering of Israel, particularly spiritual Israel—those who have come to him, the God of Israel (3 Nephi 11:14).

The Lord

It should not be surprising that the Lord and Jesus express very similar concerns in their use of the word *Israel,* for they are, in fact, the same person. Clearly, the Lord's overriding concern is with scattered Israel and the express purpose of gathering her. In the past he has sought to gather fallen and scattered Israel, including the Nephites (3 Nephi 10:4–6); in the future he will gather Israel (1 Nephi 19:16), restore her (2 Nephi 3:13), and recover her through Joseph Smith (2 Nephi 3:13; 29:1). The parable of the olive tree makes this clear (Jacob 5:3). In the meantime, he will visit the remnants of Israel with judgment in order to show mercy to the Gentiles (1 Nephi 13:33), send his words to and speak to his people (2 Nephi 29:2, 12), and see that his words are shared among the lost tribes (2 Nephi 29:13). He will do this, despite the fact that there are some who say that God will not remember his covenants, and thus they fight against the covenant people (2 Nephi 29:14; Mormon 8:21). In the end, true Israel will be composed of those who come to the Father through Christ (Ether 4:14–15), including Gentiles (2 Nephi 10:18). In the day that this occurs, the meek shall rejoice in the Holy One of Israel, and the people shall stand in awe of the God of Israel (2 Nephi 27:30, 34).

In summary, the emphasis among the divine or heavenly figures is on the people of Israel as a nation, a spiritual group, a covenantal group, or a remnant. Most striking is the likeness which is seen between the words of the Lord and those of Jesus. Since the two are indeed the same person, one should expect this, but it is doubtful that such parallels could have been constructed by a nineteenth-century author given the wide dispersion of the passages under consideration within the Book of Mormon.

Isaiah and Zenos

Not surprisingly, Isaiah speaks of Israel numerous times, in one context or another, with a rate of 4.06 uses per thousand. Zenos, another author from the plates of brass, uses *Israel* less often, but still with a use rate of 1.41 per thousand. Figure 5 shows the distribution of the word *Israel* when it is used in conjunction with other words or phrases. It is evident that Isaiah has a variety of phrases which he uses in relation to *Israel*. It would seem that his concern is with Israel as a people and with the God who is over them.

In Zenos's few uses of *Israel,* the emphasis seems to be similar. Figure 6 shows the concerns of the two authors when the meaning of *Israel* is examined. The first half of figure 6 shows Isaiah to be concerned for the nation of Israel, which, through his prophetic vision, he sees falling away from the God of Israel (1 Nephi 20:1–2). He refers especially to Israel, the northern kingdom, which is ruled by Pekah (2 Nephi 17:1; 19:12, 14). Israel despises the word of the Lord (2 Nephi 15:24), fears what it should not fear, and therefore will stumble over God (2 Nephi 18:14). In the allegory of the vineyard, God judges Israel and lays waste to her (2 Nephi 15:6–7).

There is hope, however, because Isaiah and those who heed his message are signs and wonders of God's presence in Israel (2 Nephi 18:18). The Lord will send his word to Israel (2 Nephi 7:4;[6] 19:8), Israel will burn Assyria (2 Nephi 20:17), the remnant of the deported tribes will find a highway leading out of Assyria (2 Nephi 21:16), and the Lord will choose Israel and give them their land (2 Nephi 24:1–2).

---

[6] 2 Nephi 7:4a differs from the received text in Isaiah 50:4a. While the Isaiah text preserved in Nephi states that "The Lord God hath given me the tongue of the learned, that I should know how to speak a word in season *unto thee, O house of Israel,*" the text of Isaiah 50:4a says, "The Lord God hath given me the tongue of the learned, that I should know how to speak a word in season *to him that is weary*" (emphasis added).

The possessors of the land will probably be spiritual Israel, and not merely those who have blood lineage.

	Isaiah	Zenos
House of	5	2
Tribes, house of	-	-
People, house of	-	-
Children of	-	-
12 tribes of	-	-
People of	5	-
Both houses of	1	-
Nation of	5	-
Escaped of	1	-
Preserved of	-	-
King of	1	-
Remnant of	1	-
Outcasts of	1	-
Lost tribes of	-	-
Remnant, house of	-	-
Scattered tribes of	-	-
God of	3	2
Holy One of	7	2
Redeemer of	-	-
Mighty One of	-	-
My people	-	-
My called of	-	-
My servant	-	-

Figure 5: Israel

Isaiah is also concerned for scattered Israel. The servant calls to scattered Israel and will bring Israel to God (1 Nephi 21:1, 5). The remnant will return to the Holy One of Israel (2 Nephi 20:20–22), God's ensign will assemble the outcasts of Israel (2 Nephi 21:12), and "in that day" the fruit of the land will be the pride of the survivors of Israel (2 Nephi 14:2). God, the Holy One of Israel, who accomplishes all this, counsels Israel (2 Nephi 15:19), is her Redeemer (1 Nephi 20:17; 3 Nephi 22:5) and guardian (3 Nephi 20:42), and is great (2 Nephi 22:6).

	Isaiah	Zenos
Nation	10	1
Spiritual entity	2	-
Covenant with	-	-
Scattered	5	-
Lehites, part of	-	-
People of God	-	-
Olive tree	1	-
A king of	1	-
Judged/destroyed	-	-
God redeems	4	2
God judges	1	-
God is	2	-
Jesus is God	-	-
God opposed	3	3
Praise/rejoice in	-	-
Fear God	-	-
God will reign	-	-

Figure 6: Israel

Almost all of Zenos's uses of *Israel* actually occur in the space of five verses when Nephi 1 quotes Zenos. In these verses, Zenos states that at the time of Christ's death, God will visit scattered Israel, some with his voice because of their righteousness and others with destruction because of their wickedness (1 Nephi 19:11). He further states that those in Jerusalem will crucify the God of Israel, reject his signs, and despise him, thereby guaranteeing their dispersion and suffering. When they no longer turn from the Holy One of Israel, then the Father will remember his covenants with them (1 Nephi 19:13–15). The one other instance in which Zenos uses *Israel* is at the beginning of his parable of the tame olive tree, when he calls the house of Israel to hear his words (Jacob 5:2).

In summary, both Isaiah and Zenos emphasize God's actions, which may be merciful or wrathful, in relation to disobedient and scattered Israel.

Lehi and His Sons

In the following materials, Lehi's words have limited value, simply because he uses *Israel* only four times. However, his sons, Nephi 1 and Jacob, use it a great deal and have very similar distribution patterns. Figure 7 reflects the way *Israel* is used in relation to other phrases written by the three men.

	Jacob	Lehi	Nephi 1
House of	9	2	20
Tribes, house of	-	-	-
People, house of	-	-	1
Children of	1	-	3
12 tribes of	-	-	-
People of	-	-	-
Both houses of	-	-	-
Nation of	-	-	-
Escaped of	-	-	-
Preserved of	-	-	-
King of	-	-	-
Remnant of	-	-	-
Outcasts of	-	-	-
Lost tribes of	-	-	2
Remnant, house of	-	-	-
Scattered tribes of	-	-	-
God of	1	-	2
Holy One of	17	2	10
Redeemer of	-	-	-
Mighty One of	-	-	1
My people	-	-	-
My called of	-	-	-
My servant	-	-	-

Figure 7: Israel

As with all persons who use *Israel,* the phrases "house of Israel" and "Holy One of Israel" seem to be commonplace. However, these three writers all emphasize both phrases simultaneously, which makes them different from the divine figures and from Mormon and Moroni 2, as we shall see later. However, the two Old World figures, Isaiah and Zenos, do have some similarities with Lehi and his sons.

When we turn to the distribution of the meaning of *Israel* in figure 8, the similarities between Lehi, Jacob, and Nephi 1, as well as their differences from the other writers, are heightened.

	Jacob	Lehi	Nephi 1
Nation	3	-	8
Spiritual entity	3	-	-
Covenant with	1	2	2
Scattered	1	-	6
Lehites, part of	3	-	7
People of God	-	-	-
Olive tree	1	-	2
A king of	-	-	-
Judged/destroyed	-	-	-
God redeems	8	1	2
God judges	2	-	1
God is	5	-	1
Jesus is God	-	-	2
God opposed	1	1	3
Praise/rejoice in	-	-	3
Fear God	-	-	-
God will reign	-	-	2

Figure 8: Israel

An examination of figure 8, especially the first portion which is concerned with the people of Israel, underlines the similarities between Nephi 1 and Jacob in word use. At the same time, however, it also indicates their differences. Clearly, Jacob and Nephi 1 attach many of the same meanings to the word *Israel,* whether it concerns the people or their God. However, Nephi 1 is more diffuse in the way he speaks about God, while Jacob tends to stress that God is the Redeemer and then ascribes other attributes to him. In addition, Jacob has more references to the God of Israel (16) than he does to the people of Israel (12). In contrast, Nephi 1 tends to treat Israel as a nation which is scattered, while Jacob tends to be more even in his treatment of Israel as a people. Also, Nephi 1 refers more often to the people of Israel (26) than he does to the God of Israel (14).

The divine figures are the only individuals who have similar distributions with reference to the people of Israel, but since Nephi 1 and Jacob interacted directly with the Angel and the Lord, it is not surprising to find some commonalities.

Lehi

Lehi speaks twice of the house of Israel as scattered and sees his descendants as a part of that scattering (2 Nephi 3:5, 24). He also speaks twice of the Holy One of Israel, once when he blesses his son, Joseph, telling him that if he will obey God, the New World will be a land of security (2 Nephi 3:2), and once when he states that if those who come to the New World reject the Holy One of Israel, judgment will come upon them (2 Nephi 1:10).

Jacob

Jacob speaks of Israel as a nation when he says that he will read Isaiah's words which are to all the house of Israel with whom God has covenanted (2 Nephi 6:5; 9:1), that Zenos spoke to Israel (Jacob 5:1), that God remembers Israel (Jacob 6:4), and that Jacob's people should come to Christ so that they do not have to suffer the wrath of God that the children of Israel experienced in the wilderness (Jacob 1:7). However, as the parable of the olive tree indicates (Jacob 6:1), Israel as a nation is scattered (2 Nephi 10:22), and the Nephites are part of her (2 Nephi 6:5). But there is also a spiritual Israel, composed of those who are righteous and have faith in the Holy One of Israel. Eventually, the Lamanites will become a righteous branch of this Israel (2 Nephi 9:53).

Clearly, Jacob's major interest is in how God works in relationship to Israel. First, God intends to redeem Israel. He will manifest himself to the Jews in the flesh as Jesus, through whom deliverance and resurrection will come (2 Nephi 6:9; 9:11–12, 23). Further, Jacob rejoices in the greatness and mercy of this God (2 Nephi 9:19, 25). However, some, like the Jews at Jerusalem, will oppose God and will thus necessitate that he act in judgment rather than mercy (2 Nephi 6:10; 9:15).

Of all the authors under consideration, Jacob uses the most descriptive language about God. Jacob refers to him as the God of Israel (2 Nephi 9:44), the Holy One of Israel (2 Nephi 6:15; 9:24), the God who gives breath (2 Nephi 9:26), and the God who is the keeper of the gate (2 Nephi 9:41).

Nephi 1

While using all but one of the meanings of *Israel* found in Jacob, Nephi 1 adds a few other dimensions. First, he speaks of God as the Holy One or Mighty One of Israel who redeems, because Nephi 1 knows that Moses spoke of Jesus and that nations will dwell safely in the Holy One of Israel if they will repent (1 Nephi 22:12, 21, 28). Hence, the God of Israel reigns and is worthy of praise and thanks (1 Nephi 5:9–10; 22:24, 26; 2 Nephi 31:13). This God is Christ (2 Nephi 28:5; 30:2), but he will not go unopposed. There will be those who reject Jesus, as did the first-century Jewish leaders (1 Nephi 15:17), those who trample him (1 Nephi 19:7), and who harden their hearts (1 Nephi 22:5)—all of whom God will scatter or destroy (1 Nephi 22:5, 18).

Nephi 1, however, is less concerned with the God of Israel and more concerned with the people of Israel, particularly the scattered people. Thus, Nephi 1 sees Israel as a nation brought out of bondage from Egypt (1 Nephi 17:23, 25, 29). In addition, Israel is a nation to which Nephi 1 speaks (1 Nephi 19:19; 2 Nephi 33:13), to which the words of the prophet, Isaiah, are directed (1 Nephi 19:24), which shall be nursed by the Gentiles (1 Nephi 22:6), and against which nations will conduct war (1 Nephi 22:14).

To Nephi 1 an even greater concern than Israel as a nation in the general sense is Israel as a scattered people. Israel is like an olive tree whose branches, one of which is Lehi's family (1 Nephi 15:12), are scattered across the face of the earth (1 Nephi 10:12, 14). Further, Nephi 1 sees that Israel will be scattered because of their opposition to Jesus (1 Nephi 22:3, 5, 7). Some, who are already scattered, will receive signs, like the three days of darkness, at the time of his death (1 Nephi 19:10). Scattered Israel, however, should not despair, for they will be gathered (1 Nephi 10:14), a fact of which Isaiah prophesied (1 Nephi 15:20) and which is a consequence of the Lord's covenant with Israel (1 Nephi 22:9, 11). The relevance of this to Lehi and his descendants is that they are part of scattered Israel (1 Nephi 15:12; 19:24; 2 Nephi 25:4), and therefore they will be participants in the fulfillment of the Lord's promises to Israel (1 Nephi 15:14, 16; 2 Nephi 28:2). Thus, Lehi's descendants can have hope that God will remember them in the future.

In summary, Nephi 1 and Jacob speak in very similar language about Israel and its God. However, there are clear differences between them: Jacob seems to be more concerned with the God of Israel, while Nephi 1 seems to be more concerned with the scattered people of Israel who will eventually be gathered.

	Mormon	Moroni 2
House of	8	5
Tribes, house of	-	-
People, house of	1	-
Children of	2	-
12 tribes of	-	-
People of	-	-
Both houses of	-	-
Nation of	-	-
Escaped of	-	-
Preserved of	-	-
King of	-	-
Remnant of	2	-
Outcasts of	-	-
Lost tribes of	-	-
Remnant, house of	-	-
Scattered tribes of	1	-
God of	-	-
Holy One of	-	-
Redeemer of	-	-
Mighty One of	-	-
My people	-	-
My called of	-	-
My servant	-	-

Figure 9: Israel

Israel

Moroni 2

Neither Mormon nor Moroni 2 appears to place a major emphasis on Israel. Each refers to Israel primarily as the "house of Israel," as figure 9 shows, and each speaks of Israel as a nation, as a people with whom God covenanted, and as a scattered people, as demonstrated in figure 10.

Mormon's usage is broader than Moroni 2's, as shown in figure 9, probably because Mormon simply writes more than does Moroni 2. Of greater interest is that neither writer exhibits any desire to talk about the God of Israel. This reinforces what was discovered in Mormon's and Moroni 2's uses of "earth," for Moroni 2 spoke only twice of God's creative activity and Mormon never mentioned God's work in relation to the earth.

	Mormon	Moroni 2
Nation	6	2
Spiritual entity	-	-
Covenant with	4	2
Scattered	5	-
Lehites, part of	-	1
People of God	-	-
Olive tree	-	-
A king of	-	-
Judged/destroyed	-	-
God redeems	-	-
God judges	-	-
God is	-	-
Jesus is God	-	-
God opposed	-	-
Praise/rejoice in	-	-
Fear God	-	-
God will reign	-	-

Figure 10: Israel

All of Moroni 2's references deal with the "house of Israel." Ether spoke concerning the house of Israel and Jerusalem, which will be built up for Israel (Ether 13:5). Both references are to Israel as a nation. Israel is also a people with whom the Father covenanted (Mormon 9:37; Moroni 10:31). The New Jerusalem, which is to be built in the Western Hemisphere, is for those who are washed in the blood of the Lamb and for the seed of Joseph who are numbered among the house of Israel (Ether 13:11).

Mormon

For Mormon, Israel is the nation or people to whom he writes (Mormon 3:17–18), to whom Jesus will return (3 Nephi 29:2), for whom the Gentiles will care (Mormon 5:11), among whom there was no wickedness as great as that of Mormon's day (Mormon 4:12), and among whom calamity has come (Mormon 5:11). They are a scattered people, but the three Nephites will eventually minister to all of them (3 Nephi 28:29). There is no reason to harass any of the remnant of Israel (3 Nephi 29:8), and Mormon speaks to the remnant and calls them to repentance (Mormon 7:1–3), for Israel is a covenant people of God (3 Nephi 29:1, 9). God will remember his covenant people and restore them to the lands of their inheritance (3 Nephi 29:1; Mormon 5:14).

Earlier, it was suggested that only authors or persons closely associated with Old World Israel use the word *Israel*. Obviously, Mormon and Moroni 2 are exceptions to that idea. Interestingly, Mormon mentions Israel only after he has abridged the information on the Large Plates, some of which is found in 3 Nephi. In other words, Mormon worked through the account of the resurrected Jesus' visit to the people at Bountiful, saw the Lord's emphasis on Israel as a scattered covenant people who would be gathered, realized the importance of those ideas for persons who would later read his work, and incorporated those ideas into his final reflections. Moroni 2, following in his father's footsteps, does likewise. Even so, neither author seems to feel the attachment to Israel that earlier writers like Nephi 1 and Jacob do.

Conclusions

Author Individuality

It has been shown that there are clearly individual traits among the authors, even when they speak from similar perspectives. The divine figures speak primarily about the people of Israel but reflect different emphases between them. So do Lehi and his sons. There is amazing congruence between Nephi 1 and Jacob in both the language used and the meanings attached to *Israel*. Yet they are also distinct, for Jacob speaks about what the God of Israel does in relation to the people of Israel, while Nephi 1 reverses that emphasis and speaks more about the people of Israel in the midst of earthly life.

Mormon and Moroni 2 show no interest in speaking about the "God of Israel" but demonstrate a concern for the people, with a slight emphasis by Mormon on the gathering of the scattered remnant. However, Israel is not, proportionately, of great importance to either. Finally, Isaiah shows a great deal of variety in his language about Israel and indicates a concern for Israel as a nation, as well as for its scattering. He also speaks of God as the one who will redeem Israel and not forget her. Zenos, in his few references, appears concerned with the God of Israel who is opposed by some, but who will ultimately redeem his people.

Theological Implications

The theme of the scattering and gathering of Israel is an important one, for it indicates that although the people of God have been judged, and as a result scattered, they have not been forgotten. If God were to forget his covenant people, he would be an untrustworthy God. If he could promise to remember Israel forever, and yet walk away from her when she became disobedient, then his promises to those who live in the latter days would be suspect. He has not done that, however, for he continues to love Israel and will slowly, through Jesus Christ, bring her back to the fold.

It is exciting that the persons he gathers are not merely related to Israel by blood but may be adoptees like the Gentiles. No one who comes to Christ is excluded from Israel, but at the same time, it is only within spiritual Israel—those who follow Christ—that salvation may be found. In the end, Israel is simply the name for the covenant family of God, while the historical nation of Israel is the means through which God chose to summon his family to return to him.

6

Land and Lands

The concept of *Land* is critical to an understanding of the Old Testament. Since land was among the blessings of Israel's covenant with the Lord, it is as much a matter of doctrine as a matter of society. Land plays an important role in God's interaction with his people. Abraham was promised a land by the Lord. Moses led the children of Israel to the promised land. Joshua defeated the inhabitants of the promised land and took possession of it. The people were exiled from the land by the Assyrians and the Babylonians, yet there was hope of return. A remnant of the Jews returned to the land of Israel under Zerubbabel and others. The Maccabees regained the land from Syria, and the Jews had to flee the land after the fall of Jerusalem in A.D. 70.

Given these precedents, it is important that we examine the use of the terms *Land* and *Lands* within the Book of Mormon to determine how these words were understood among the people of Israel who dwelt in the New World.

Most of the authors within the Book of Mormon use the word *Land*. Abinadi never uses it, while Enos uses it only once, Amulek twice, and Zenos three times. Figure 1 shows the use per thousand words of author text, from the highest usage to the lowest, as well as the actual number of times the word *Land* appears in a particular author.

18.64	Zeniff	(34)
7.11	Mormon	(696)
5.93	Mosiah	(7)
5.62	Moroni 2	(108)
5.52	Lehi	(26)
5.48	Father	(6)
5.33	Helaman	(27)
4.89	Lord	(56)
4.81	Ammon	(11)
3.58	Moroni 1	(11)
2.70	Nephi 2	(6)
2.66	Isaiah	(19)
2.27	Samuel	(7)
2.22	Nephi 1	(63)
1.94	Lord-Isa	(9)
1.93	Angel	(4)
1.69	Alma 2	(34)
1.45	Jesus	(14)
1.42	Benjamin	(6)
1.00	Enos	(1)
0.70	Zenos	(3)
0.70	Jacob	(6)
0.63	Amulek	(2)

Figure 1: Land

We will examine *Land* and *Lands* under two headings: a geographical grouping and a special grouping. In the first group we will examine those instances where *Land* or *Lands* refers to a geographical region, while in the second group we will examine those instances in which *Land* or *Lands* is defined in a way which appears to transcend a purely geographical meaning. We will discuss the authors in the same order that we did in chapter 5 on "Israel"—considering the divine figures, the prophetic figures from the plates of brass, Lehi and his sons and grandson, and Mormon and Moroni 2. However, because *Land* and *Lands* were more widely used by the Book of Mormon authors than was *Israel,* it is necessary to add other authors: the earlier figures of the Zarahemla period (Zeniff, Benjamin, Mosiah, Ammon, Alma 2, and Amulek), and later persons of Zarahemla (Captain Moroni, Helaman, Nephi 2, Samuel).

Geographical References

The divine figures (Nephi's angel, the Father, Jesus, the Lord, and the Lord in Isaiah), make a number of references to *Land* in a geographical sense, as figure 2 indicates. "Land of" means that the author specifies a particular land by name, e.g., land of Zarahemla, land of Nephi, land of Gideon, etc. "Region" indicates that the author uses *Land* by itself to indicate some region, the context determining what that area might be. Canaan and Judea are regions but were considered separately because they are Old World regions. "Territory" is basically an unspecified region, while "New World" refers to the Western Hemisphere. "Directions" means that the author uses compass directions with the word *Land,* e.g., land northward, land southward, land south, etc. The other headings, such as "borders of" and "round about," are phrases used by the authors to describe the geographical dimensions of the land of which they speak.

	Angel	Father	Jesus	Lord	Lord-Isa
Land of	-	1	1	9	2
Region	-	-	1	6	4
Borders of	-	-	-	-	-
Round about	-	-	-	-	-
Part(s) of	-	-	-	-	-
Quarter of	-	-	-	-	-
Territory	-	-	-	-	-
Strange	-	-	-	-	-
Canaan	-	-	-	-	-
Judea	-	-	1	-	-
New World	1	2	4	25	-
Directions	-	-	-	-	-

Figure 2: Land

Clearly, the use distribution of the divine figures falls into the categories of "Land of," "Region," and "New World." We will examine how the word *Land* is used within each of these groups and determine what similarities or differences there may be between the various figures.

Angel

Of the four times that the Angel uses the word *Land,* only once does he use it as a geographical region. In doing so he specifically refers to the New World upon which the Gentiles have been given power by God. This land is choice above all other lands (1 Nephi 13:30)—the one instance in which the Angel uses the word *Lands.*

Father

Of the six times the Father uses *Land,* three refer to geographical areas. Once he speaks of the land of Jerusalem, to which Israel will be gathered (3 Nephi 20:29), and twice he speaks of the New World, upon which the Gentiles have scattered and scourged God's people (3 Nephi 16:8; 20:28).

The Lord

Of all the divine personages, the Lord deals most extensively with the concept of *Land,* and slightly over 70 percent of his usages relate to geography. He refers four times to the land of Jerusalem as a land of wickedness from which he delivered Lehi's family (e.g., 1 Nephi 17:14) just as he delivered Israel from the land of Egypt (2 Nephi 3:10; Mosiah 12:34). In a New World context, he commands Ammon not to go to the land of Nephi, where his life will be endangered, but to go to the land of Middoni where his brothers are imprisoned (Alma 20:2, 5).

The references to land as a region, with one exception, refer to New World localities: the valley of Alma (Mosiah 24:23), Ani-Anti, and Nephi (Alma 27:12), all of which the Lord commands the people to abandon in order that they may not perish. The Lord also pronounces a woe upon the area around Zarahemla because of the wickedness that is present there (Helaman 13:16). The single exception to the New World localities is Abinadi's quoting of the fifth of the Ten Commandments, in which the Lord commands that persons honor their fathers and mothers. If the people obey, then they will have a long life in the land which God has given them (Mosiah 13:20)—a message as relevant for the delivered Nephites as it was for the Israelites coming out of Egypt.

A dominant concern to the Lord in the Book of Mormon seems to be the New World, since it accounts for 62.5 percent of the Lord's geographical references. Lehi reminds his sons that the Lord has promised that when they obey God, they will prosper in the land (2 Nephi 1:20; see also 2 Nephi 4:4; Jacob 2:29; Enos 1:10; Jarom 1:9; Omni 1:6; Alma 9:13; 50:20). By this time, Lehi's family is well established in the New World, and thus the land to which the promise refers has to be the Western Hemisphere. According to Jacob, God promised that the New World would be a land of inheritance, a land of liberty, a land without kings, a land fortified against other nations, a land consecrated to Lehi's seed, and even a land upon which the Gentiles would be blessed (2 Nephi 10:10-12, 19). Abinadi and Samuel, however, quote the Lord as saying that if there is no obedience or repentance, the people will be cursed and destroyed from off the land; however, a record of those fallen people will be preserved for those who later inhabit the land (Mosiah 12:8; see also Alma 37:25; 45:16; Helaman 13:17-19). It is precisely because the people did not repent, as the Lord reminded the Nephites, that destruction came at the time of Christ's crucifixion (3 Nephi 9:12). Finally, the Lord tells both Israel and the Gentiles that when the Book of Mormon comes forth, the Father's work will have begun once again on this hemisphere (Ether 4:17).

Jesus

When Jesus appeared to the Nephites at the temple in Bountiful, he told them that the Father had not given him permission to tell any of the persons in the Old World about the scattered tribes which the Father had led out of the land, i.e., out of the northern kingdom, Jerusalem, Judea, and their environs (3 Nephi 15:15; 16:1). These verses constitute Jesus' geographical references to the Old World. Not all Jesus' sheep reside either in the Old World or in Lehi's land of inheritance (3 Nephi 16:1), but for those who do or will live in the Western Hemisphere, the Father will establish them, both Israelite and Gentile, and will establish the New Jerusalem for them (3 Nephi 20:22; 21:4).

The Lord in Isaiah

Not surprisingly, all geographical references of the Lord in Isaiah refer to the Old World. In 1 Nephi 21:12 the Lord refers to the gathering of Israel, one reference point being the land of Sinim, which refers to Aswan on the Nile. The same chapter states that Israel will return to her land, which had previously been devastated, and prosper in it (1 Nephi 21:12, 19). When the Lord refers to *Land* as regions, he signifies Judah twice (2 Nephi 16:11-12) and the destruction of Babylon once (2 Nephi 23:9).

In summary, there are some observable differences in the way the various divine figures speak with respect to geography. For the Father, Israel will be gathered *to* Jerusalem, while the Lord speaks of delivering portions of Israel *from* Jerusalem. Similarly, Jesus speaks of the people who have been taken out of Jerusalem, and the Lord in Isaiah speaks only of the Old World. When the New World is discussed, the Angel says that the Gentiles will be given power over it. Similarly, the Father indicates that the Gentiles will scatter Lehi's descendants upon the New World. The Lord led various groups out of Jerusalem to preserve them and commands various people to leave New World regions where they are in danger. If the people obey his commandments, they will have a long life in the land. Finally, Jesus indicates that the New World is the place where the New Jerusalem will be established.

Prophets of the Plates of Brass

The two prophets of the plates of brass who use the word *Land* are Isaiah and Zenos. Their geographical uses are shown in figure 3.

Zenos's use of *Land* is almost incidental and is rather generic. Three occurrences are found in the parable of the tame olive tree. *Land* simply refers to the various portions of the vineyard—the world (Jacob 5:21, 43, 69).

	Isaiah	Zenos
Land of	7	-
Region	6	2
Borders of	-	-
Round about	-	-
Part(s) of	-	1
Quarter of	-	-
Territory	-	-
Strange	-	-
Canaan	-	-
Judea	-	-
New World	-	-
Directions	-	-

Figure 3: Land

Isaiah, however, speaks of a number of Near Eastern lands: Assyria (2 Nephi 17:18), Zebulun (2 Nephi 19:1), Naphtali (2 Nephi 19:1), and Egypt (2 Nephi 21:16). When he uses the word to mean "regions," those regions are also Near Eastern: Ephraim, Judah, and Syria (2 Nephi 17:16, 22, 24; 19:19). He also speaks of the "land of the shadow of death," perhaps meaning those people of Israel and Judah who were under Assyrian domination or threat (2 Nephi 19:2). In like manner, he speaks of the "land of the Lord," meaning Israel (2 Nephi 24:2). Isaiah also speaks poetically of being cut off from the land of the living, referring to death (Mosiah 14:8). Finally, Isaiah uses *Land* to mean the world or the earth, which is how some translations render the original Hebrew word in Isaiah 10:23 (2 Nephi 20:23) and 14:21 (2 Nephi 24:21). In the first instance, the Lord will bring his work with Israel to an end in the midst of the earth. In the second instance, slaughter is prepared for those who do evil, for they cannot inherit the earth. Thus, whether his language is poetic, prophetic, or historical, Isaiah's geographical orientation is on the Near East.

Lehi

In figure 4 we find the geographical distribution of terms among Lehi, his sons, and his grandson.

	Enos	Jacob	Lehi	Nephi 1
Land of	-	-	2	18
Region	-	-	-	7
Borders of	-	-	-	-
Round about	-	-	-	-
Part(s) of	-	-	-	-
Quarter of	-	-	-	-
Territory	-	-	-	-
Strange	-	-	-	-
Canaan	-	-	-	3
Judea	-	-	-	-
New World	-	2	13	10
Directions	-	-	-	-

Figure 4: Land

Nephi 1 speaks most frequently about the land in a geographical way, but this is not surprising, for he was the narrator who enabled us to follow the wanderings of his family and gave us the various signposts which they encountered. Of all the family, he writes the longest text. But even so, Lehi makes a significant contribution to the study of the word *Land,* for he has a use rate of 5.52 per thousand words of text and makes a number of references to *Land,* by which he means the New World.

Lehi refers twice to the land of Jerusalem. In the first instance, it is the land from which the Lord removed his family (2 Nephi 1:30). In the second use the Lord promised, according to Lehi, that anyone who is brought from Jerusalem to the New World and who keeps God's commandments will prosper in the land (2 Nephi 1:9). However, the bulk of Lehi's geographic uses of *Land* refer to the New World. It is a land which the Lord gave to Lehi and his children (2 Nephi 1:5), the knowledge of its existence being kept from others

(2 Nephi 1:8). The people who come to this land will be those whom the Father brings (2 Nephi 1:6-7). If the people become wicked, the land will be cursed (2 Nephi 1:7, 31), but if they are righteous they will be safe and prosper in the land (2 Nephi 1:9, 32). Sam's and Zoram's seed shall be among those who inherit the land and prosper in it (2 Nephi 1:31; 4:11). Thus, it is a special land for Lehi's descendants, as we shall see when we consider the other uses of *Land*.

Nephi 1

Nephi 1 refers to the land of Jerusalem as that from which he and his family fled (1 Nephi 2:11; 16:35; 18:24; 2 Nephi 1:1, 3), as that to which he and his brothers return (1 Nephi 3:9-10; 5:6; 7:2), as that to which some desired to return (1 Nephi 7:7), and as that to which the Jews will one day return (2 Nephi 25:11). When he speaks of *Land* as a region, in five instances the referent is the land of Jerusalem (1 Nephi 3:18-19; 7:14-15).

Other lands to which Nephi 1 refers are Egypt, from which Israel was delivered (1 Nephi 5:15; 17:40; 2 Nephi 25:20), and Canaan, which is not mentioned by name but is the land the Lord gave to the children of Israel (1 Nephi 17:32-33, 35). The mention of Egypt and the reference to Canaan had relevance for Lehi's family since they understood themselves as being delivered by the Lord from an unrighteous people and being carried to a new and promised land. Nephi 1 also mentions Bountiful, where the ship which brought Lehi and his family to the New World was built (1 Nephi 17:5, 7)—a place that was perhaps seen in retrospect as a precursor of the promised land that was yet to come. Nephi 1 also notes that where there are wicked persons, the Lord curses their land (1 Nephi 17:38). Nephi 1's only other reference to a region refers to the land of Nephi over which he gave authority to Jacob and Joseph to be teachers (2 Nephi 5:26).

Nephi 1 is also concerned about the New World. He notes that the people prospered in the New World (2 Nephi 5:13), although in building their temple, they did not have access to many of the precious things that Solomon had (2 Nephi 5:16). Nephi 1 sees in a vision the wars that will occur between the Nephites and the Lamanites in the New World (1 Nephi 12:3, 20) and the ultimate destruction which will attend the people's wickedness (1 Nephi 22:18; 2 Nephi 27:1). He sees the Gentiles prospering in the Western Hemisphere (1 Nephi 13:20; 22:7). The plates are written to instruct Nephi 1's people, who will possess the land (1 Nephi 19:3). Many Jews shall be gathered in the New World (2 Nephi 30:7). Thus, according to Nephi 1, the New World is a place of blessing for those who follow the Lord and a place of destruction for those who do not.

Nephi 1 uses the word *Lands* geographically three times. He recounts how he read from the plates of brass to his brothers so that they might know how the Lord had worked in other lands (1 Nephi 19:22). He also prophesies that in the last days, the Gentiles and Jews alike will be wicked in the New World as well as in other lands or nations (2 Nephi 27:1).

Jacob

Jacob refers twice to the New World. First, he indicates that the people have sought precious metals which were abundant in the New World and have consequently become proud as they accrued wealth (Jacob 2:12–13). Second, he states that those who do evil will find the land cursed because of them (Jacob 3:3).

In summary, Lehi refers mostly to the New World as a special land for his descendants. Nephi 1 refers to the Old World as a place from which they have fled, and refers to the New World as a place of blessing. Jacob warns against pride in the New World and warns those who do evil that the land will consequently be cursed.

Zeniff

From figure 5, it appears that the concept of New World lands begins to diminish, especially with Zeniff, Ammon, and Amulek. We will attempt to determine why the New World is part of Alma 2's thinking, and precisely what he means by it.

	Alma 2	Ammon	Amulek	Benjamin	Mosiah	Zeniff
Land of	7	5	1	1	-	9
Region	10	2	1	4	1	16
Borders of	-	-	-	-	-	-
Round about	-	-	-	-	-	-
Part(s) of	-	-	-	-	-	-
Quarter of	-	-	-	-	-	-
Territory	-	-	-	-	-	-
Strange	1	2	-	-	-	-
Canaan	-	-	-	-	-	-
Judea	-	-	-	-	-	-
New World	11	-	-	1	4	-
Directions	-	-	-	-	-	-

Figure 5: Land

Zeniff's interest in the land focuses primarily on the land of Nephi, since he was primarily interested in getting back to his roots. When Zeniff speaks in regional terms, Nephi is the land which he wished to possess (Mosiah 9:3, 5, 7, 10; 10:1), the land the Lamanite king gave him (Mosiah 9:7), the land in which the people prospered (Mosiah 9:9, 11; 10:5), the land for which the Lamanites after twelve years of Nephite possession began to contend (Mosiah 9:14; 10:2), and the land which came into bondage under the Lamanites (Mosiah 10:18). Localities to which Zeniff refers directly are the lands of Zarahemla, from which he left (Mosiah 9:2), Nephi (or Lehi–Nephi), to which he was going and in which there was warfare (Mosiah 9:1, 6, 14), and Shilom, a land which he also received from the Lamanite king (Mosiah 9:6, 14). In addition, he refers to the lands of Shemlon and Shilom as places of confrontation between his people and the Lamanites (Mosiah 10:7–8). Finally, Zeniff mentions Old World Jerusalem in explaining why the Lamanites harbored hard feelings toward the Nephites: they believed they were driven from Jerusalem because of the iniquities of their fathers (Mosiah 10:12).

Benjamin

All of Benjamin's uses of *Land* are geographic. In the one instance when he refers to the land where the Nephites are, he promises that they will prosper in the land if they keep the Lord's commands (Mosiah 2:22). The land to which Benjamin refers is simply that in which the people are living, most particularly the land of Zarahemla (Mosiah 1:7, 10; 2:31). However, he still retains the memory of the Old World, for his one specific reference to a land other than his own is to the land of Jerusalem, out of which the Lord led the people (Mosiah 1:11).

Mosiah

Benjamin's son Mosiah seems to be a bit further removed from the Old World in his use of *Land*. In one instance, the word appears to refer to the region of Zarahemla, throughout which Mosiah had sought to establish peace (Mosiah 29:14). The four references to the New World lands seem to refer essentially to the land in which the people are living, with less sense of an Old World/New World separation. Certainly the consciousness of being separated from a homeland as found in Lehi, Nephi, and Jacob is absent. Mosiah warns that if the people choose iniquity, the judgments of God will come upon the land (Mosiah 29:27). He also desires that inequality should be banished from the land, and that it should be a land of liberty (Mosiah 29:32).

Ammon

When one turns to Ammon, Mosiah's son, four references to the land of Zarahemla and one to the land of Nephi are found. Zarahemla is the land which Ammon and his brothers left to go on their mission to the land of Nephi (Alma 26:1, 9), a mission that was jeered by the inhabitants of Zarahemla (Alma 26:23). When he writes of regions, he expresses his amazement at the miracles the Lord had worked in Ishmael and Nephi (Alma 26:12), as well as at the love he found exhibited by the Lamanite converts, a love that could find no equal either in the land of Zarahemla or anywhere in Lamanite territory (Alma 26:33). He is not, however, unaware of the people's separation from Israel, for both Nephites and Lamanites are wanderers in a "strange land"—a branch of Israel lost from its root (Alma 26:36).

Alma 2

When Alma 2 speaks geographically, he speaks specifically of various lands, referring sometimes to locations in the New World and at other times to Old World places. In the first group are the lands of Mormon, Manti, Nephi, and Siron. He speaks of his father establishing a church in the land of Mormon and then refers to it as a region (Alma 5:3). When Zoram, the commander of the Nephite armies, asks Alma 2 where he should seek for the Nephites taken captive by the Lamanites, Alma 2 tells him to go above Manti on the east of the river Sidon, and there he will recover those individuals taken captive (Alma 16:6). Alma 2 rejoices at the success of the sons of Ammon in preaching the gospel in the land of Nephi (Alma 29:14) and sorrows at Corianton's immorality with the harlot Isabel in the land of Siron (Alma 39:3). In addition, he refers to old Jerusalem, mentioning to the people of Ammonihah (Alma 9:9) and to his son, Helaman (Alma 36:29), that their fathers had been delivered from Jerusalem by the Lord. Alma 2 also mentions Salem—the city over which Melchizedek was king—as he challenges the people of Ammonihah to humble themselves as Abraham did before Melchizedek (Alma 13:17–18).

When Alma 2 uses *Land* to mean a region, it is simply a way to avoid repeating the name of the land about which he is speaking—the same kind of usage one finds in other authors. As noted above, Alma 2 speaks of the land of Mormon as the place where his father first established a church (Alma 5:3). He refers to the land of Zarahemla as the place to which the Lord brought his father's people and where his father began to work to establish the church more strongly (Alma 5:5). Alma 2 is called to preach to the people of Zarahemla (Alma 5:49) and to be high priest over the church in the land (Alma 8:23), i.e., the land of Zarahemla, which encompasses many smaller lands. He preaches to the people in Ammonihah and refers to their land as "this land" (Alma 8:24). Finally, in his defense to Korihor, Alma 2 states that he always supported himself with his own hands, despite his extensive travel around the land of Zarahemla (Alma 30:32).

When we turn to the New World idea in Alma 2, it is interesting to observe that only he and his friend Ammon speak of being wanderers in a "strange land," i.e., a land separated from their land of origin (Alma 13:23). It seems to be more than a coincidence that *no one* in the Book of Mormon uses this phrase except these two closely associated friends.

In considering the passages that have been designated as "New World" references, it should be said that these designate less of an Old World consciousness as opposed to the New, but more of a sense of land which transcends specific geographical boundaries and includes the lands of the Nephites and Lamanites. In this sense, then, there is a difference between Lehi and his sons, who have a sharp sense of difference between the Old and New Worlds, and Alma 2, who still recognizes this difference but who does not particularly make the differentiation. For example, as he speaks to the people in Ammonihah, Alma 2 states that the Lamanites were cut off from the presence of the Lord since the beginnings of their transgressions in the land (Alma 9:14). This is an object lesson to the people of Ammonihah, showing that if they continue in their present path, they will not prosper in the land—the land in which they are living—any more than the Lamanites have. However, because of their ignorance, the Lamanites are far better off than the people of Ammonihah, for God will have mercy on the Lamanites and prolong their days in the land, but no such promise is given to the people of Ammonihah (Alma 9:16–18). In other references to the land in which the people are living, Alma 2 seems to be very close to Lehi. The people will prosper in the land if they are obedient to the Lord's commands (Alma 36:1, 30; 37:28; 38:1; 45:8, 16), but if they are disobedient, the land will be cursed (Alma 37:28, 31; 45:16).

Amulek

The two references to *Land* by Amulek are both geographical. In the first instance, he reminds the people of Ammonihah that Lehi came out of the land of Jerusalem (Alma 10:3). In the second case, he tells them that the only reason destruction had not already fallen on Ammonihah was because of the prayers of the few righteous in the land (Alma 10:22).

In summary, the focus of these earlier Nephite writers was primarily on the geography of the New World, with Zeniff and Ammon particularly concerned with the land of Nephi, while the others focused primarily on Zarahemla. The others have not forgotten their roots in Israel, but this dimension has clearly diminished in importance.

Captain Moroni (Moroni 1)

Figure 6 indicates the geographical references of later individuals in Zarahemla's history.

	Helaman	Moroni 1	Nephi 2	Samuel
Land of	17	2	2	-
Region	2	2	2	5
Borders of	-	2	-	-
Round about	1	-	-	-
Part(s) of	3	-	-	-
Quarter of	2	-	-	-
Territory	-	-	-	-
Strange	-	-	-	-
Canaan	-	-	-	-
Judea	-	-	-	-
New World	-	-	-	2
Directions	-	-	-	-

Figure 6: Land

Essentially, the same categories are present that were seen with the previous writers; there is an emphasis on the naming of particular places and references to particular regions. However, Helaman seems to have a broader vocabulary than do the previous writers.

All of Captain Moroni's geographical uses of *Land* refer to places in the New World. He has deep concern for Nephite lands, for it was those lands that he had to protect. The Title of Liberty calls people to defend the Nephite lands (Alma 46:20). Also, Moroni 1 writes to Pahoran, the governor of those lands (Alma 60:1). Apart from Mormon, Captain Moroni is the only writer who uses the phrase "borders of," for he indicates that the Lamanites are encroaching upon the land "in the borders by the west sea"[1] (Alma 52:11), and he notes in his letter to Pahoran that thousands are dying defending the borders of the land (Alma 60:22). In naming specific places, Moroni 1 demands that Ammoron return to the land of Nephi (Alma 54:6) and threatens to come down to the land of Zarahemla if Pahoran does not respond to his needs (Alma 60:30).

Helaman

Helaman's basic orientation is clearly toward Zarahemla, to which he refers specifically twelve times. It seems, however, that the land of Zarahemla, as Helaman understands it, is the localized region around the city of Zarahemla rather than a broader region of Nephite lands. Perhaps this is so, because by Helaman's day the Nephite lands extended from the East Sea to the West Sea and included everything in between. With this in mind, Helaman receives supplies and troops from Zarahemla and the "land round about" (Alma 56:28; 57:6; 58:3–4), sends prisoners to Zarahemla (Alma 56:57; 57:6, 11, 15–16, 28), and marches toward Zarahemla (Alma 58:23–24). There is one regional reference to this localized Zarahemla (Alma 57:29), again having a concern with sending prisoners there. However, the other regional reference seems to imply a broader range of Nephite lands from which the Lamanites took prisoners (Alma 58:30).

Other references which imply that the Nephite lands were no longer limited to the area of the city of Zarahemla are references to a "part," "parts," or a "quarter" of the land where some event takes place. Thus Helaman writes to Captain Moroni, telling him how things are progressing in his part of the land (Alma 56:2, 9), noting that since he could not take Manti, he devoted his troops to maintaining that portion of the land which they still held (Alma 58:3). Finally,

---

[1] This could also qualify as a directional reference since it refers to the West Sea.

Helaman tells Captain Moroni that the Lamanites have pulled out of his area, that his troops have regained possession of many of their "lands" (Alma 58:33),[2] but that he still needs supplies (Alma 58:30). He does not, however, wish to trouble Moroni 1 unduly in the event that the Lamanites had entered the quarter of the land that Moroni 1 was trying to defend (Alma 58:35).

In addition to Zarahemla, Helaman names other specific places which all seem to be references to localized lands. He names Nephi as the land from which the people of Ammon came (Alma 56:3) and to which captured Nephite chief captains were probably taken (Alma 56:12). He also speaks of the "land of Manti, or the city of Manti, and the city of Zeezrom, and the city of Cumeni, and the city of Antiparah" as captured cities (Alma 56:14). His clarification that Manti should be spoken of as a city rather than as a land reinforces the premise that Helaman sees the Nephite lands composed of many regions or cities.

Nephi 2

Nephi 2 casts an eye back to old Jerusalem when he wishes that he had lived in the days of Nephi 1, when the people were slow to do iniquity (Helaman 7:7). As he speaks to the less-than-righteous people of his day, he reminds them of all the prophetic voices that had testified of Jerusalem's destruction and of Christ's coming. For those who doubted Jerusalem's fall, he cites the presence of Zedekiah's descendants who came through Mulek and who were still among his listeners, even in a day which was far removed from Jerusalem's fall to the Babylonians (Helaman 8:21). When he uses *Land* in a regional manner, Nephi 2 refers twice to Zarahemla, asking God to bring a famine on the land and then to remove the famine as the people begin to change their lives (Helaman 11:4, 13).

Samuel

Samuel never mentions a specific geographical place by name and is thus somewhat different from the writers we have just examined. However, all of his regional references seem to be to Zarahemla,

---

[2] This represents Helaman's two geographical uses of the word *Lands*.

since it is to the people of Zarahemla that he is speaking. The Lord has cursed the land of Zarahemla because of the people's wickedness (Helaman 13:23, 30, 35–36). Samuel's New World references are to the lands of both the Nephites and Lamanites; however, he does not seem to be concerned about differentiating between the Old World and the New, but concerns himself with the signs of Jesus' birth and death that will occur in the land of the Nephites and the Lamanites (Helaman 14:20, 28).

In summary, the basic concern of these authors is with Zarahemla, but perhaps with an understanding of the lands of the Nephites as being a collection of cities or localized lands which make up a broader whole. This certainly seems to be the case with Helaman, and his expanded vocabulary tends to undergird this suggestion. The Old World context seems more diminished in these authors than in any of the previous ones, with the exception of Nephi 2, who refers to Lehi's escape from Jerusalem and the city's subsequent destruction.

	Mormon	Moroni 2
Land of	293	9
Region	256	44
Borders of	13	-
Round about	12	-
Part(s) of	17	1
Quarter of	4	1
Territory	2	-
Strange	-	-
Canaan	-	-
Judea	-	-
New World	7	25
Directions	56	5

Figure 7: Land

Mormon and Moroni 2

When we turn to Mormon and Moroni 2, we come to the Book of Mormon geographers *par excellence,* especially in the case of Mormon. Of all Mormon's references to *Land,* 94.7 percent deal with geography. Only Zeniff uses the word with a higher use rate per thousand words of text (18.64) than does Mormon (7.11). Moroni 2 uses it at a rate of 5.62 per thousand. Thus, for these two authors *Land* is a highly important word. Figures 7 and 8 show the distribution of their use for both *Land* and *Lands.* Since our focus in this section is on geography, we will only deal with the geographic references to *Lands.*

	Mormon	Moroni 2
Regions	8	2
Other	-	-
Lamanites'	1	-
Zarahemla	1	-
Roundabout	-	-
Foreign	-	1
Precious	-	-
Inheritance	7	-
Choice	-	5
Of possession	4	-
Promised	-	-
Of my people	-	-
Your	-	-
Our	1	-
Your own	-	-
Their	24	-
Own	1	-
Their own	9	-
Whatsoever	1	-

Figure 8: Lands

Obviously, there are too many instances in which the word *Land* is used by Mormon and Moroni 2 to cite them all. However, we will look at Mormon's and Moroni 2's geographic concerns, their areas of stated interest, and some phraseology that is unique to them. Even without breaking their usage down, there are some unique elements already visible between them from figure 7. For example, Moroni 2 is far less specific in the places he names than is Mormon, and this may be due, in part, to the fact that Moroni 2 edits Ether and does not have the clear knowledge of the Jaredite lands that he and his father had of the Nephite and Lamanite lands. He therefore tends to speak of unnamed regions. Moroni 2 also places a decidedly greater emphasis on the New World than does Mormon, but as we have seen in other authors, this emphasis in Moroni 2 is not so much a distinction between Old and New worlds as a way of talking about both the Jaredite and Nephite/Lamanite lands as a whole. Even so, Moroni 2 does refer explicitly to the Old World. Finally, it is interesting to note that only Mormon and Moroni 2 associate directions with the lands of which they speak. When *Lands* is considered from a geographical standpoint, both Mormon and Moroni 2 use the word with a couple of individual variations to refer to regions.

Moroni 2

Specific New World lands which Moroni 2 names are Nehor (Ether 7:4), Moron (Ether 7:5-6; 14:6, 11), Desolation (Ether 7:6), Heth (Ether 8:2), and Corihor (14:27). He refers also to the Old World when he notes that Joseph took his father into Egypt, as the Lord brought Lehi out of Jerusalem, in order that Joseph's seed would not perish (Ether 13:7).

Since most of the names of the Jaredite lands were apparently not known to Moroni 2, when he speaks of people leaving a land, giving a law in the land, etc., he does so with a nonspecific, regional meaning to the word *Land*. For example, Moroni 2 says that king Shule issued a law throughout the land which permitted the prophets to travel where they pleased (Ether 7:25). Omer is warned to depart out of the land (Ether 9:3). Nimrah fled from the land (Ether 9:9). There is war in the land (Ether 10:8, 15). Morianton gains power over the land (Ether 10:8-10). People prosper in the land (Ether 10:16). Forests and animals cover the land (Ether 10:19).[3] Moroni 2 uses

---

[3] For other examples of this same type of use, see Ether 10:33; 11:4; 12:1; 15:12, 14.

Lands in a similar way. The great sea divided the "lands," i.e., probably the Pacific Ocean dividing the Asian continent from the American continent (Ether 2:13). Anyone who participates in secret combinations seeks to overthrow the freedom of lands, nations, and countries (Ether 8:25). The restoration will occur when one hears of fires, tempests, and smoke in foreign lands (Mormon 8:29).

Moroni 2 also speaks of the land northward and the land southward, the former being the inhabited land of the Jaredites (Ether 10:21) and the latter being a place to which people fled before serpents (Ether 9:31–32), the place of the Jaredite hunting grounds (Ether 10:19, 21), and the place which the Nephites called Zarahemla (Ether 9:31). The two lands were separated by a narrow neck of land (Ether 10:20).

As noted above, Moroni 2 believes the New World lands are special, as we shall see more fully later. That identification with the lands of the Western Hemisphere is underlined in two ways: (1) by speaking generally about events that cut across regional boundaries but which clearly are related to the broad region inhabited by Jaredites or Nephites and Lamanites; and (2) by speaking regionally with essentially the same meaning. These two are not always easy to separate, but Moroni 2 seems to make this subtle distinction, especially when he refers to "this land" which should be understood as a specific reference to the New World in which events cut across regional boundaries. It would not, then, be inappropriate (see figure 7) to take the twenty-four regional references, which I believe refer to the lands of the New World, and add them to the twenty-five New World references, thereby giving us a total of forty-nine New World references and twenty regional references. To do so only heightens the already strong sense of New World orientation that one finds in Moroni 2.

When we consider Moroni 2's New World references, we see that he is clearly conscious of others who have possessed the land before him and whose words will pass to later generations (Mormon 8:23; 9:36). He also denotes Jesus as the God of this land (Ether 2:12). This land is a promised land upon which the Jaredites bowed down (Ether 6:12), upon which they planted their crops (Ether 6:13), and upon which they began to spread (Ether 6:18). Orihah exercised his rule wisely over the land (Ether 7:1). The land can be cursed because of wickedness (Ether 7:23) or blessed because of righteousness (Ether 7:26). Prophets work in the land (Ether 9:28), and if the inhabitants are not righteous, other people may possess it (Ether 11:21). This land is the place where the New Jerusalem will be built (Ether 13:4, 6), where the remnant of the house of Joseph will grow (Ether 13:8), and where the three Nephites tarried before they were taken by the Lord (Mormon 8:10).[4]

When we consider Moroni 2's regional references to the New World lands, we find him lamenting that the land is covered with robbery, murder, and bloodshed (Mormon 8:8–9), noting that the wicked shall be swept off the land (Ether 2:10–11), citing the fact that there was peace in the land under Emer and Coriantum (Ether 9:15, 22), and noting that people began to die quickly because of drought and poisonous snakes in the land (Ether 9:30–31).[5]

Thus, Moroni 2 has a strong identification with the Western Hemisphere, whether he is talking about the Jaredites or the final destruction of the Nephites. He is fully aware, however, that the Nephites and Lamanites are a separated branch of Israel.

Mormon

As indicated above, Mormon is *the* geographer of the Book of Mormon. Without him we would know virtually nothing about the Book of Mormon lands. It is in Mormon that we find the names of the Book of Mormon cities and regions and the differentiation made between lands north and south. While it is beyond the scope of this study, it is important to note that Mormon is also the one who mentions the mountains, seas, directions, and animals. However, we need to be careful as we study his knowledge of the Book of Mormon lands, because he did not always have personal knowledge of the lands of which he wrote, particularly those in the land of Nephi. Hence, Mormon may have been dependent upon sources himself,

---

[4] For other usages in this same vein, see Ether 7:11; 9:16, 20, 26; 10:4; 13:2.

[5] For similar references see Ether 10:4; 11:6–7; 13:25–26, 31; 14:1, 17–19, 21–23.

thereby necessitating that we distinguish between first- and second-hand knowledge when we try to use his descriptions of the land.

Mormon names forty-one different lands, many of them several times.[6] For example, he mentions the land of Nephi forty-three times, Zarahemla seventy-three times, Bountiful twenty-one times, Ammonihah eleven times, and Jershon eighteen times. As far as I can determine, these references are simply the product of a writer who wants to let people know where things took place. For Mormon, God worked in real history and among real people, all of whom lived in real places; Mormon had visited many of these places and had personal knowledge of them. This is an emphasis that runs through Mormon's entire work, beginning with Words of Mormon 1:13 and ending with Mormon 6:6.

To avoid constantly repeating a place name, Mormon often refers to the land as a region, permitting the context to determine to which specific land he is speaking. Once again, however, the list is long, for he mentions twenty-eight such regions.[7] The most dominant region is Zarahemla (155 times) which often appears to encompass all Nephite lands rather than merely being a local designation. For Mormon, Zarahemla had become a designation for the whole Nephite land.

Also important to Mormon among the regional designations are the land of Nephi (27) and a broad designation, appearing primarily in 4 Nephi, which seems to include the lands of both the Nephites and

---

[6] The lands which Mormon mentions are (in alphabetical order): Ammonihah (11), Amulon (3), Antionum (4), Between Zarahemla (1), Bordering on the wilderness (1), Bountiful (21), Cumorah (4), David (1), Desolation (10), Father's nativity (1), Gideon (7), Helam (9), His nativity (1), Ishmael (11), Jashon (1), Jershon (18), Jerusalem (7), Joshua (1), Lamanites (2), Lehi (4), Lehi-Nephi (2), Manti (7), Many waters (1), Melek (5), Middoni (8), Midian (1), Morianton (2), Mormon (1), Moroni (5), Near Bountiful (1), Neck of (1), Nephi (43), Nephihah (4), Nephites (1), Noah (2), Shem (1), Shemlon (4), Shilom (8), Sidom (4), Zarahemla (73), Zoramites (1).

[7] In alphabetical order the regions are: Ammonihah (5), Antionum (4), Antum (1), By the seashore (1), Desolation (1), Fortified land in Zarahemla (2), Gideon (1), Helam (3), Ishmael (4), Jershon (3), Jerusalem (1), Lamanite lands (1), Lamanite and Nephite lands (26), Lehi and Melek (1), Manti (1), Melek (1), Middoni (1), Mormon (1), Moroni (1), Nephi (27), Nephi, Zarahemla, and land northward (1), Nephihah (1), Nephite lands (2), New World (1), Northward (10), Region (2), Sidon (1), Zarahemla (155).

Lamanites (26). After these two, other specific regional areas are mentioned much less frequently. In addition, Mormon uses a variety of expressions to denote various portions of the land: "borders of,"[8] "round about,"[9] "part(s) of,"[10] and "quarters of."[11]

When Mormon speaks regionally and uses *Lands,* he speaks in much the same way as he did with *Land.* The Lamanites had taken possession of Shemlon, Shilom, and Amulon and had appointed kings over these lands (Mosiah 24:2). Helaman recaptured many of the Nephite lands (Alma 59:1) and, in the fifty-eighth year of the judges, the Nephites succeeded in regaining the lands around Zarahemla. In addition, Mormon speaks of the lands which were called Mulek in the north and Lehi in the south, noting that they were rich in gold and silver (Helaman 6:10-11). Finally, he narrates the events in which Lachoneus gathered the people to one place, leaving the lands in the north and in the south to the Lamanites, but leaving them deserted and without game (3 Nephi 4:1–2). Later, the Nephites give lands of their own from the midst of the Nephite lands to ex-Gadianton robbers who were Lamanites (3 Nephi 6:3).

Mormon is also the only writer, apart from his son, Moroni 2, who uses directional designations with respect to various land regions. He refers to the land northward (33), the land southward (12), the land south (5), the land north (5), and the land on the south by the sea (1). The difference between Mormon and Moroni 2 is that all of Mormon's references are to Nephite and Lamanite lands, while those of Moroni 2 are to Jaredite lands.

Of major interest for this study is the unique language that Mormon and Moroni 2 share in referring to the lands of which they speak. No other author uses the phrases listed in figure 9 with any

---

[8] E.g., Mosiah 18:4, 31; 19:6; 21:2, 26; 23:25; Alma 2:36; 3:23; 8:5; 16:2; 27:14; 51:14; 52:15.

[9] E.g., Mosiah 11:12; 21:2, 20; 23:25; 27:2; Alma 21:21; 24:1; 48:8; 49:13; 50:9; 59:2, 6.

[10] Alma 52:5, 13; 53:8; 59:3, 6; 62:42; Helaman 1:23, 27; 3:6, 23; 4:9; 6:7; 11:6, 33; 3 Nephi 7:12; Moroni 8:28.

[11] E.g., Mosiah 27:6; Alma 43:26; 52:10; 56:1.

consistency.[12] Where they do appear they are very isolated instances. Figure 9 shows these phrases and the frequency with which they appear in Mormon and Moroni 2.

	Mormon	Moroni 2
Throughout all the land	24	1
Over all the land	7	2
Throughout the land	11	1
Through all the land	1	1
In all the land	23	2
Through the land	2	-
All the land	3	-
Throughout all his land	1	-
Against all the land	1	-
[Throughout] all the face of the land	12	9
The whole face of the land	4	2
[Throughout] the face of all the land	3	-
The face of the [this] land	10	15
The face of the whole land	1	-

Figure 9

There seems to be a tendency, particularly throughout Mormon, to use language that is expansive and inclusive.[13] Only Moroni 2 regularly uses similar language, but there are clearly differences between father and son. Moroni 2 seems to like the phrase "the face

---

[12] The exceptions are Alma 2 ("upon all this land"—Alma 37:28), Ammon ("in all the land"—Alma 26:33), Isaiah ("[in] all the land"—2 Nephi 17:24; 20:23), Lord in Isaiah ("the whole land"—2 Nephi 23:5), Lehi ("the face of this land"—2 Nephi 1:9, 31), Lord ("all the face of the earth"—Ether 1:43), Mosiah ("throughout the land"—Mosiah 29:14; "the face of the land"—Mosiah 29:32), Nephi 1 ("the face of the [this] land"—1 Nephi 12:4, 20; 22:7; 2 Nephi 30:7); Samuel ("the face of the land"—Helaman 14:20; "all the face of this land"—Helaman 14:28), Zenos ("all the land of the [my] vineyard"—Jacob 5:21, 69).

[13] See as examples of Mormon's use of these expansive phrases: Mosiah 2:1; 27:2, 32; 29:1; Alma 1:16; 2:5; 5:1; 8:5; 16:15; 23:3; 43:29; 49:13; 59:2; 62:46; Helaman 3:31; 6:28, 38; 11:1, 32; 16:22–23; 3 Nephi 1:7; 2:11; 6:3, 5; 8:3, 22; 28:18, 23; 4 Nephi 1:18, 23, 46; Mormon 1:13, 19; 2:8, 15; Moroni 9:19. For examples of Moroni's use see Mormon 8:8–10; Ether 2:3; 6:12–13, 18; 7:25; 9:28, 31; 11:6; 13:2, 31; 14:22; 15:14. The above lists are not exhaustive. It should be noted that the inclusive phrases are not used by Moroni 2 in the book of Moroni.

of the [this] land," while Mormon likes to include the word "all" in the various phrases he uses. In these phrases, we have the clear fingerprints of Mormon and Moroni.

In summary, both Mormon and Moroni 2 provide geographical details, but it is Mormon who is the most interested by far in geographical notes. Clear differences are detectable, however, and lie particularly in the way the two use expansive phrases when talking about the land, a practice that is virtually unique to the two of them.

	Angel	Father	Jesus	Lord	Lord-Isa
Promised	1	1	-	4	-
Covenant	1	-	-	-	-
Choice	-	-	-	5	-
Holy	-	-	-	1	-
Prepared	-	-	-	1	-
Chosen	-	-	-	-	-
Liberty	-	-	-	1	-
Inheritance	1	-	7	3	-
Our possession	-	-	-	-	-
Our	-	-	-	-	-
Own	-	-	-	-	1
Our fathers'	-	1	-	-	-
Whatsoever	-	-	-	-	-
Better	-	-	-	-	-
A	-	-	-	-	-
Their	-	-	-	1	-
Thy	-	1	-	-	1
My	-	-	-	-	1
His	-	-	-	-	-
Ground	-	-	-	-	-
Earth	-	-	-	-	-
As verb	-	-	-	-	-

Figure 10: Land

Special Meanings to the Word *Land*

This portion of the chapter will deal with generally nongeographical uses of the word *Land*. As can be seen in figure 10, these have to do with the ways in which *Land* is defined or described. Some of these uses identify the land as a special gift from God. Others designate the land as the possession of the people who speak of it. Some miscellaneous designations of the land are also included.

Figure 10 shows how the divine or heavenly beings use *Land*. Clearly, the emphasis is on *Land* being a place of inheritance, a choice land, and a promised land, especially in the words of the Lord and of Jesus. When we couple this emphasis with the already observed emphasis on the land of the New World, it is clear that the divine figures proclaim the Western Hemisphere to be a special place.

Angel

The Angel speaks of the "land" of the New World, indicating to Nephi 1 that it is a choice land which has been promised to Lehi for his descendants' inheritance (1 Nephi 13:30). Even the Gentiles, if they do not harden their hearts, will be blessed upon this promised land (1 Nephi 14:2).

Father

The Father's words are quoted by Jesus when he appeared at the temple in Bountiful. These quoted words deal with the Father's promises to the patriarchs of Israel, i.e., that the Father would remember and gather Israel, that he would give them their land of inheritance and their land of promise which is Jerusalem (3 Nephi 20:29), and that the Gentiles may be participants in this process. However, if the Gentiles do not repent, their cities in the New World will be destroyed (3 Nephi 21:15). Thus, the Father ties together the covenants made with Abraham, Isaac, and Jacob with the new work in the latter days which will fulfill those original covenants.

The Lord

The Lord captures, in one verse, his view of the land to which he is bringing Lehi and his family. It is a land of promise (twice designated as "promised land" and twice as "land of promise"), a land prepared by the Lord, and a choice land (1 Nephi 2:20). These themes echo throughout all his words. It is a promised land to those who keep his commandments (1 Nephi 4:14; 17:13), and when Lehi's family arrives in the promised land, they will know that the Lord is God (1 Nephi 17:14). It is the land of inheritance for Lehi's seed and those who will become part of that seed (2 Nephi 10:10, 19). It is a choice land, not only for Lehi's seed, but also for the Jaredites (2 Nephi 10:19; Ether 1:42; 2:15). It is a holy land (Enos 1:10). It is a land of liberty for the Gentiles (2 Nephi 10:11). The one use that falls outside the above sense of a "promised land" is the prophecy of Abinadi, when he, using the Lord's words, reveals that plagues will come upon the people in King Noah's land and that insects will pester "their" land (Mosiah 12:6).

The Lord in Isaiah (Lord-Isa)

The words of the Lord as recorded in Isaiah reflect an Old World context. In the first instance, because the people of Judah fear the alliance of Syria and Ephraim (Israel or the Northern kingdom) and do not trust the Lord, God's people in the land of Judah will be overrun and almost demolished by Assyria (2 Nephi 18:8). Second, those who oppress God's people, particularly the Babylonians and Assyrians, will eventually flee to their own lands or be trampled by the Lord (2 Nephi 23:14; 24:25).

Jesus

Apart from the geographical references already examined, all Jesus' references are to a "land of inheritance." He tells the people at Bountiful (the descendants of Lehi and Mulek) that this land (the New World) is the land of their inheritance (3 Nephi 15:13; 16:16; 20:14). But it is also a land of inheritance for the Gentiles, if they will but come to Christ (3 Nephi 21:22). Old Jerusalem and its environs, however, are to be the inheritance of scattered Israel (3 Nephi 20:33, 46). There is one final reference in which the location of the land of inheritance is not clearly specified, but it refers to the gathering of scattered Israel to a land (3 Nephi 21:28).

In addition to the singular form of *Land,* the divine figures also speak of *Lands* as figure 11 shows.

Land and Lands 131

	Angel	Lord
Regions	-	-
Other	1	-
Lamanites'	-	-
Zarahemla	-	-
Roundabout	-	-
Foreign	-	-
Precious	-	-
Inheritance	-	2
Choice	-	3
Of possession	-	1
Promised	-	-
Of my people	-	1
Your	-	-
Our	-	-
Your own	-	-
Their	-	-
Own	-	-
Their own	-	-
Whatsoever	-	-

Figure 11: Lands

As noted in the geographic section, the Angel's one use of *Lands* is geographic. However, the Lord's use of *Lands* is solely theological. First, the New World is a land that is choice above all other lands (1 Nephi 2:20; 2 Nephi 10:19; Ether 2:15). Second, the Jews shall one day be restored to the lands of their inheritance (2 Nephi 10:7-8), as will all scattered Israel (2 Nephi 29:14). Finally, God has heard the mourning of his daughters, "in all the lands of my people," because of the wickedness of their husbands (Jacob 2:31). This is probably a reference to scattered Israel.

In summary, all the divine figures are primarily concerned about *Land* as a land of promise and inheritance, either for Lehi's descendants or for the scattered tribes.

Prophets of the Plates of Brass

Not too surprisingly, Isaiah's focus is not on lands of promise. Instead, he has some miscellaneous references to *Land,* as figure 12 shows. All of Zenos's references to land are geographic.

	Isaiah	Zenos
Promised	-	-
Covenant	-	-
Choice	-	-
Holy	-	-
Prepared	-	-
Chosen	-	-
Liberty	-	-
Inheritance	-	-
Our possession	-	-
Our	-	-
Own	1	-
Our fathers'	1	-
Whatsoever	-	-
Better	-	-
A	-	-
Their	3	-
Thy	-	-
My	-	-
His	-	-
Ground	1	-
Earth	-	-
As verb	-	-

Figure 12: Land

In two verses, Isaiah mentions scattered Israel returning to her lands,[14] along with strangers, and possessing those lands (2 Nephi 24:1-2). Isaiah, in a prayer, refers three times to "their" land, meaning the land of Judah which has been polluted by intermarriage, soothsayers, the search for wealth, and idol worship (2 Nephi 12:7-8). Thus, the Lord has forsaken his people temporarily. Finally, Isaiah uses *Land* to refer to solid ground (2 Nephi 15:30).

Lehi

Figure 13 gives the distribution of the special uses of *Land* among Lehi and his immediate descendants.

---

[14] Isaiah has one reference to *Lands,* and it is in the context of Israel being gathered to her lands of promise (2 Nephi 24:2).

Land and Lands 133

	Enos	Jacob	Lehi	Nephi 1
Promised	-	1	4	18
Covenant	-	-	1	-
Choice	-	-	1	-
Holy	-	-	-	-
Prepared	-	-	-	-
Chosen	-	-	-	-
Liberty	-	-	1	-
Inheritance	-	2	4	6
Our possession	-	-	-	-
Our	-	-	-	-
Own	-	-	-	-
Our fathers'	-	-	-	-
Whatsoever	-	-	-	-
Better	-	1	-	-
A	-	-	-	-
Their	-	-	-	-
Thy	-	-	-	-
My	-	-	-	-
His	-	-	-	-
Ground	1	-	-	1
Earth	-	-	-	-
As verb	-	-	-	-

Figure 13: Land

Obviously, Lehi, Nephi 1, and Jacob emphasize the New World land as a promised land or a land of inheritance.

Lehi rejoices in the fact that he has obtained a land of promise which is choice and precious (1 Nephi 5:5; 2 Nephi 1:10) and meant for those who will be obedient to the Lord (2 Nephi 1:10). God's agent in bringing Lehi's family to the promised land was Nephi (2 Nephi 1:24). That land will be an inheritance for Lehi's sons' descendants (2 Nephi 3:2). It is also a land which the Lord covenanted to give Lehi (2 Nephi 1:5) and will remain a land of liberty unless the people become unrighteous (2 Nephi 1:7).

Nephi 1

Like the Lord, Nephi 1 uses two phrases that have been designated "promised land" in figure 13. They are "promised land" (six times) and "land of promise" (nine times). All four of Lehi's references are to the "land of promise." However, there seems to be no significant difference between the meanings of the two phrases.

Nephi 1 sets the stage for his emphasis on a promised land when he includes a note in the preface to 1 Nephi stating that God was leading Lehi's family to a "promised land." He tells of the land's importance and of the events that will occur on it. Nephi 1 tells us that because of the Lord's wisdom, Lehi's family was commanded to take both their wives and the plates of brass to the promised land (1 Nephi 5:22; 7:1) and that if they were faithful, they would reach that land (1 Nephi 7:13). He also tells of Lehi's understanding that Israel would be scattered and ultimately gathered, and that their trek to the promised land was a part of that scattering (1 Nephi 10:13). Nephi 1 himself had a vision of the promised land in which he saw many cities in the land, a mist of darkness settling on the land (1 Nephi 12:4), and Columbus coming to the land (1 Nephi 13:12).

When Lehi's family finally leaves the Old World for the promised land, the winds drive them toward it (1 Nephi 18:8), they sail toward it after Laman and Lemuel's rebellion (1 Nephi 18:22-23), and they arrive at it and name it "the promised land" (1 Nephi 18:23). Nephi 1 relates that Lehi told Laman and Lemuel how blessed they were to have been brought by the Lord from Jerusalem to the promised land (2 Nephi 1:3). Nephi 1 speaks of a promised land one more time, when, in the face of Laman and Lemuel's rebellions, he reminds them that the Israelites, despite their wickedness, were led out of Egypt to the promised land by Moses (1 Nephi 17:42).

Nephi 1 gives an interesting twist to the idea of a "land of inheritance." In five out of six instances, this phrase does not refer to the New World. Three times the "land of inheritance" refers to Lehi's properties near Jerusalem. Lehi and his family leave the land of his inheritance (1 Nephi 2:4, 11), yet the sons return to it to gather the wealth left there in order to attempt to buy the plates of brass from Laban (1 Nephi 3:16, 18). Nephi 1's other uses of "inheritance" refer to the exiled Jews in Babylon returning to the land of their inheritance (1 Nephi 10:3) and to the Gentiles prospering in their land of inheritance, i.e., the New World (1 Nephi 13:15). Nephi 1, like Isaiah, refers once to *Land* as that which is opposite to the sea. The "mother Gentiles" battle on land and sea against those Gentiles who have come to the New World (1 Nephi 13:17).

Jacob and Enos

As already seen, Jacob's use of *Land* is sparse when compared to that of Lehi and Nephi 1. He speaks, as did Nephi 1, of the family having been driven out of their land of inheritance to a better land (2 Nephi 10:20). That better land was the land of promise which had great deposits of precious ores (Jacob 2:12). However, if the people of Nephi in Jacob's day did not cease their wickedness, their land of inheritance would be given to the Lamanites (Jacob 3:4).

Enos uses the word *Land* only once, in a wholly unique way. He tells us that the Nephites tilled the land, i.e., the ground, in order to raise grain and fruit (Enos 1:21).

When we turn to *Lands* as used by Lehi and his sons, we find many of the same emphases that we have already observed, as shown in figure 14.

When Lehi uses *Lands,* he refers to the New World. It is a land which is choice above all other "lands." Thus, Lehi uses the word in a comparative sense (2 Nephi 1:5). However, when Lehi's descendants become wicked, the lands of their "inheritance"[15] will be given to other nations (2 Nephi 1:11).

Nephi 1 uses "lands of inheritance" as he used "land of inheritance," i.e., to refer to Old World lands. Israel will be gathered together to her lands of inheritance (1 Nephi 22:12), as will those who were "carried away captive" to Babylon (2 Nephi 25:11). In like manner, Jacob indicates that when the Jews come to Christ, they will be gathered to the lands of inheritance and promise, which would be Old World lands (2 Nephi 6:11; 9:2).

---

[15] There is a difference here between the word "inheritance," as found in the printer's manuscript, and the word "possessions," as found in the 1981 Book of Mormon.

	Jacob	Lehi	Nephi 1
Regions	-	-	1
Other	-	-	2
Lamanites'	-	-	-
Zarahemla	-	-	-
Roundabout	-	-	-
Foreign	-	-	-
Precious	-	-	1
Inheritance	2	1	2
Choice	-	1	-
Of possession	-	-	-
Promised	1	-	-
Of my people	-	-	-
Your	-	-	-
Our	-	-	-
Your own	-	-	-
Their	-	-	-
Own	-	-	-
Their own	-	-	-
Whatsoever	-	-	-

Figure 14: Lands

In summary, the emphasis among Lehi and his sons is on the promised land and the land of inheritance. However, there is a distinct difference between Lehi and Nephi 1 on what constitutes the land of inheritance. For Lehi it is the New World lands, while for Nephi 1 it predominantly refers to the land near Jerusalem from which they came. When Jacob uses the word *Lands,* it is with this same Old World sense.

Zeniff

The use of *Land* takes on a different complexion for the writers in Zarahemla. Figure 15 displays those differences.

Most of Zeniff's references are to the land of Nephi; this is what he means when he refers to land of "our fathers." He and his people seek to return to Nephi and repossess it (Mosiah 9:3-4; 10:3). It is also what he calls "our" land, a land which his people had to defend against the Lamanites so that they could live in peace (Mosiah 9:18; 10:20–21).

Land and Lands 137

	Alma 2	Ammon	Amulek	Benjamin	Mosiah	Zeniff
Promised	4	-	-	-	-	1
Covenant	-	-	-	-	-	-
Choice	-	-	-	-	-	-
Holy	-	-	-	-	-	-
Prepared	-	-	-	-	-	-
Chosen	-	-	-	-	-	-
Liberty	-	-	-	-	1	-
Inheritance	-	-	-	-	1	1
Our possession	-	-	-	-	-	-
Our	1	-	-	-	-	3
Own	-	-	-	-	-	-
Our fathers'	-	-	-	-	-	4
Whatsoever	-	1	-	-	-	-
Better	-	-	-	-	-	-
A	-	-	-	-	-	-
Their	-	1	-	-	-	-
Thy	-	-	-	-	-	-
My	-	-	-	-	-	-
His	-	-	-	-	-	-
Ground	-	-	-	-	-	-
Earth	-	-	-	-	-	-
As verb	-	-	-	-	-	-

Figure 15: Land

Zeniff, at one point, explains why the Lamanites were so angry with the Nephites. In doing so, he mentions the "land of their first inheritance" (Mosiah 10:13) which refers to the region where Lehi and his family first landed in the promised land (Mosiah 10:15) and where the Lamanites believed their fathers had been wronged by Nephi 1 and those who followed him (Mosiah 10:13).

Mosiah

Mosiah expresses his wishes for his people near the end of his life. These include the desire that the people might continue in the land and *inherit* it (note the verb form) and that it might be a land of liberty without inequality (Mosiah 29:32).

Ammon

Ammon joyfully tells us that God is conscious of people in "whatsoever" land he may find them (Alma 26:37). He obviously evokes this exclamation because of the Lamanites's response to the gospel. He then tells the Anti-Nephi-Lehies that he will go into the land of Zarahemla to see if the people will be willing to have the converted Lamanites dwell in "their" land (Alma 27:15).

Alma 2

Alma 2 has a mixed use of *Land* meaning a promised land. In one instance he refers to God leading the people of Israel out of Egypt into the promised land (Alma 36:28). In two other instances he refers to the New World as the promised land to which the Liahona directed Lehi's family. The Liahona, however, is used as a type for those who adhere to Christ's words and consequently find "a far better land of promise" (Alma 37:44–45). Finally, God, through his angels, is declaring glad tidings to all those scattered on the face of the earth, and thus, says Alma 2, angels are declaring this good news in "our" land (Zarahemla) (Alma 13:24).

Only Zeniff and Alma 2 use the word *Lands*. Zeniff refers once to his people tilling their "lands" on the south of the land of Shilom (Mosiah 9:14). Alma 2 closes his sermon to the people of Gideon by blessing their houses and their lands (Alma 7:27).

In summary, the idea of the New World as a promised land, while not having fully disappeared, has certainly diminished among these earlier writers of the Zarahemla period. There is a much greater consciousness, particularly for Zeniff, of "our" land.

Captain Moroni (Moroni 1)

The above emphasis on "our land" becomes even more apparent in the later Zarahemla writers, although their use of *Land* for other than geographic reasons is limited. Figure 16 shows the use distribution.

Land and Lands

	Helaman	Moroni 1	Nephi 2	Samuel
Promised	-	-	1	-
Covenant	-	-	-	-
Choice	-	-	-	-
Holy	-	-	-	-
Prepared	-	-	-	-
Chosen	-	-	-	-
Liberty	-	-	-	-
Inheritance	-	1	-	-
Our possession	-	-	1	-
Our	2	3	-	-
Own	-	1	-	-
Our fathers'	-	-	-	-
Whatsoever	-	-	-	-
Better	-	-	-	-
A	-	-	-	-
Their	-	-	-	-
Thy	-	-	-	-
My	-	-	-	-
His	-	-	-	-
Ground	-	-	-	-
Earth	-	-	-	-
As verb	-	-	-	-

Figure 16: Land

Captain Moroni (Moroni 1) has a clear sense that the land upon which he lives is Nephite land or "our land." He will defend that land against those who would invade it (Alma 60:2). Moroni 1 tells Pahoran that unless aid is forthcoming, he will leave forces to defend that part of "our" land where he is and come down to stir up an insurrection against those who so negligently administer the government (Alma 60:25–27). But his concept of land goes beyond Zarahemla, for he has not forgotten that the land of Nephi was the land of "our first inheritance." Thus, he tells the Lamanite leader, Ammoron, that if he does not withdraw from the Nephite lands, he, Moroni 1, will push Ammoron back into his own land, the land of their first inheritance (Alma 54:12).

Helaman and Nephi 2

Helaman makes two references to "our" land. He writes to Moroni 1, telling him that his troops are holding all that portion of the land around Manti that they can and that he has sent messengers to the governor of "our" land, i.e., Zarahemla, to inform him of the situation and to request supplies and men. However, when that aid was not sent, he begins to despair that the judgments of God might be upon his ("our") land (Alma 58:4, 9).

	Helaman	Moroni 1	Nephi 2
Regions	2	-	-
Other	-	-	-
Lamanites'	-	-	-
Zarahemla	-	-	-
Roundabout	-	-	-
Foreign	-	-	-
Precious	-	-	-
Inheritance	-	1	-
Choice	-	-	-
Of possession	-	1	-
Promised	-	-	-
Of my people	-	-	-
Your	-	-	1
Our	3	3	-
Your own	-	2	-
Their	-	-	-
Own	-	-	-
Their own	-	-	-
Whatsoever	-	-	-

Figure 17: Lands

Nephi 2 speaks once of the "land of our possession" which he tells the people of Zarahemla will be taken from them if they do not repent (Helaman 7:22). He also speaks of the promised land, meaning the New World, when he wishes that he could have lived in the land in the days of Nephi 1 (Helaman 7:7).

When we consider the use of *Lands,* we see a continuing emphasis on "our" land, especially with Captain Moroni and Helaman.

Captain Moroni was determined to keep his ("our") lands from being overrun by the Lamanites (Alma 44:5; 54:10; 60:17). To that end, he tells Zerahemnah to return to his own lands and possessions. If he does not do so, then the Nephites would be compelled to take over their own lands of inheritance, once again meaning the Lamanite lands in Nephi (Alma 54:6–7, 13). Helaman, for his part, is also determined to keep the Nephite lands (Alma 58:10, 12, 38). Finally, Nephi 2 tells the people of Zarahemla that if they do not repent, their lands will be taken from them (Helaman 7:28).

In summary, as was suggested at the beginning of this section, there is a distinct sense of "our" land that runs through these later writers.

Mormon and Moroni 2

As figures 18 and 19 show, Mormon and Moroni 2 have a much richer use of language in this "special" area than do the other writers we have so far examined. Given Mormon's and Moroni 2's high rates per thousand words of text and the length of their texts, this is not surprising. Their use of *Lands* will be integrated into the discussions on *Land,* hence the inclusion of figure 19 in this section.

Note both the similarities and the differences between Mormon and Moroni 2 in their choice of descriptive words with reference to *Land.* Moroni 2 speaks of a promised or choice land, while Mormon shows almost no interest in that theological area. Both, however, speak of a land of inheritance. In addition, they are the only persons in the entire Book of Mormon who use *Land* as a verb. Further, Mormon has uses of *Land* that are unique to him. When Mormon's and Moroni 2's uses of *Lands* are considered, there continue to be differences, the most obvious being that Moroni 2 continues to prefer to speak of "choice" lands, an expression that Mormon never uses.

	Mormon	Moroni 2
Promised	-	10
Covenant	-	-
Choice	-	3
Holy	-	-
Prepared	-	-
Chosen	1	1
Liberty	1	-
Inheritance	3	4
Our possession	-	-
Our	1	-
Own	4	-
Our fathers'	-	-
Whatsoever	-	-
Better	-	-
A	5	-
Their	10	-
Thy	-	-
My	-	-
His	3	-
Ground	-	-
Earth	-	1
As verb	1	1

Figure 18: Land[16]

Moroni 2

Moroni 2 explains his understanding of the promised land succinctly in Ether 2:7–12. There he states that the New World, to which the Jaredites were brought, is a choice land that God had preserved for a righteous people. In fact, it is a land choice "above all other lands" (Ether 2:7, 10; 9:20; 10:28; 13:2). All who live in this land must serve God, and if they do not, they will be swept from the land—a threat that Moroni 2 makes three times in these six verses.

---

[16] If one adds together the numbers for Mormon in figures 7 and 18, the total is 689 as opposed to the actual 696 uses of *Land* by Mormon. It has not been worth the effort to try to find those seven "lost" references, because they make no ultimate difference to the point of the study.

Those who possess the land will be free from bondage or captivity if they serve the God of the land, Jesus Christ. Moroni 2 addresses these words particularly to the Gentiles who will live in the land, so that they may be warned of the conditions associated with inhabiting this New World land and not suffer the consequences of disobedience to which the previous inhabitants had been subjected.

	Mormon	Moroni 2
Regions	8	2
Other	-	-
Lamanites'	1	-
Zarahemla	1	-
Roundabout	-	-
Foreign	-	1
Precious	-	-
Inheritance	7	-
Choice	-	5
Of possession	4	-
Promised	-	-
Of my people	-	-
Your	-	-
Our	1	-
Your own	-	-
Their	24	-
Own	-	-
Their own	10	-
Whatsoever	1	-

Figure 19: Lands

After describing the requirements for possession of the land, Moroni 2 then recounts the travel of the Jaredites across the great sea, during which they were blown toward and finally reached the promised land (Ether 6:5, 7, 12). Upon arriving, the Jaredites bowed down upon the land and thanked the Lord for their safe passage (Ether 6:12). Moroni 2 also notes that the number of people who started the journey with Jared and his brother was twenty-two; they had begotten children before coming to the promised land, thus they rapidly grew in number (Ether 6:16). Therefore, it would seem that more than twenty-two

Jaredites landed on the shores of the New World. Moroni 2 mentions the promised land one more time when he says that Shule reigned in righteousness and remembered the great things the Lord had done in bringing his fathers to the promised land (Ether 7:27).

As seen above, Moroni 2 also understood that the Western Hemisphere was choice land. For example, the people who lived under Lib's reign could not have been happier, for they lived in a choice land (Ether 10:28). Moroni 2 tells us that after the waters of the great flood receded, this land became a choice and chosen land above all others (Ether 13:2).

Moroni 2 uses the phrase "land of their inheritance" in three ways. First, it designates regions of the New World that the Jaredites had possessed, from which they had been driven, and to which they had again returned. Thus, Noah regains the land of his first inheritance (Ether 7:16), as does Omer (Ether 9:13). Second, Coriantumr would live to see another people receive the Jaredite land for their inheritance (Ether 13:21). Third, the New World will be the land of inheritance for the remnant of the house of Joseph and the place where a holy city like old Jerusalem will be built (Ether 13:8). Hence, there is no question that Moroni 2 understands the New World lands to be very special in the eyes of the Lord.

Finally, Moroni 2 once uses *Land* to mean the earth or the world. He says that the Jaredites gathered bees and "all manner of that which was upon the face of the land," such as seeds (Ether 2:3). He uses *Land* once more, but this time as a verb, telling us that the Jaredites landed on the shores of the promised land (Ether 6:12).

Mormon

Interestingly, Mormon shows almost no interest in the theological implications of *Land*. As indicated earlier, he is the geographer *par excellence*. Even his few references in the "special use" category are, for the most part, geographic in nature. This trend also holds true when we consider *Lands*.

We do, however, get a small glimpse of his theological understanding of the land when he refers to a "land of inheritance." Surprisingly, his references are to Israel returning to their land of inheritance, which seems to imply not a New World land, but an Old

World land (Mormon 3:17; 5:14). The New World is not wholly neglected by Mormon, however. It is a very localized area to which Mormon refers when he reports that after Captain Moroni prayed, he set aside all the land south of the land of Desolation as a chosen land of liberty (Alma 46:17). Mormon's one other reference to "land of inheritance" is similarly localized, when he reports that Lamoni and Ammon returned from Middoni to Ishmael, the land of their inheritance (Alma 21:18). The same is true when "lands of inheritance" or "lands of possessions" are considered. King Benjamin fought the Lamanites until they were driven out of the lands of the Nephite inheritance, i.e., the city and region of Zarahemla (Words of Mormon 1:14). The people of Ammon received the poor Zoramites and gave them lands for their inheritance in Jershon (Alma 35:9, 14), just as the Nephites had received the people of Ammon and had given them land (Alma 43:12). In contrast to "lands of inheritance" is Mormon's phrase "land of possession." The former seems to be legitimate property, while the latter is not. Captain Moroni seeks to cut off the supplies of the Lamanites in their lands of possession (Alma 50:12), i.e., those lands they had taken from the Nephites. Similarly, the Lamanites gave their lands of possession to the Nephites (Helaman 5:52), although the antecedent of "their" is unclear and could refer to the Nephites and the lands they originally possessed.

All of Mormon's other references in the "special use" category seem to be the product of his editorial work. Essentially, he is an observer standing outside the events he records. Thus, he speaks of other people's land as "their" land or lands. For example, Limhi's people go to war against the Lamanites to drive them out of "their" (the Nephites') land (Mosiah 21:7; see also Alma 3:21). Similarly, Mormon reports that the Lamanite king sent out an edict that the sons of Mosiah should be permitted to preach the gospel in any part of "their" (the Lamanites') land (Alma 23:1). The same pattern holds true when we examine Mormon's references to "their [own] lands."[17]

---

[17] For references to "their lands" or "their own lands," see: Alma 3:1; 8:7; 16:8, 11; 35:14; 43:9, 26, 30, 47–48; 44:23; 48:8, 10; 50:7, 36; 51:1; 52:13; 63:15; Helaman 1:18; 4:13, 16, 19; 11:29, 31; 3 Nephi 2:17; 4:3, 16; 5:26; 6:1–2; Mormon 3:1, 7; 4:15.

In like manner, the Lamanites return to their "own" land (Mosiah 20:26) and scatter Nephite flocks to drive them into their "own" land (Alma 18:7). Samuel the Lamanite, after being rejected by the people of Zarahemla, was about to return to his "own" land (Helaman 13:2). Further, Limhi's search party finds "a" land covered with bones (Mosiah 21:26) and Alma 1 finds "a" land, i.e., the land of Helam, which is beautiful and pleasant (Mosiah 23:4). Mormon also states that a Lamanite king had the right to cast foreigners out of "his" land (Alma 17:20) and that Amalickiah was gathering soldiers from all parts of "his" land (Alma 51:9).

Shortly before the final destruction of the Nephites, Mormon reports that the Nephite defenders of the city of Jordan prevented the Lamanites from entering "our" land (Mormon 5:4), and Mormon fortifies the narrow neck of land to prevent the Lamanites from getting any of their ("our") lands (Mormon 3:6). Finally, Mormon, like Moroni 2, uses *Land* once as a verb, telling us that those who accept the word of God may "land" their souls at the right hand of God (Helaman 3:30). The contrast is, of course, that Moroni 2 refers to landing on the shore of the promised land whereas Mormon refers to landing on the right hand of God.

In summary, there is a clear distinction between Mormon and Moroni 2. Moroni 2 concentrates on the New World as a land of promise and inheritance, while Mormon has almost no emphasis in the theological arena, continuing primarily to focus on land as a geographic, and often localized, entity.

Conclusions

Author Individuality

There are clear distinctions between the various writers considered above which may be cited, and here we will try to define the major distinctions.

The Father focuses on the Old World, stating that Israel will be gathered to her old lands. However, the covenant that the Father made with Abraham, Isaac, and Jacob will find its culmination in his new work in the latter days. In contrast, the focus of the Lord and Jesus is on the New World. People have been taken from the Old World and brought to the New World, which is a prepared, preserved, and choice land for all who will be obedient to the Lord, including the Gentiles.

Lehi's focus is primarily on the New World as the promised land, a theme which Nephi 1 echoes. For both Lehi and Nephi 1, the New World is a land to which God will bring various peoples, all of whom will prosper if they are but obedient to the Lord. However, Nephi 1 looks back more than does Lehi, seeing Jerusalem and its environs as that from which his family had been delivered and as that to which the Jews will one day return. Nephi 1 also has a panoramic view which looks forward, for he sees the destruction of the Nephites because of their disobedience. There is one very clear distinction between Lehi and Nephi 1, and that relates to their understanding of "land of inheritance." For Lehi it is the New World, while for Nephi 1 it refers predominantly to Jerusalem, where Lehi's original lands of inheritance were, to which the Babylonian exiles would return, and to which Israel would ultimately be gathered.

Among the earlier inhabitants of Zarahemla, there are some interesting trends. Zeniff speaks almost exclusively of the land of Nephi. The one exception, and it is unique to Zeniff, is a reference to the place where Lehi first landed—the land of first inheritance. All Benjamin's uses of land are geographic and refer to Zarahemla, while his son Mosiah wishes for a land of liberty and equality and sees wickedness as something which could lead to destruction in the land. Mosiah's son Ammon speaks of Zarahemla predominantly as that land which he left in order to go to the land of Nephi as a missionary. Alma 2 focuses on the New World, but not as something which stands separated from the old one. Rather he views himself as a man of the land upon which he lives. He does, however, recognize that his fathers were delivered from Jerusalem and uses Abraham and Melchizedek as examples in his preaching. He also develops a distinctive connection between the Lord's bringing Israel out of Egypt, bringing Lehi out of Jerusalem, and bringing people who believe in Christ out of this world to a better land (heaven). Finally, Alma 2 and Ammon, two close friends, share the only two references to being inhabitants of a "strange land," i.e., one separated from the Nephites' original home.[18] One has to ask whether this is only coincidence or a product of Joseph Smith's editing. I do not believe either is a sufficient explanation but rather that the references are small glimpses at the accuracy of the Book of Mormon, which occasionally preserves even small linguistic commonalities between friends.

Among the earlier Nephites, there was a diminishing sense of New World versus Old World. This continues among the later Nephite writers, with a corresponding increase in identity with "our" land. Thus, Zarahemla is the primary focus for these writers, although Captain Moroni has not forgotten that the Nephites once lived in the land of Nephi. For him it is still the land of their inheritance. For all these writers, there is a conception of expanded Nephite lands, and thus one sees, particularly in Helaman, a growing sense of various "lands" which make up *the* land.

There are some distinct contrasts between Mormon and Moroni 2. First, Mormon lists many specific place names, while Moroni 2 lists very few. Second, Mormon exhibits almost no interest in a theology of *Land,* while Moroni 2 has a strong sense of the New World as a promised land preserved by God for the righteous. Those who live in the land must serve God or be destroyed. In articulating this, Moroni 2's prime example is the Jaredites. Further, according to Moroni 2, this land is a land of inheritance for Jaredites, Nephites, Lamanites, and Gentiles, if and when they are obedient to the Lord. It will be the site of the New Jerusalem and the place where the remnant of Joseph will prosper.

Mormon stands in sharp contrast to this. As already mentioned, his interests seem almost entirely geographic, but there may be a theological reason for all his geography. It has always been a fundamental tenet of Judeo-Christian theology that God works in real human history. It would seem that Mormon's geographical emphasis admirably demonstrates God's intervention in the history of the Nephite and Lamanite peoples.

---

[18] Jacob has a similar thought, but not similar language, in Jacob 7:26.

The "land" that receives the most attention from Mormon is Zarahemla, but rather than being a local designation, it appears to be the name which covers most of the Nephite lands. Thus there seems to have been a progression from the earlier writers who viewed Zarahemla as their rather localized dwelling place to the later writers who viewed Zarahemla as a land among lands, and finally to Mormon who seems to have viewed Zarahemla as a name covering all Nephite lands.

Mormon's understanding of "land of inheritance" is different from that of Moroni 2, for it seems to reflect a localized area. Israel will return to Jerusalem, its land of inheritance. Captain Moroni dedicated the land south of Desolation as a land of inheritance. Lamoni and Ammon returned to Ishmael, their land of inheritance. Mormon also differentiates between a land of "inheritance" and a land of "possession," the latter designating an illegal ownership.

Finally, it should be noted that Mormon and Moroni 2 are the only authors who give compass directions related to the lands of which they speak. Mormon does this extensively with regard to Lamanite and Nephite lands, while Moroni 2 does it a few times with reference to Jaredite lands. In addition, there is one other small but marked commonality between Mormon and Moroni 2 in which father and son are the only persons in the Book of Mormon who use *Land* as a verb. Moroni 2 tells us that the Jaredites "landed" in the New World, and Mormon suggests that one may "land" in heaven. Perhaps once again there has been preserved for us a small but significant congruence between these two individuals.

Of much greater and clearer significance than these last two similarities, however, is the unique descriptive phraseology used with *Land* which is very apparent in Mormon and somewhat present in Moroni 2. Mormon's expansive and inclusive language which refers to "all the land," or other related phrases, simply cannot be explained as a coincidence. It permeates Mormon's language, no matter which author he is editing. Of the few instances where similar phrases in other authors occur, most appear in the material which Mormon edits and may well be his phrase rather than the original author's. As seen above, Moroni 2 uses some of this same language, but at a reduced level. Apparently he picked it up from his father, but it was not as ingrained in his basic language structure as it was in Mormon's.

In summation, it does not seem probable that one author, such as Joseph Smith, could have produced what has been observed with these expansive phrases. Rather, these are clear marks of the editor over against every other author. Lest some suggest that Joseph Smith may have been that editor, it should be pointed out that Larsen and Rencher have clearly distinguished through wordprint between Joseph Smith and all Book of Mormon authors.[19]

Theological Implications

There are a number of implications that may be drawn from this study of *Land*. First, it is not simply the New World that is important in God's overall scheme of things, for Jerusalem is the place to which the tribes of Israel, at least some of them, and the Jews will finally be gathered. For many others, however, the New World is immensely important. It is the place to which God led some select peoples that they might be preserved when the cultures around them were falling apart. Sadly, they did not learn well the lessons of history and were themselves either destroyed or polluted to the degree that others took over their lands in the Western Hemisphere. But even that was part of God's plan, for it opened up the blessings of the gospel, not only to the people of Israel but also to the Gentiles, for whom the New World was and is a land of promise if they will be obedient to God and serve him in it. Those of Israel who have the closest identification with the lands of the New World, who will be strengthened in those lands, are the descendants of Joseph, I suspect, both literal and adoptive. For those of us whose lineage is traced to either Ephraim or Manasseh, this land is a special land of both opportunity and obligation. It is through these descendants of Abraham, Isaac, and Jacob that the covenants God made with the early patriarchs will be fulfilled in the last days.

---

[19] Wayne A. Larsen and Alvin C. Rencher, "Who Wrote the Book of Mormon? An Analysis of Wordprints," in *Book of Mormon Authorship: New Light on Ancient Origins*, ed. Noel B. Reynolds (Provo, Utah: Religious Studies Center, Brigham Young University, 1982), 172–80.

7

Summary Tests of a Method

My research began in 1987. It sprang from my personal belief that the Book of Mormon is precisely what The Church of Jesus Christ of Latter-day Saints says it is: an ancient book written by various ancient authors over approximately a one-thousand-year period and delivered to Joseph Smith by the angel Moroni in 1827. But for many, both outside and inside the Latter-day Saint community, merely to assert this belief is insufficient. Hence, theories have been developed by some to demonstrate that the Book of Mormon is in reality a nineteenth-century writing.

It seemed to me that there ought to be a way of responding to these alternative views in a reasoned manner, for I do not believe that faith and reason are antithetical. One may not be able to create faith through reason, but certainly faith can utilize and be supported by it, for the mind and the spirit are both integral elements of what it is to be human. Therefore, I wondered if it would be possible to provide some empirical data that would support the position that the Book of Mormon is an ancient book.

As noted earlier, I began with the hypothesis that if the Book of Mormon were written by a variety of authors, then it might be possible, on the basis of the vocabulary used by the various authors, to distinguish between them. I had no idea whether one could demonstrate any differences in content word usage between the authors, but I knew that "wordprints" had made such discriminations using the small words. Thus, it seemed that one could do something similar with the content words in their literary context. The methodology has developed over time, but the end result of all the various approaches articulated in the preceding chapters is that there are indeed identifiable differences between the various authors on a variety of subjects, differences that I do not believe could have been created by a nineteenth-century author or editor.

In this concluding chapter, I will not try to summarize all that has been shown in the previous chapters. For details, one can turn to the preceding chapters and to the summaries at the end of each. However, the hypothesis that different authors contributed to the Book of Mormon can be emphasized by reviewing how pairs of authors, each of whom has texts in the Book of Mormon in excess of ten thousand words in length, deal with the words that have been considered. We will begin by contrasting Nephi 1 and Alma 2, authors whose wordprints show them to be totally different persons and in whom we have already seen clear differences in chapter 1 when their use of the various word clusters was considered. We will determine whether this difference is maintained for each of the words we have considered after chapter 1. Following this analysis of Nephi 1 and Alma 2, we will follow the same comparative procedure in examining Alma 2 and Mormon, Alma 2 and Moroni 2, and Nephi 1 and Moroni 2. We will conclude with an examination of Nephi 1 and Mormon, a pair that John Hilton has found hard to differentiate fully by using wordprints. Perhaps we can shed some light on the question of whether they are different through comparing Nephi 1's and Mormon's word usages considered in this study.

Nephi 1 and Alma 2

When the null-hypothesis rejections which compare Nephi1:S and Alma2:S are examined, it is seen that there are four rejections. The number of rejections suggests a significant difference between the two authors. When we then examine the two authors' use of the word clusters discussed in chapter 1, we find that Nephi1:S and Alma 2 are once again shown to be quite different. In fact, as figure 1 demonstrates, their interests are almost reversed.

Nephi1:S	Alma 2
2.9 Ancient Near East	2.5 Eschatology
2.2 Gathering	1.8 Spiritual
1.8 Prophecy	1.7 Slavery
1.6 Editing	1.7 Ethics
1.5 Xology	1.6 Xology
1.4 God	1.6 Trouble
1.4 Creation	1.5 Evil
1.2 Spiritual	1.4 God
1.1 Eschatology	0.8 Prophecy
1.1 Evil	0.6 Creation
0.9 Ethics	0.4 Gathering
0.8 Slavery	0.4 Ancient Near East
0.7 Trouble	0.3 Editing

Figure 1

When we compared Alma 2's and Nephi 1's use of the Near East word cluster, a similar difference was observable. Alma 2 had little concern for the cluster, while Nephi 1 had great concern for it, as the normalized numbers in figure 2 clearly show.

Author	Length	Number	Per 1000, author text	Per 1000, BofM text	Normalized
Alma 2	20,227	37	1.83	4.38	0.42
Nephi1:N1	10,238	51	4.98	4.38	1.14
Nephi1:S	17,982	195	10.8	4.38	2.47

Figure 2

Law/Command Complex

When we turn to the content words, the picture is less clear if one simply looks at the numbers and categories in the various tables. However, the issue, as we have seen in all the above chapters, is not whether authors use the same words or phrases, but rather what the authors *mean* by those words and phrases. Thus, while there are similarities, as seen in figure 3, in the words of the Law/Command complex used by Nephi 1 and Alma 2, the real issue is how they used the words. Even so, figure 3 shows that there are differences in the emphases each author puts on various expressions.

	Alma 2	Nephi 1
Command	11	2
Commanded	7	33
Commandest	-	-
Commandeth	2	5
Commanding	-	-
Commandment	-	7
Commandments	29	26
Commands	-	-
Law	13	23
Law of Moses	-	4
Laws	-	-
Come unto	9	7

Figure 3: Law/Command

One observable difference between Nephi 1 and Alma 2 (see figure 3) is that Alma 2 uses the present tense *Command,* while Nephi 1 uses the past tense *Commanded.* Only Nephi 1 speaks of the singular *Commandment* or mentions the Law of Moses.

When we examine the way the complex is used in Alma 2, we see an integration of a strong ethical consciousness with the realization of the necessity of Christ's atonement. By contrast, in Nephi 1 we find the complex referring to the Lord's daily commandments, perhaps best understood as "instructions." They both use *Law* to refer to the Law of Moses, but for Alma 2 *Law* may also mean secular law. For both authors, Christ is the culmination of the law or commandments. Even so, it is difficult not to affirm that there are clear differences between the two authors in the Law/Command complex.

Church/Churches

Nephi 1 and Alma 2 could hardly be more different in their use of the words *Church* and *Churches.* As figure 4 indicates, they focus on quite different things: Nephi 1 is concerned primarily about the great and abominable church, while Alma 2 sees the church as both a localized group of people and as an entity which exists in the Old and New Worlds and cuts across all boundaries. In addition, only Nephi 1 uses the word *Churches* in an entirely negative sense, thus supporting the emphasis he has laid on the great and abominable church. Hence, the differences between the two authors are clear when *Church* and *Churches* are considered.

	Alma 2	Nephi 1
Christ's church in New World	5	-
Local church	3	-
God's church outside New World	2	-
Great and abominable	-	6
Of the Lamb	-	3
Of the devil	-	-
Universal	4	1
Not true church	-	-
New World/universal	1	-
Jews	-	1

Figure 4: Church

Earth

When we consider the word *Earth,* differences between the two authors continue to be evident. In figure 5 it is clear that Nephi 1 places a greater emphasis on God's activities in relation to the earth than does Alma 2.

The only instance in which Alma 2 appears to speak of God being actively involved with the earth is under the heading "God shakes." However, when the passages are examined, one discovers that it is really the voice of the angel, who appears to Alma 2 and the sons of Mosiah, that shakes the earth. In contrast, Nephi 1 demonstrates an awareness of God's lordship over the earth.

	Alma 2	Nephi 1
God comes to/in	-	-
God Father of	-	1
God creates	-	1
God's mercy over	-	-
God over	-	-
God smites	-	1
God of	-	-
God commands	-	-
God has power over	-	-
God's footstool	-	1
God's will done in	-	-
God lord of	-	-
God's purposes on	-	-
God rules	-	-
God shakes	3	1

Figure 5: Earth—God's Acts

When the earth as the "globe" is considered, figure 6 seems to show greater congruence between the two authors.

	Alma 2	Nephi 1
Face of (positive)	3	4
Face of (negative)	6	5
Ends of	1	2
Planet	1	8
Witnesses to God	1	-
Four corners of	-	-
At rest	-	-
Treasures of	-	-
Be joyful	-	-
Four parts of	-	-
Swear by	-	-
New	-	-
Four quarters of	-	1
World	-	3

Figure 6: Earth—Globe

Summary Tests of a Method

However, when one looks at the way "face of" is used, it is clear that there are real differences. Alma 2's use of the phrase is generally negative, indicating that people may be cut off from the face of the earth for transgression. Nephi 1 is concerned with Israel being scattered across the face of the earth. Nephi 1 clearly has an emphasis on the earth as "planet" that Alma 2 does not. For Nephi 1 the earth will pass away, its end will be revealed, and Joseph's seed will continue as long as the earth remains. Alma 2 indicates once that the earth will pass away. Thus, once again significant differences are seen between the two authors, differences that are clearly maintained in figure 7.

	Alma 2	Nephi 1
Will see salvation	-	-
Abr's seed blesses	-	-
People of	-	-
Midst of	-	-
Trouble	-	-
Meek of	-	-
Chief ones of	-	-
People of tremble	-	-
Nation(s) of/on	-	-
Salt of	-	-
Remnant of	-	-
Gathered people of	-	-
Inhabitants of	-	1
Family of	-	-
Kindreds of	-	2
Smite the	-	-
Seal on	-	-
Loose on	-	-
Wickedness of	-	-
Land(s) of	-	1
(Die) like other people	-	-
Multitudes of	-	3

Figure 7: Earth—Inhabitants of

The differences continue when *Earth* is used to mean "ground."

	Alma 2	Nephi 1
Fall to	3	3
Smite to	-	-
As dust of	-	-
Return to	-	-
Face to	-	-
Till	-	-
Man from	-	-
Prostrate on	-	-
Raise from	-	-
Bowed to	-	-
Level to (kill)	-	-
Cut down to (kill)	-	-
Kneel upon	-	-
Sit on	-	-

Figure 8: Earth—As Related to Humans

	Alma 2	Nephi 1
In ground	-	1
Caves of	-	-
Fruit of	-	-
Surface of	-	-
Seeds of	-	-
Dirt	-	3
Face of	-	-
Is smitten	-	-
Ground	-	1
Smite	-	-
God shakes	3	1

Figure 9: Earth—Ground as Ground

In figure 8 it appears that Alma 2 and Nephi 1 use the same language. However, Alma 2 indicates that following the appearance of the angel, *he* fell to the earth, while Nephi 1 talks of *other* persons or things falling to the earth: Laban, cities, and the great whore. As shown in figure 9, Alma 2 does not even mention the ground as ground, except to note that the angel's voice shook it. In contrast,

Nephi 1 mentions that those who persecute the prophets will be swallowed in the earth, and that his family began to cultivate the earth; these examples underscore the differences between the two authors.

Israel

Little needs to be said about the authors and their views on Israel, for Israel is immensely important to Nephi 1, as figures 10 and 11 show, but the word is not even mentioned by Alma 2.

	Nephi 1
House of	20
Tribes, house of	-
People, house of	1
Children of	3
12 tribes of	-
People of	-
Both houses of	-
Nation of	-
Escaped of	-
Preserved of	-
King of	-
Remnant of	-
Outcasts of	-
Lost tribes of	2
Remnant, house of	-
Scattered tribes of	-
God of	2
Holy One of	10
Redeemer of	-
Mighty One of	1
My people	-
My called of	-
My servant	-

Figure 10: Israel

	Nephi 1
Nation	8
Spiritual Entity	-
Covenant with	2
Scattered	6
Nephites and Lamanites part of	7
People of God	-
Olive tree	2
A king of	-
Judged/destroyed	-
God redeems	2
God judges	1
God is	1
Jesus is God	2
God opposed	3
Praise/rejoice in	3
Fear God	-
God will reign	2

Figure 11: Israel

Land

Figure 12 indicates some commonalities between Nephi 1 and Alma 2 when the geographical uses of *Land* are considered, but just as the apparent similarities above show, the numbers are deceptive.

	Nephi 1	Alma 2
Land of	18	7
Region	7	10
Borders of	-	-
Round about	-	-
Part(s) of	-	-
Quarter of	-	-
Territory	-	-
Strange	-	1
Canaan	3	-
Judea	-	-
New World	10	11
Directions	-	-

Figure 12: Land—Geographical

Nephi 1's orientation is very much toward the Old World, with Jerusalem being of principal concern to him, for it is from Jerusalem that his family fled, to Jerusalem that they returned for the plates of brass and for wives, and to Jerusalem that the Jews will one day return. The mentioning of Egypt and Canaan seems to provide examples of the way in which God can lead people to a promised land. When Nephi 1 does refer to the New World, it is to a land in which the righteous will prosper, a land where his people will finally be destroyed, and a land where the Gentiles will prosper.

Alma 2, however, speaks primarily of New World localities, e.g., Zarahemla, Mormon, and Manti, while recognizing that his fathers were delivered from Jerusalem. He also uses Melchizedek, king of Salem, as a sermon example. There is less consciousness of the Old World as opposed to the New World in Alma 2 than in Nephi 1.

In the special categories related to land, figure 13 shows differences between Alma 2 and Nephi 1.

Summary Tests of a Method

	Nephi 1	Alma 2
Promised	18	4
Covenant	-	-
Choice	-	-
Holy	-	-
Prepared	-	-
Chosen	-	-
Liberty	-	-
Inheritance	6	-
Our possession	-	-
Our	-	1
Own	-	-
Our fathers'	-	-
Whatsoever	-	-
Better	-	-
A	-	-
Their	-	-
Thy	-	-
My	-	-
His	-	-
Ground	1	-
Earth	-	-
As verb	-	-

Figure 13: Land—Special

Obviously, Nephi 1 is much more concerned for the promised land and the land of inheritance than is Alma 2. The promised land for Nephi 1 is the New World, to which his family travels and about which he had visions. As we have seen, his references to "land of inheritance" have an Old World orientation. Alma 2's references to "promised land" refer to Canaan, to the New World toward which the Liahona guided Lehi's family, and to heaven. Finally, when the two authors' uses of *Lands* in figure 14 are examined, one sees further differences between Nephi 1 and Alma 2.

Nephi 1 has an Old World orientation and reads Isaiah to his brothers so they will know how God has dealt with his children in other lands. Alma 2 ends a sermon in Gideon by blessing the people and their lands.

	Nephi 1	Alma 2
Regions	1	-
Other	2	-
Lamanites'	-	-
Zarahemla	-	-
Roundabout	-	-
Foreign	-	-
Precious	1	-
Inheritance	2	-
Choice	-	-
Of possession	-	-
Promised	-	-
Of my people	-	-
Your	-	1
Our	-	-
Your own	-	-
Their	-	-
Own	-	-
Their own	-	-
Whatsoever	-	-

Figure 14: Lands

Summary

We began this section on Nephi 1 and Alma 2 by noting that wordprints had clearly differentiated between the two authors, and we wanted to determine whether that difference was consistently present with the content words we have been examining. In every instance, differences are clear in word usage and meaning between these two authors, thus strongly supporting the wordprint delineations.

Alma 2 and Mormon

We turn now to a comparison of Alma 2 and Mormon, two writers who have texts of significant length. Alma 2 has 20,227 words and Mormon writes 97,515 words. We will follow the same format in comparing Alma 2 and Mormon that we followed above with Nephi 1 and Alma 2.

Word Clusters

In the case of Mormon:S and Alma2:S, the number of null-hypothesis rejections was 0, meaning that a clear statistical delineation between the two authors could not be made on the basis of the word clusters. However, figure 15 compares the word clusters that are of importance in Alma 2 and Mormon. Since Mormon's work can be divided into sermonic, first-person narrative, and third-person narrative, these divisions have been retained and may prove to be instructive.

Alma 2		Mormon:S		Mormon:N1		Mormon:N3	
2.5	Eschatology	3.2	Xology	3.5	Numbers	1.8	Money
1.8	Spiritual	2.8	Gathering	2.3	Editing	1.8	Directions
1.7	Slavery	2.4	Spiritual	2.2	Directions	1.8	Contention
1.7	Ethics	2.1	Eschatology	2.0	Military	1.6	Military
1.6	Xology	2.0	Sacramental	1.5	Neg. emotions	1.6	Government
1.6	Trouble					1.5	Numbers
1.5	Evil						

Figure 15

Initially, there appear to be some similarities between Alma 2 and Mormon:S in their use of clusters. Eschatology is important in both, as is the Spiritual cluster. The Christology cluster also appears in both but is of significantly less importance in Alma 2 than it is in Mormon:S. Beyond these similarities, however, the commonalities cease. The word clusters Slavery, Ethics, Trouble, and Evil do not appear in Mormon's writings at a significant level. Similarly, the majority of Mormon's clusters do not appear at a significant level in Alma 2. Thus, based on the various clusters and their importance to the two authors, it can be said that there are greater differences than there are similarities.

Law/Command

Turning to the Law/Command complex, we see in figure 16 the following distribution.

	Alma 2	Mormon
Command	11	20
Commanded	7	78
Commandest	-	-
Commandeth	2	1
Commanding	-	1
Commandment	-	7
Commandments	29	53
Commands	-	5
Law	13	64
Law of Moses	-	16
Laws	-	17
Come unto	9	16

Figure 16: Law/Command

An examination of the above numbers indicates both similarities and differences between Alma 2 and Mormon. There is common stress on *Command, Commanded, Commandments, Law,* and *Come unto*. But even with these commonalities, we must also note that the ratio between *Command* and *Commanded* is reversed and that there is proportionately greater stress on *Law* by Mormon. Perhaps even more important are the words which Mormon uses and Alma 2 does not: *Commanding, Commandment, Commands, Law of Moses,* and *Laws*.

When we turn to the meanings attached to the word group, we see, as already noted above, that Alma 2 integrates a strong sense of ethics with roots in spirituality, while *Law* is primarily secular law.

Mormon, on the other hand, has some unique usages in this complex. First, he uses *Command* to mean "leadership" and is completely unique in this usage. Second, most of his uses are secular in nature, i.e., secular leaders give various commands. The exception to this is when Mormon is not editing and speaks for himself—in that case the Lord commands. In his edited material, *Law* and *Laws* refer to secular law, while in his sermonic material, Mormon uses *Law* either to mean the Law of Moses or what Latter-day Saints call "the plan of salvation." *Commandments* can be understood as a way of talking about the Christian life. In speaking of the Law of Moses, Mormon always points it forward to Christ. Thus Mormon's understanding of the Law/Command complex is quite different from that of Alma 2.

Church/Churches

Figure 16 shows how Alma 2 and Mormon use the word *Church*. Alma 2 never uses the word *Churches,* while Mormon uses it primarily to indicate local or denominational entities. Since Alma 2 does not use the word, no chart is included for *Churches*.

	Alma 2	Mormon
Christ's church in New World	5	80
Local church	3	20
God's church outside New World	2	-
Great and abominable	-	-
Of the Lamb	-	-
Of the devil	-	-
Universal	4	44
Not true church	-	3
New World/universal	1	-
Jews	-	-

Figure 17: Church

As seen in figure 17, Alma 2 uses *Church* to refer to Christ's universal church in the New World, which manifests itself in local congregations. Mormon's uses of *Church* are very similar, with a very clear emphasis on the New World church. Thus there is not a clear difference between Alma 2 and Mormon in relationship to *Church,* except that Mormon stresses the New World church and uses *Churches* while Alma 2 does not.

Earth

When we consider Alma 2's and Mormon's uses of the word *Earth,* there are some similarities between them, but we will see also that there are some distinct differences. Figure 18 demonstrates both the similarities and the differences between the two.

Clearly, neither of the authors speaks of God's acts in relation to the earth. However, the similarity that God shakes the earth is only apparent, because in Alma 2 it is the voice of the Angel which shakes the earth, while in Mormon it is God's power that shakes it.

	Alma 2	Mormon
God comes to/in	-	-
God Father of	-	-
God creates	-	-
God's mercy over	-	-
God over	-	-
God smites	-	-
God of	-	-
God commands	-	-
God has power over	-	-
God's footstool	-	-
God's will done in	-	-
God Lord of	-	-
God's purposes on	-	-
God rules	-	-
God shakes	3	10

Figure 18: Earth—God's Acts

	Alma 2	Mormon
Face of (positive)	3	2
Face of (negative)	6	2
Ends of	1	2
Planet	1	10
Witnesses to God	1	-
Four corners of	-	-
At rest	-	-
Treasures of	-	-
Be joyful	-	-
Four parts of	-	-
Swear by	-	-
New	-	-
Four quarters of	-	2
World	-	-

Figure 19: Earth—Globe

Figure 19 shows additional similarities in phraseology but not necessarily in meaning. Alma 2 uses "face of" primarily in a negative vein, i.e., people will be cut off from the face of the earth. However, Mormon's uses are more concerned with people being scattered across the earth and the ministry to those peoples. He also uses *Earth* several times to mean planet, an emphasis not found in Alma 2.

Summary Tests of a Method 167

	Alma 2	Mormon
Will see salvation	-	-
Abr's seed blesses	-	-
People of	-	-
Midst of	-	-
Trouble	-	-
Meek of	-	-
Chief ones of	-	-
People of tremble	-	-
Nation(s) of/on	-	-
Salt of	-	-
Remnant of	-	-
Gathered people of	-	-
Inhabitants of	-	-
Family of	-	-
Kindreds of	-	-
Smite the	-	-
Seal on	-	-
Loose on	-	-
Wickedness of	-	-
Land(s) of	-	-
(Die) like other people	-	4
Multitudes of	-	-

Figure 20: Earth—Inhabitants of

Figure 20 shows that neither author is concerned with speaking of the inhabitants of the earth. Mormon, however, does say that people "go the way of all the earth" in reference to death.

Any similarities between Alma 2 and Mormon break down quickly when we consider the use of *Earth* to mean "ground." Mormon is virtually unique in this usage, as figures 21 and 22 demonstrate.

Thus, while there are some similarities between Alma 2 and Mormon, those similarities diminish in importance when viewed in light of Mormon's uniqueness in using *Earth* to mean "ground."

	Alma 2	Mormon
Fall to	3	26
Smite to	-	3
As dust of	-	3
Return to	-	-
Face to	-	-
Till	-	2
Man from	-	-
Prostrate on	-	4
Raise from	-	2
Bowed to	-	4
Level to (kill)	-	2
Cut down to (kill)	-	1
Kneel upon	-	4
Sit on	-	1

Figure 21: Earth—As Related to Humans

	Alma 2	Mormon
In ground	-	7
Caves of	-	-
Fruit of	-	-
Surface of	-	1
Seeds of	-	-
Dirt	-	9
Face of	-	3
Is smitten	-	2
Ground	-	5
Smite	-	1
God shakes	3	10

Figure 22: Earth—Ground as Ground

Israel

As with Alma 2 and Nephi 1, little needs to be said here, for as noted before, Alma 2 does not use the word *Israel*. While it is not a very important word in Mormon's text, he does use it, as figures 23 and 24 show.

Land/Lands

As one examines figures 25, 26, and 27, it is hard to see any particular similarities between Alma 2 and Mormon. With only minor exceptions in every category, they are different. For a detailed analysis, the chapter on *Land/Lands* can be consulted.

Summary

As with Nephi 1 and Alma 2, clear differences between Alma 2 and Mormon are apparent. Only with *Earth* were there some small similarities, but those quickly evaporated in light of Mormon's unique use of *Earth* to mean "ground."

Summary Tests of a Method 169

	Mormon
House of	8
Tribes, house of	-
People, house of	1
Children of	2
12 tribes of	-
People of	-
Both houses of	-
Nation of	-
Escaped of	-
Preserved of	-
King of	-
Remnant of	2
Outcasts of	-
Lost tribes of	-
Remnant, house of	-
Scattered tribes of	1
God of	-
Holy One of	-
Redeemer of	-
Mighty One of	-
My people	-
My called of	-
My servant	-

Figure 23: Israel

	Mormon
Nation	6
Spiritual entity	-
Covenant with	4
Scattered	5
Nephites and Lamanites part of	-
People of God	-
Olive tree	-
A king of	-
Judged/destroyed	-
God redeems	-
God judges	-
God is	-
Jesus is God	-
God opposed	-
Praise/rejoice in	-
Fear God	-
God will reign	-

Figure 24: Israel

	Alma 2	Mormon
Land of	7	293
Region	10	255
Borders of	-	13
Round about	-	12
Part(s) of	-	17
Quarter of	-	4
Territory	-	2
Strange	1	-
Canaan	-	-
Judea	-	-
New World	11	7
Directions	-	56

Figure 25: Land—Geographical

	Alma 2	Mormon
Promised	4	-
Covenant	-	-
Choice	-	-
Holy	-	-
Prepared	-	-
Chosen	-	1
Liberty	-	1
Inheritance	-	3
Our possession	-	-
Our	1	1
Own	-	4
Our fathers'	-	-
Whatsoever	-	-
Better	-	-
A	-	5
Their	-	10
Thy	-	-
My	-	-
His	-	3
Ground	-	-
Earth	-	-
As verb	-	1

Figure 26: Land—Special

	Alma 2	Mormon
Regions	-	8
Other	-	-
Lamanites'	-	1
Zarahemla	-	1
Roundabout	-	-
Foreign	-	-
Precious	-	-
Inheritance	-	7
Choice	-	-
Of possession	-	4
Promised	-	-
Of my people	-	-
Your	1	-
Our	-	1
Your own	-	-
Their	-	24
Own	-	1
Their own	-	9
Whatsoever	-	1

Figure 27: Lands

Alma 2 and Moroni 2

The null-hypothesis rejections found between Alma2:S and Moroni2:N3 showed a huge difference with seven rejections. However, no clear statistical difference could be shown between Alma2:S and Moroni2:S. In figure 28, however, we see the more important word clusters in Alma 2 and Moroni 2. As with Mormon, we are able to divide Moroni 2 into sermonic and narrative materials. However, there is not as much difference between these materials in Moroni 2 as there is in Mormon.

Alma 2	Moroni 2:S	Moroni 2:N3
2.5 Eschatology	3.2 Xology	3.2 Animals
1.8 Spirituality	2.0 Sacramental	2.0 Sacramental
1.7 Slavery	1.8 Spirituality	1.8 Spirituality
1.7 Ethics	1.8 God	1.8 Eschatology
1.6 Xology	1.8 Eschatology	
1.6 Trouble		
1.5 Evil		

Figure 28

When the word clusters are considered, both similarities and differences are apparent between Alma 2 and Moroni 2. There are common emphases on Eschatology, Spirituality, and Christology. In Alma 2, however, the clusters concerning Slavery, Ethics, Trouble, and Evil are unique, while the clusters dealing with God, Animals, and the Sacramental found in Moroni 2 are not present at all in Alma 2.

	Alma 2	Moroni 2
Command	11	-
Commanded	7	16
Commandest	-	-
Commandeth	2	2
Commanding	-	-
Commandment	-	4
Commandments	29	1
Commands	-	-
Law	13	4
Law of Moses	-	1
Laws	-	1
Come unto	9	11

Figure 29: Law/Command

Law/Command

Figure 29 shows that Alma 2 and Moroni 2 apparently have different tastes in language when the *Law/Command* group is considered.

Alma 2 seems to prefer *Command* and *Commandments,* neither of which is used much by Moroni 2. In contrast, Moroni 2 uses *Commanded* and *Commandment,* along with *Law of Moses* and *Laws,* neither of which Alma 2 uses. From the standpoint of meaning, Alma 2, once again, is concerned with ethics in a spiritual context, while law is primarily a secular notion or may possibly mean the Law of Moses. Moroni 2's concern is predominantly with the commands of the Lord, with little concern for the words related to law. Hence, there is a difference between the two writers.

Church/Churches

This complex is not of great importance to either Alma 2 or Moroni 2, as figure 30 shows.

	Alma 2	Moroni 2
Christ's church in New World	5	-
Local church	3	7
God's church outside New World	2	-
Great and abominable	-	-
Of the Lamb	-	-
Of the devil	-	-
Universal	4	2
Not true church	-	-
New World/universal	1	-
Jews	-	-

Figure 30: Church

As we noted earlier when we studied *Church,* Moroni 2's main concern is with the local church, though he recognizes that there is a universal church which transcends all boundaries. Alma 2's concerns are very similar, but with a stronger emphasis on the church in the New World. Moroni 2 uses *Churches* seven times, also with a local emphasis, compared to Alma 2, who never uses the word. However, little definite can be said about similarities or differences between the two authors on the basis of their use of these words.

Summary Tests of a Method 173

	Alma 2	Moroni 2
God comes to/in	-	-
God Father of	-	-
God creates	-	2
God's mercy over	-	-
God over	-	-
God smites	-	-
God of	-	-
God commands	-	-
God has power over	-	-
God's footstool	-	-
God's will done in	-	-
God lord of	-	-
God's purposes on	-	-
God rules	-	-
God shakes	3	2

Figure 31: Earth—God's Acts

	Alma 2	Moroni 2
Face of (positive)	3	1
Face of (negative)	6	7
Ends of	1	3
Planet	1	2
Witnesses to God	1	-
Four corners of	-	-
At rest	-	-
Treasures of	-	-
Be joyful	-	-
Four parts of	-	-
Swear by	-	1
New	-	1
Four quarters of	-	1
World	-	-

Figure 32: Earth—Globe

Earth

A bit more information is available for the word *Earth*, but not in great abundance. Again, neither Moroni 2 nor Alma 2 is particularly concerned with the word.

Figure 31 shows that Moroni 2 mentions God's creative activity and the fact that persons can shake the earth. Clearly, Alma 2 differs, since it is the Angel's voice, or wishfully his own, that shakes the earth—not others' voices. However, there are so few usages in this category that it is difficult to draw firm conclusions.

Figure 32 shows the authors' uses of *Earth* to mean the "globe."

As noted before, Alma 2 uses the phrase "face of" primarily in a negative way, but Moroni 2's use is even more negative. People are scattered on the "face of the earth" at the time of the great tower. No rain falls, and thus great destruction is present on the earth. No one repents, and the Book of Mormon will appear when great pollutions cover the earth. In addition, Moroni 2 has a few other uses that are not found in Alma 2. No absolutely clear distinction can be made between Alma 2 and Moroni 2 in this instance.

Figure 33, once again, shows that neither author has a particular interest in the grouping of earth's inhabitants, and they are therefore quite similar.

The two instances of Moroni 2's use are insufficient to draw any conclusions.

	Alma 2	Moroni 2
Will see salvation	-	-
Abr's seed blesses	-	-
People of	-	-
Midst of	-	-
Trouble	-	-
Meek of	-	-
Chief ones of	-	-
People of tremble	-	-
Nation(s) of/on	-	-
Salt of	-	-
Remnant of	-	-
Gathered people of	-	-
Inhabitants of	-	1
Family of	-	-
Kindreds of	-	-
Smite the	-	-
Seal on	-	-
Loose on	-	-
Wickedness of	-	-
Land(s) of	-	-
(Die) like other people	-	1
Multitudes of	-	-

Figure 33: Earth—Inhabitants of

In figures 34 and 35, differences appear a bit more clearly.

	Alma 2	Moroni 2
Fall to	3	2
Smite to	-	-
As dust of	-	-
Return to	-	-
Face to	-	-
Till	-	3
Man from	-	1
Prostrate on	-	-
Raise from	-	-
Bowed to	-	-
Level to (kill)	-	-
Cut down to (kill)	-	-
Kneel upon	-	-
Sit on	-	-

Figure 34: Earth—As Related to Humans

	Alma 2	Moroni 2
In ground	-	5
Caves of	-	-
Fruit of	-	-
Surface of	-	-
Seeds of	-	-
Dirt	-	2
Face of	-	-
Is smitten	-	-
Ground	-	-
Smite	-	-
God shakes	3	2

Figure 35: Earth—Ground as Ground

As noted previously, Alma 2 falls to the ground when the angel appears to him, for the angel is shaking the earth with his voice. Moroni 2, by contrast, speaks of others falling to the earth, of others tilling the earth, of humans being created from the dust of the earth, of the record he is writing being drawn from the earth, and of ore being mined from the earth. He also states that persons who have faith can cause the earth to shake.

In summary, there are both similarities and differences between Alma 2 and Moroni 2 concerning the word *Earth*. Moroni 2 speaks briefly about God as creator, while Alma 2 does not mention anything about God's activity in relation to the earth. Neither author speaks in any significant way about categories under "inhabitants of the earth." Both speak of the earth as a "globe." There is a stronger and broader emphasis in Moroni 2 on negative aspects of scattering. As with the comparison between Alma 2 and Mormon, however, deeper differences appear when the earth means "ground." The points of contact between Moroni 2 and Alma 2 lie in the falling to the earth and in the shaking of the earth. Even so, the meanings are different, for Alma 2 himself falls to the earth while Moroni 2 speaks of others falling to the earth. Similarly, the angel's voice shakes the earth in Alma 2's writing, while persons of faith may shake it in Moroni 2's. In addition, Moroni 2 speaks of the ground in other ways that are simply not represented in Alma 2. In conclusion, despite some similarities in the use of *Earth,* the differences still outweigh them, and it must be said that the authors display differences that one would expect to find between the writings of two different people.

Israel

Since Alma 2 never uses the word *Israel* and Moroni 2 uses it several times, it is clear that Alma 2 and Moroni 2 are different with respect to this word.

Land

When the geographical use of *Land* is considered, we find the differences in usage as indicated in figure 36.

Clearly, the word *Land* is of much greater importance to Moroni 2 than it is to Alma 2, for Moroni 2's use per thousand words of text is almost four times as great as that of Alma. There are similarities in the major categories used, but Moroni 2 has a much greater use of "region," a much clearer focus on the New World, and a greater

	Alma 2	Moroni 2
Land of	7	9
Region	10	44
Borders of	-	-
Round about	-	-
Part(s) of	-	1
Quarter of	-	1
Territory	-	-
Strange	1	-
Canaan	-	-
Judea	-	-
New World	11	24
Directions	-	5

Figure 36: Land—Geographical

	Alma 2	Moroni 2
Regions	-	2
Other	-	-
Lamanites'	-	-
Zarahemla	-	-
Roundabout	-	-
Foreign	-	1
Precious	-	-
Inheritance	-	-
Choice	-	5
Of possession	-	-
Promised	-	-
Of my people	-	-
Your	1	-
Our	-	-
Your own	-	-
Their	-	-
Own	-	-
Their own	-	-
Whatsoever	-	-

Figure 37: Lands

concern for directions than does Alma 2. For Moroni 2, the New World, as opposed to the Old World, is very special as a promised land. When *Lands* is considered, the differences between Moroni 2 and Alma 2 are only heightened, as figure 37 illustrates.

Summary

The examination of the similarities and differences in word usage between Alma 2 and Moroni 2 shows more differences than similarities. Significant differences are found in the authors' use of *Law/Command, Earth, Israel,* and *Land/Lands*. Their use of *Church* shows the greatest similarities, but there are few times that the word is used by either.

Nephi 1 and Moroni 2

Word Clusters

Nephi1:S		Moroni2:S		Moroni2:N3	
2.9	Ancient Near East	3.2	Xology	3.2	Animals
2.2	Gathering	2.0	Sacramental	2.0	Sacramental
1.8	Prophecy	1.8	Spiritual	1.8	Spiritual
1.6	Editing	1.8	God	1.8	Eschatology
1.5	Xology	1.8	Eschatology		

Figure 38

The differences between Nephi 1 and Moroni 2 in the word clusters most important to each are clear. The only common one is Christology, which is more important to Moroni 2 than to Nephi 1. All other clusters are unique to the individual authors. Thus, on the basis of word clusters, a clear difference is seen between the two. The null-hypothesis rejections are not as clear, however. Nephi1:N3 and Moroni2:S show two rejections. Nephi1:S and Moroni2:S show no rejections, and Nephi1:N1 and Moroni2:S show two rejections. While these figures suggest differences, they are only marginal for delineation.

Law/Command

As figure 39 shows, there is considerably more congruence between Nephi 1 and Moroni 2 in the Law/Command group than was seen in the other word clusters.

Clearly, the language of Nephi 1 and Moroni 2 is very similar in this group. The weighting given to the various words is certainly different, but they use virtually the same vocabulary with only one word unique to Nephi 1 and one unique to Moroni 2. Hence, if there is a difference between the two, it must lie in the way the words are used, and this is the case. For Nephi 1, commands are daily "instructions," while for Moroni 2 they are the commands of the Lord in a broader sense. Nephi 1 uses *Law* predominantly to refer to the Law of Moses which culminates in Christ. Moroni 2 has little concern for law, but where he does use it, it refers either to "father-in-law," to secular law, or to the Law of Moses.

Summary Tests of a Method 179

	Nephi 1	Moroni 2
Command	2	-
Commanded	33	16
Commandest	-	-
Commandeth	5	2
Commanding	-	-
Commandment	7	4
Commandments	26	1
Commands	-	-
Law	23	4
Law of Moses	4	1
Laws	-	1
Come unto	7	11

Figure 39: Law/Command

Church/Churches

When Church/Churches is considered, we see the distributions as shown in figures 40 and 41.

As far as the word *Church* is concerned, there is a clear difference between Nephi 1 and Moroni 2. Nephi 1's concern is primarily with the great and abominable church, while Moroni 2's is with the local congregation. Their concerns coincide, however, when *Churches* is

	Nephi 1	Moroni 2
Christ's church in New World	-	-
Local church	-	7
God's church outside New World	-	-
Great and abominable	6	-
Of the Lamb	3	-
Of the devil	-	-
Universal	1	2
Not true church	-	-
New World/universal	-	-
Jews	1	-

Figure 40: Church

	Nephi 1	Moroni 2
Other churches	-	-
Two churches	-	-
Local	-	-
Local/denominational	6	7

Figure 41: Churches

considered. For both, *Churches* refers to local entities in conflict with one another and the true church. They are characterized by pride, wealth, and false doctrine. Thus, there is a balance between similarities and dissimilarities when the *Church/Churches* material is examined.

Earth

A similar pattern of similarities and differences arises between Nephi 1 and Moroni 2 when *Earth* is considered. For example, Nephi 1 appears a bit more concerned with God's acts in relation to the earth than does Moroni 2, as figure 42 shows.

The only significant difference is that Nephi 1 says that God shook the earth, while Moroni 2 holds that people of faith may cause it to shake.

When the earth is considered as the globe, distribution is as shown in figure 43.

While the phrases are essentially the same, there are differences in what Nephi 1 and Moroni 2 stress. For Nephi 1, Israel is scattered on the earth and the church of the Lamb covers the earth. In addition,

	Nephi 1	Moroni 2
God comes to/in	-	-
God Father of	1	-
God creates	1	2
God's mercy over	-	-
God over	-	-
God smites	1	-
God of	-	-
God commands	-	-
God has power over	-	-
God's footstool	1	-
God's will done in	-	-
God lord of	-	-
God's purposes on	-	-
God rules	-	-
God shakes	1	2

Figure 42: Earth—God's Acts

	Nephi 1	Moroni 2
Face of (positive)	4	1
Face of (negative)	5	7
Ends of	2	3
Planet	8	2
Witnesses to God	-	-
Four corners of	-	-
At rest	-	-
Treasures of	-	-
Be joyful	-	-
Four parts of	-	-
Swear by	-	1
New	-	1
Four quarters of	1	1
World	3	-

Figure 43: Earth—Globe

"planet" is stressed, i.e., it may end. For Moroni 2, it is not Israel that is scattered, but people at the time of the great tower. Further, there is destruction and lack of repentance, and there are great pollutions at the time the Book of Mormon appears. Thus the ideas attached to the earth as a globe are different between the two authors.

Figure 44 shows the distribution of *Earth* when related to its inhabitants.

	Nephi 1	Moroni 2
Will see salvation	-	-
Abr's seed blesses	-	-
People of	-	-
Midst of	-	-
Trouble	-	-
Meek of	-	-
Chief ones of	-	-
People of tremble	-	-
Nation(s) of/on	-	-
Salt of	-	-
Remnant of	-	-
Gathered people of	-	-
Inhabitants of	1	1
Family of	-	-
Kindreds of	2	-
Smite the	-	-
Seal on	-	-
Loose on	-	-
Wickedness of	-	-
Land(s) of	1	-
(Die) like other people	-	1
Multitudes of	3	-

Figure 44: Earth—Inhabitants of

In this category, Nephi 1 seems to use a richer vocabulary. There is only one commonality between the two: both use "inhabitants of," Nephi 1 referring to judgments upon the inhabitants of the earth, and Moroni 2 referring to the brother of Jared being shown the inhabitants of the earth. Nephi 1 has concerns that go beyond this one concept.

Moroni 2, like his father, uses "dust of the earth" as a poetic way of speaking about death.

Figures 45 and 46 show the distribution of word use when earth means "ground."

	Nephi 1	Moroni 2
Fall to	3	2
Smite to	-	-
As dust of	-	-
Return to	-	-
Face to	-	-
Till	-	3
Man from	-	1
Prostrate on	-	-
Raise from	-	-
Bowed to	-	-
Level to (kill)	-	-
Cut down to (kill)	-	-
Kneel upon	-	-
Sit on	-	-

Figure 45: Earth—As Related to Humans

	Nephi 1	Moroni 2
In ground	1	5
Caves of	-	-
Fruit of	-	-
Surface of	-	-
Seeds of	-	-
Dirt	3	2
Face of	-	-
Is smitten	-	-
Ground	1	-
Smite	-	-
God shakes	1	2

Figure 46: Earth—Ground as Ground

When the earth is related to its inhabitants, Moroni 2 has a few more references than does Nephi 1. However, the language is very similar when figure 46 is considered, with a somewhat higher emphasis by Moroni 2 on things buried in the earth, especially the record upon which he is working. Hence, there are some commonalities and some differences when *Earth* meaning "ground" is under consideration.

In summary, there are not sharp distinctions between Nephi 1 and Moroni 2 with regard to *Earth*. Yet the differences are probably greater than the similarities.

Israel

As already seen, *Israel* is a very important word for Nephi 1. It is significantly less important to Moroni 2, as figures 47 and 48 indicate.

Clearly, the differences in relation to *Israel* are immense. For further details, chapter 5 concerning *Israel* can be consulted.

	Nephi 1	Moroni 2
House of	20	5
Tribes, house of	-	-
People, house of	1	-
Children of	3	-
12 tribes of	-	-
People of	-	-
Both houses of	-	-
Nation of	-	-
Escaped of	-	-
Preserved of	-	-
King of	-	-
Remnant of	-	-
Outcasts of	-	-
Lost tribes of	2	-
Remnant, house of	-	-
Scattered tribes of	-	-
God of	2	-
Holy One of	10	-
Redeemer of	-	-
Mighty One of	1	-
My people	-	-
My called of	-	-
My servant	-	-

Figure 47: Israel

	Nephi 1	Moroni 2
Nation	8	2
Spiritual entity	-	-
Covenant with	2	2
Scattered	6	-
Nephites and Lamanites part of	7	1
People of God	-	-
Olive tree	2	-
A king of	-	-
Judged/destroyed	-	-
God redeems	2	-
God judges	1	-
God is	1	-
Jesus is God	2	-
God opposed	3	-
Praise/rejoice in	3	-
Fear God	-	-
God will reign	2	-

Figure 48: Israel

	Nephi 1	Moroni 2
Land of	18	9
Region	7	44
Borders of	-	-
Round about	-	-
Part(s) of	-	1
Quarter of	-	1
Territory	-	-
Strange	-	-
Canaan	3	-
Judea	-	-
New World	10	24
Directions	-	5

Figure 49: Land—Geographical

	Nephi 1	Moroni 2
Promised	18	10
Covenant	-	-
Choice	-	3
Holy	-	-
Prepared	-	-
Chosen	-	1
Liberty	-	-
Inheritance	6	4
Our possession	-	-
Our	-	-
Own	-	-
Our fathers'	-	-
Whatsoever	-	-
Better	-	-
A	-	-
Their	-	-
Thy	-	-
My	-	-
His	-	-
Ground	1	-
Earth	-	2
As verb	-	1

Figure 50: Land—Special

Land/Lands

Figures 49–51 show the distributions for *Land* and *Lands*. Differences are evident between Nephi 1 and Moroni 2 in figures 49–51, especially when the meanings of words are emphasized. As seen previously, Nephi 1 strongly emphasizes Old World lands, underlined by relating "land of inheritance" and *Lands* to the Old World. While the New World is the promised land for him, there is no comparison to the emphasis that Moroni 2 places on the New World. Moroni 2, like his father, also adds directional notes that are not found in Nephi 1. Differences are, therefore, greater than similarities when *Land/Lands* is examined.

	Nephi 1	Moroni 2
Regions	1	2
Other	2	-
Lamanites'	-	-
Zarahemla	-	-
Roundabout	-	-
Foreign	-	1
Precious	1	-
Inheritance	2	-
Choice	-	5
Of possession	-	-
Promised	-	-
Of my people	-	-
Your	-	-
Our	-	-
Your own	-	-
Their	-	-
Own	-	-
Their own	-	-
Whatsoever	-	-

Figure 51: Lands

Summary

The differences between Nephi 1 and Moroni 2 are not as sharp as those between Nephi 1 and Alma 2 or Alma 2 and Mormon. However, they are quite different on the word clusters Israel and Land/Lands and somewhat different on Law/Command and Earth. They are closest to one another with regards to Church/Churches. On balance, the differences between the two outweigh their similarities.

Nephi 1 and Mormon

When we consider Nephi 1 and Mormon, we begin a comparison of the two authors with the longest texts in the Book of Mormon. Mormon writes 97,515 words or 36 percent of the total book. Nephi 1 writes 28,637 words or 11 percent of the book. Hence it will be interesting to see how these two authors compare to one another. We begin with the word clusters from chapter 1.

Some differences are visible in figure 52. Neither the Ancient Near East cluster nor the Prophecy cluster, found in Nephi 1, is part of Mormon's five or six top clusters. Similarly, Christology is significantly less important in Nephi 1 than it is in Mormon:S. In terms of similarities, the Gathering cluster is of greater importance in Mormon than in Nephi 1, but for each it is important. The Editing cluster is also important. The contrasts, however, far outweigh the similarities, since the majority of Mormon's concerns are quite different from those of Nephi 1.

Nephi1:S		Mormon:S		Mormon:N1		Mormon:N3	
2.9	Ancient Near East	3.2	Xology	3.5	Numbers	1.8	Money
2.2	Gathering	2.8	Gathering	2.3	Editing	1.8	Directions
1.8	Prophecy	2.4	Spiritual	2.2	Directions	1.8	Contention
1.6	Editing	2.1	Eschatology	2.0	Military	1.6	Military
1.5	Xology	2.0	Sacramental	1.5	Neg. emotions	1.6	Government
1.4	God					1.5	Numbers
1.4	Creation						

Figure 52

The null-hypothesis rejections between the two are not conclusive. Nephi1:N1 versus Mormon:S gives one rejection, while Nephi1:S versus Mormon:S gives no rejections.

	Mormon	Nephi 1
Command	20	2
Commanded	78	33
Commandest	-	-
Commandeth	1	5
Commanding	1	-
Commandment	7	7
Commandments	53	26
Commands	5	-
Law	64	23
Law of Moses	16	4
Laws	17	-
Come unto	16	7

Figure 53: Law/Command

Law/Command

In figure 53 we see the numerical comparison between Nephi 1 and Mormon regarding the Law/Command complex.

The most obvious items of note are that Mormon uses the word *Command* significantly more than does Nephi 1, and with the unique meaning of "leadership." Second, Mormon uses the word *Laws* seventeen times, while Nephi 1 does not use the word at all. Third, Nephi 1 uses *Commandeth* proportionately more than does Mormon, who uses it only once. The greater difference, however, lies in what these words signify. For Nephi 1 there is an emphasis upon God's commandments in daily life, and *Law* refers to the Law of Moses. Mormon's emphasis in his editorial writings, by contrast, is primarily secular. The commands of which he speaks are principally royal and secular in nature, and the laws are either Mosiah's laws or tribal laws. His use of *Commandments* seems to refer to the Christian life, and his references to *Law* generally mean the Law of Moses. In this he is similar to Nephi 1. Similarly, in his sermonic material, Mormon speaks of God commanding, but his sermonic material does not have the orientation toward day-by-day items, as Nephi 1's does. Thus, Mormon and Nephi 1 are quite different in the Law/Command complex.

	Mormon	Nephi 1
Christ's church in New World	80	-
Local church	20	-
God's church outside New World	-	-
Great and abominable	-	6
Of the Lamb	-	3
Of the devil	-	-
Universal	44	1
Not true church	3	-
New World/universal	-	-
Jews	-	1

Figure 54: Church

	Mormon	Nephi 1
Other churches	-	-
Two churches	-	-
Local	10	-
Local/denominational	5	6

Figure 55: Churches

Church/Churches

Figures 54 and 55 show the word distribution for the words *Church* and *Churches*.

Clearly, there are great differences between Mormon and Nephi 1 in the use of *Church* and *Churches*. They are concerned with totally different uses of the word, with only one similarity. Nephi 1 refers once to the universal church. Otherwise, Nephi 1 is concerned about the conflict between the great and abominable church and the church of the Lamb. Mormon, on the other hand, is concerned about the

	Mormon	Nephi 1
God comes to/in	-	-
God Father of	-	1
God creates	-	1
God's mercy over	-	-
God over	-	-
God smites	-	1
God of	-	-
God commands	-	-
God has power over	-	-
God's footstool	-	1
God's will done in	-	-
God Lord of	-	-
God's purposes on	-	-
God rules	-	-
God shakes	10	1

Figure 56: Earth—God's Acts

	Mormon	Nephi 1
Face of (positive)	2	4
Face of (negative)	2	5
Ends of	2	2
Planet	10	8
Witnesses to God	-	-
Four corners of	-	-
At rest	-	-
Treasures of	-	-
Be joyful	-	-
Four parts of	-	-
Swear by	-	-
New	-	-
Four quarters of	2	1
World	-	3

Figure 57: Earth—Globe

church in the New World, local churches, and the universal church. The sense of local churches continues for Mormon in his use of *Churches*. In the book of Mosiah he speaks of churches being established throughout the land, and all are positive references. In 4 Nephi, however, his references to churches are negative, for churches are now being built in opposition to Christ's true church. Nephi 1 uses *Churches* in much the same way. Overall, however, there are major differences between Mormon and Nephi 1 in the uses of these words.

Earth

While a few similarities are apparent between Mormon and Nephi 1 when *Earth* is considered, we will see that once again the differences overshadow the similarities. Figure 56 shows their use of words related to God's acts.

Apart from affirming that God has power to shake the earth, Mormon uses none of the concepts associated with this category. While Nephi 1 does not express very many of the ideas in the group, he makes it clear that God is in control of the earth.

Figure 57 shows the two authors' uses of earth as "globe." Clearly, there are significant similarities in word use. Yet, Mormon and Nephi 1 are quite different in what they understand these categories to signify. Considering "face of," Mormon speaks once of Israel's scattering and once of the scattering that occurred at the time of the great tower. He also mentions Jesus explaining the earth's history to its end and mentions the Three Nephites ministering on the face of the earth. Nephi 1 is primarily concerned with the scattering of Israel and with the great and abominable church and the church of the Lamb being spread upon the earth.

With regards to the earth meaning "planet," Nephi 1 tends to stress theology: God's power can cause the earth to pass away, what is sealed on earth is sealed in heaven, Joseph's seed will not pass away as long as the earth continues, etc. In contrast, Mormon is more event-oriented: the earth can be commanded to stand still, Nehor is killed between heaven and earth, Jesus' garments are whiter than anything found on earth, etc. Thus, differences in meaning are greater than shown in the numerical accounting of figure 57.

Figure 58 examines the earth with reference to its inhabitants.

	Mormon	Nephi 1
Will see salvation	-	-
Abr's seed blesses	-	-
People of	-	-
Midst of	-	-
Trouble	-	-
Meek of	-	-
Chief ones of	-	-
People of tremble	-	-
Nation(s) of/on	-	-
Salt of	-	-
Remnant of	-	-
Gathered people of	-	-
Inhabitants of	-	1
Family of	-	-
Kindreds of	-	2
Smite the	-	-
Seal on	-	-
Loose on	-	-
Wickedness of	-	-
Land(s) of	-	1
(Die) like other people	4	-
Multitudes of	-	3

Figure 58: Earth—Inhabitants of

Neither writer makes much use of this category, but what little they use is distinct to each.

Finally, the dominant difference between Mormon and Nephi 1 appears in figures 59 and 60.

	Mormon	Nephi 1
Fall to	26	3
Smite to	3	-
As dust of	3	-
Return to	-	-
Face to	-	-
Till	2	-
Man from	-	-
Prostrate on	4	-
Raise from	2	-
Bowed to	4	-
Level to (kill)	2	-
Cut down to (kill)	1	-
Kneel upon	4	-
Sit on	1	-

Figure 59: Earth—As Related to Humans

	Mormon	Nephi 1
In ground	7	1
Caves of	-	-
Fruit of	-	-
Surface of	1	-
Seeds of	-	-
Dirt	9	3
Face of	3	-
Is smitten	2	-
Ground	5	1
Smite	1	-
God shakes	10	1

Figure 60: Earth—Ground as Ground

The differences here are so evident that it is only necessary to show the two tables. In conclusion, there are no significant similarities between Nephi 1 and Mormon in any of the categories related to the word Earth.

Israel

With regards to the word *Earth,* particularly when "ground" is meant, Mormon is dominant in his use. Concerning the word *Israel,* the reverse is seen. For Nephi 1, *Israel* is highly important, as figures 61 and 62 show.

Figure 61 shows some common language between Mormon and Nephi 1 concerning "house of," "people of the house of," and "children of." However, their uses of the rest of the phrases are clearly different. The two authors differ in what they stress as they write about Israel. Mormon understands himself to be writing to scattered Israel. Nephi 1, while sharing this view to a degree, has a much stronger sense of historical Israel which God brought out of bondage in Egypt and which was later scattered.

	Mormon	Nephi 1
House of	8	20
Tribes, house of	-	-
People, house of	1	1
Children of	2	3
12 tribes of	-	-
People of	-	-
Both houses of	-	-
Nation of	-	-
Escaped of	-	-
Preserved of	-	-
King of	-	-
Remnant of	2	-
Outcasts of	-	-
Lost tribes of	-	2
Remnant, house of	-	-
Scattered tribes of	1	-
God of	-	2
Holy One of	-	10
Redeemer of	-	-
Mighty One of	-	1
My people	-	-
My called of	-	-
My servant	-	-

Figure 61: Israel

Summary Tests of a Method 193

Figure 62 shows that Mormon uses absolutely no language referring to God in relation to Israel. Thus, Mormon and Nephi 1 are again significantly different in their language and usage.

	Mormon	Nephi 1
Nation	6	8
Spiritual Entity	-	-
Covenant with	4	2
Scattered	5	6
Nephites and Lamanites part of	-	7
People of God	-	-
Olive tree	-	2
A king of	-	-
Judged/destroyed	-	-
God redeems	-	2
God judges	-	1
God is	-	1
Jesus is God	-	2
God opposed	-	3
Praise/rejoice in	-	3
Fear God	-	-
God will reign	-	2

Figure 62: Israel

	Mormon	Nephi 1
Land of	293	18
Region	255	7
Borders of	13	-
Round about	12	-
Part(s) of	17	-
Quarter of	4	-
Territory	2	-
Strange	-	-
Canaan	-	3
Judea	-	-
New World	7	10
Directions	56	-

Figure 63: Land—Geographical

Land/Lands

We turn finally to the use of *Land* and *Lands,* as found in Mormon and Nephi 1. Figure 63 shows the word distribution with reference to geography.

Mormon's language is clearly much broader than that of Nephi 1, and there are no directions mentioned by Nephi 1, an area clearly stressed by Mormon. Thus, the differences are very clear. Figure 64 compares the Special category.

Significant differences are once again evident. The only common ground surrounds the concept of "land of inheritance," but Nephi

1 speaks predominantly about the lands from which his father came, while Mormon indicates that Israel will be gathered to her lands of inheritance, i.e., the Old World.

	Mormon	Nephi 1
Promised	-	18
Covenant	-	-
Choice	-	-
Holy	-	-
Prepared	-	-
Chosen	1	-
Liberty	1	-
Inheritance	3	6
Our possession	-	-
Our	1	-
Own	4	-
Our fathers'	-	-
Whatsoever	-	-
Better	-	-
A	5	-
Their	10	-
Thy	-	-
My	-	-
His	3	-
Ground	-	1
Earth	-	-
As verb	1	-

Figure 64: Land—Special

	Mormon	Nephi 1
Regions	8	1
Other	-	2
Lamanites'	1	-
Zarahemla	1	-
Roundabout	-	-
Foreign	-	-
Precious	-	1
Inheritance	7	2
Choice	-	-
Of possession	4	-
Promised	-	-
Of my people	-	-
Your	-	-
Our	1	-
Your own	-	-
Their	24	-
Own	1	-
Their own	9	-
Whatsoever	1	-

Figure 65: Lands

Figure 65 displays Mormon's and Nephi 1's uses of the word *Lands*.

As in previous instances, the differences are clear. To see the specific differences or similarities, consult chapter 6.

Summary

Interestingly, the clearest differences among all the pairs of authors considered probably lie between Mormon and Nephi 1. Differences between the two are marked on the word clusters and on each word considered. Thus, where wordprint may not be as clear as we could wish, the above comparisons affirm the individuality of Mormon and Nephi 1. It would appear that Mormon did not inject himself in any significant way into Nephi's work.

Conclusion

The basic question to be answered by this study was whether one could ascertain clear differences between the authors within the Book of Mormon on the basis of content words. The answer is a resounding "yes." Everything that has been done in this study has an empirical foundation, and any other researcher can reproduce what has been done here. Subjectivity has been kept to a minimum. Certainly, persons may disagree with the way words were categorized or with my interpretation of how a word was used in a particular instance. Overall, however, the cumulative evidence is virtually overwhelming in indicating that many authors are the source for the Book of Mormon. There are simply too many cumulative differences between authors, and these differences have been checked in too many ways to conclude otherwise.

We have seen, in all chapters, precisely what we would expect if the Book of Mormon were in fact an ancient book written by a number of authors. We have observed similarities between them because they speak of the same God, many of the same events, and from a common faith. At the same time, we see distinct differences, no matter what word clusters or individual words we examined. Homogeneity is not a characteristic of the Book of Mormon. Perhaps the most impressive finding is just how different Mormon is from all other writers, even when he inserts himself in the midst of someone else's writings. Examples of this include his use of *Command* to mean "leadership," his use of *Earth* to mean "ground," his almost exclusive use of directional notations, and his expansive language associated with *Land* and *Lands*. No single nineteenth-century author could have produced the linguistic and thematic consistency found in Mormon, a consistency that runs through his work whether he is offering editorial comment within the body of another's narrative, or writing his own personal account.

Since the appearance of the Book of Mormon, some persons have contended that Joseph Smith wrote it and that it is thus a nineteenth-century writing. For many outside The Church of Jesus Christ of Latter-day Saints, this may be a position that they will always take, and it is understandable. More recently, however, there are some Latter-day Saints who claim that the Book of Mormon, either wholly or in part, was written by Joseph Smith and reflects not ancient times but rather the religious climate of the early nineteenth century. Clearly, this position says more about such persons' individual beliefs than it does about their serious investigation of the Book of Mormon.

When I was a graduate student at Duke University, I assisted in teaching an Old Testament course in the Divinity School. On the front of the course syllabus was a cartoon which showed a student lying on the floor thumbing through his Bible. His wife was standing over him, and the caption read, "Go away. Leave me alone. I'm looking for a biblical text to support my preconceived notion." Those Latter-day Saints who are claiming that the Book of Mormon is a nineteenth-century work begin from the presupposition, as do so many contemporary Bible scholars, that God cannot reveal or show the future to his prophets. Thus they assert that writings which address modern concerns must have been written in the modern times. Since the Book of Mormon speaks in part to problems found in the nineteenth century, some say by the above logic that Joseph Smith or some other author, whom Joseph Smith copied, must have written the Book of Mormon.

On the basis of this research, I have no reluctance whatsoever in asserting that no one person could possibly have written the Book of Mormon. Either it is the product of massive collusion among numerous nineteenth-century persons, or it is precisely what it claims to be—an ancient book written by ancient people. There is simply no viable middle ground.

The above chapters stress another element that is critical to scriptural interpretation: any interpreter must deal with the *text* of scripture. I simply had no idea what I would find when I began this work. I let the text say what it would. I have reported only that which

I have found and can support from computer studies of the text. I could not have made these findings without the aid of the computer, for it would have been virtually impossible to separate the authors or gather the texts in which the words under examination occurred. With the computer, however, I was able to collect all the passages, by author, in which the words under examination appeared, thereby enabling me to compare word usage relatively easily. Having done so, I am convinced that this research relates what the Book of Mormon authors have to say on their own behalf, when select words or word clusters are examined. I have simply had the privilege of being the facilitator in that process. I stand amazed before the clarity with which the individuality of the authors has come through the pages of the Book of Mormon.

My testimony of the Book of Mormon was not and is not based on this study. Even if I had not been able to distinguish between the authors as clearly as has been done here, I would still know that the Book of Mormon is an ancient book. But faith can lead one to seek a deeper understanding of those things in which one believes through the application of reason, and in this case through the application of sophisticated twentieth-century technology used in conjunction with reason. Thus, my faith invited me to apply my intellect to an exploration of the authors of the Book of Mormon. That search has been rewarded far beyond my expectations, and my faith has been deepened as I have immersed myself for the last six years in the book which is the keystone of our religion. I hope others will take up the search and expand what has only been initiated in this work.

Appendix

Below are listed all the words that make up the word clusters used and discussed in chapter 1. Printed with each word is the number of times it appears in the Book of Mormon. Thirty-four of the words are used in more than one cluster. The clusters are listed in alphabetical order.

Agriculture (60 words)

Acres 1	Dunged 2	Grafts 1	Planted 11	Shearer 1
Barley 4	Eggs 1	Grain 28	Plants 1	Shearers 1
Barns 1	Field 15	Grapes 5	Prune 6	Sow 6
Blossoms 2	Fields 11	Groves 1	Pruned 5	Straw 2
Branch 21	Figs 1	Harvest 3	Pruning 1	Till 22
Branches 53	Flock 7	Herds 23	Reap 13	Tilling 3
Butter 3	Flocking 1	Hoe 1	Ripened 4	Vine 4
Cedars 3	Flocks 79	Honey 6	Ripeness 1	Vines 1
Chaff 6	Garden 11	Mattock 1	Ripening 4	Vineyard 102
Corn 3	Graft 14	Milk 3	Root 19	Vineyards 2
Crops 1	Grafted 10	Neas 1	Roots 20	Wheat 2
Dung 2	Grafting 1	Plant 11	Seeds 9	Wool 1

Ancient Near East (109 words)

Abel 1	Cain 3	Eve 3	Jews 76	Nazareth 2
Abraham 29	Carchemish 1	Gad 1	John 3	Nob 1
Adam 26	Chaldeans 2	Galilee 1	Jonas 2	Olive 16
Amen 42	Chaldees' 1	Gentile 2	Jordan 4	Ophir 1
Amos 6	Cherubims 3	Gentiles 141	Joseph 43	Pharaoh 3
Anathoth 1	Circumcision 1	Gomorrah 1	Joshua 1	Philistines 3
Ancient 12	Cubit 1	Hebrew 3	Jot 3	Rahab 1
Ancients 3	Cush 1	Horeb 1	Judah 22	Sabbath 5
Arabian 1	Damascus 4	Hosanna 3	Judea 5	Sackcloth 4
Ark 1	David 7	Immanuel 2	Lebanon 4	Samaria 7
Asp 2	Eden 6	Isaac 13	Levi 5	Sarah 1
Ass 5	Edom 1	Isaiah 24	Malachi 2	Saul 1
Asses 1	Egypt 18	Israel 211	Manna 2	Sinai 2
Assyria 8	Egyptian 2	Israelites 1	Medes 1	Sinim 1
Assyrian 3	Egyptians 9	Jacob 100	Melchizedek 5	Sodom 2
Babylon 11	Elam 1	Jehovah 2	Messiah 31	Solomon 6
Bashan 1	Elijah 1	Jeremiah 6	Midian 2	Solomon's 1
Bethabara 1	Ephah 1	Jesse 2	Moses 72	Sycamores 1
Boaz 1	Ephraim 12	Jew 12	Moses' 3	Syria 5

Syrians 1   Tabret 1   Tittle 3   Viol 1   Zedekiah 8
Tabael 1   Tarshish 1   Uriah 1   Viols 1   Zion 45
Tabernacle 4   Teil 1   Uzziah 2   Zechariah 1

Animals (63 words)

Animal 1   Calves 2   Dove 2   Horses' 1   Serpent's 1
Animals 5   Cattle 7   Dragon 1   Insects 1   Serpents 9
Asp 2   Chickens 4   Dragons 3   Kid 2   Sheep 26
Ass 5   Cockatrice 1   Elephants 2   Lambs 1   Sheep's 1
Asses 1   Cockatrice's 2   Fish 3   Leopard 2   Swine 2
Bats 1   Cow 4   Fowl 3   Lion 10   Vultures 2
Beast 2   Cows 1   Fowls 3   Lions 3   Whale 2
Beasts 34   Creature 8   Goat 3   Moth 5   Wolf 4
Bee 2   Creatures 3   Goats 3   Owls 1   Wolves 2
Bees 1   Cumoms 2   Hen 4   Ox 4   Worm 2
Breast 3   Cureloms 2   Hoofs 2   Oxen 2   Worms 2
Bull 1   Dog 1   Horse 1   Roe 1
Calf 2   Dogs 4   Horses 12   Serpent 7

Body (51 words)

Arm 39   Feet 54   Head 67   Mouth 67   Teeth 3
Bowels 8   Finger 14   Heads 37   Mouths 10   Thigh 1
Breasts 2   Fingers 3   Heart 165   Neck 9   Tongue 24
Cheek 3   Fists 1   Hearts 277   Necks 7   Tongues 20
Cheeks 6   Flesh 86   Joint 2   Nose 1   Tooth 2
Ear 14   Foot 10   Joints 1   Nostrils 1   Womb 5
Ears 10   Foreheads 3   Knee 1   Palms 1   Wrists 1
Eye 36   Hair 8   Knees 2   Shoulder 3
Eyes 89   Hairs 1   Legs 2   Shoulders 8
Face 185   Hand 194   Lips 6   Sinew 1
Faces 6   Hands 199   Loins 34   Skin 7

Christology (58 words)

Alpha 1   Crucified 3   Lamb 77   Redeem 25   Savior 7
Ascend 4   Crucify 6   Mary 2   Redeemed 34   Savior's 2
Ascended 9   Forgive 17   Mediator 1   Redeemer 51   Saviour 5
Ascendeth 7   Forgiven 4   Mercies 18   Redeemeth 4   Spirit 276
Ascension 4   Forgiveness 5   Merciful 47   Redeeming 3   Transfiguration 2
Atone 4   Grace 31   Mercy 84   Redemption 51   Transfigured 1
Atonement 28   Immanuel 2   Merit 2   Remission 28   Virgin 6
Atoneth 4   Intercession 4   Merits 5   Resurrection 81   Virgins 1
Atoning 3   Jesus 187   Messiah 31   Salvation 88   Wash 1
Christ 386   Justified 2   Nativity 2   Sanctification 2 Washed 7
Christ's 2   Justifieth 3   Nazareth 2   Sanctified 10
Christs 1   Justify 3   Omega 1   Saving 4

Church (73 words)

Apostle 3   Assemblies 1   Bless 32   Church 227   Converted 28
Apostles 13   Assembling 2   Blessed 139   Churches 32   Covenant 100
Appoint 11   Assembly 2   Blessing 19   Congregation 1   Covenanted 21
Appointed 61   Authority 48   Blessings 15   Congregations 1   Covenanteth 1
Assemble 18   Believers 4   Brethren 549   Conversion 5   Covenanting 2
Assembled 7   Bible 11   Christians 4   Convert 3   Covenants 30

Appendix

Disciple 1	Ministering 7	Persecutions 12	Priest's 1	Scriptures 41
Disciples 54	Ministers 3	Preach 87	Priesthood 8	Seer 10
Doctrine 25	Ministry 17	Preached 16	Priests 79	Sermon 1
Doctrines 4	Pastors 1	Preacher 1	Sabbath 5	Synagogue 4
Elder 8	Persecute 13	Preachers 1	Saint 1	Synagogues 22
Elders 9	Persecuted 6	Preaching 31	Saints 28	Temple 22
Gospel 41	Persecuteth 1	Preachings 1	Sanctuaries 8	Temples 9
Minister 35	Persecuting 1	Preside 1	Sanctuary 2	
Ministered 14	Persecution 4	Priest 29	Scripture 4	

Contention (22 words)

Contend 44	Contentions 57	Disputings 1	Dissenter 1	Rebelleth 4
Contended 6	Disputation 1	Dissension 4	Dissenters 20	Rebelling 2
Contendeth 2	Disputations 10	Dissensions 20	Dissenting 1	
Contending 5	Dispute 9	Dissent 1	Rebel 14	
Contention 31	Disputing 1	Dissented 10	Rebelled 9	

Creation (72 words)

Air 13	Flint 3	Mount 25	Seasons 4	Thunder 10
Beach 1	Forest 9	Mountain 15	Shore 2	Thunderings 8
Briers 6	Forests 5	Mountains 32	Shores 1	Timber 5
Bushes 1	Fountain 11	Oak 1	Snow 1	Tree 113
Cloud 16	Fountains 1	Oaks 1	Star 2	Trees 21
Clouds 2	Grass 2	Planets 1	Stars 5	Valley 41
Dawn 2	Gravel 1	Rain 10	Stones 42	Valleys 3
Daylight 1	Hail 2	Rains 1	Storm 10	Whirlwind 5
Dew 1	Heavens 38	Reed 1	Streams 1	Whirlwinds 4
Dust 36	Hill 27	River 44	Sun 14	Wind 15
Earth 296	Hills 9	Rivers 3	Thicket 1	Winds 9
Earthquake 1	Lake 10	Rocks 10	Thickets 2	World 169
Earthquakes 4	Lilies 1	Sea 96	Thistle 1	
Fir 1	Moon 4	Seashore 26	Thistles 1	
Firmament 1	Moons 1	Season 20	Thorns 9	

Directions (10 words)

East 48	North 37	Northernmost 1	South 36	Southward 20
Eastward 3	Northern 1	Northward 45	Southeast 1	West 42

Editing (21 words)

Abridged 1	Book 76	Engraving 1	Write 122	Written 170
Abridging 1	Books 6	Engravings 12	Writeth 1	Wrote 29
Abridgment 3	Engrave 1	History 6	Writing 16	
Account 78	Engraved 1	Record 134	Writings 1	
Author 3	Engraven 31	Records 76		

Emotions, Negative (62 words)

Afraid 13	Ashamed 11	Despair 3	Envy 4	Feareth 1
Anger 90	Cried 44	Despise 7	Envying 2	Fearful 3
Angry 71	Cries 18	Despised 10	Envyings 8	Fearing 7
Anguish 11	Cry 116	Embarrassments 1	Fear 113	Frighten 2
Anxious 1	Crying 8	Envieth 1	Feared 23	Frightened 11

Furious 1	Hate 8	Mourn 25	Sorrow 51	Wail 2
Fury 9	Hated 8	Mourned 4	Sorrowed 1	Wailing 2
Grief 5	Hatred 19	Mourning 20	Sorroweth 2	Weep 5
Griefs 1	Jealous 3	Mournings 1	Sorrowful 19	Weeping 3
Grieve 1	Lament 2	Passion 1	Sorrowing 3	Wept 4
Grieved 13	Lamentation 8	Passions 1	Sorrows 6	
Grieves 1	Lamentations 3	Rage 1	Terror 8	
Grieveth 15	Lamenting 2	Sad 2	Unhappy 2	

Emotions, Positive (36 words)

Amazed 2	Delight 11	Glad 20	Lovest 1	Rejoice 72
Amazement 4	Delighted 7	Happiness 30	Loveth 6	Rejoiced 9
Astonished 25	Delighteth 13	Happy 9	Loving 1	Rejoiceth 4
Astonishing 1	Desire 83	Joy 136	Merry 5	Rejoicing 10
Astonishment 18	Desires 44	Joyful 3	Pity 4	
Cheer 3	Enjoy 2	Joyous 1	Pleased 6	
Cheerfully 1	Enjoyed 2	Love 57	Pleasing 12	
Compassion 12	Enjoyment 1	Loved 10	Pleasure 17	

Eschatology (18 words)

Endless 24	Eternity 9	Immortal 10	Last 117	Visitation 3
Endlessly 1	Everlasting 59	Immortality 9	Perdition 2	Visitations 1
Eternal 89	Everlastingly 1	Incorruptible 2	Restore 4	
Eternally 6	Forever 99	Incorruption 6	Restored 40	

Ethics (38 words)

Abhor 1	Admonitions 1	Covet 3	Obedient 11	Virtue 2
Abhorrence 2	Adultery 11	Deed 4	Obey 15	Worthiness 2
Abhorrest 1	Chaste 1	Deeds 6	Obeyed 1	Worthy 4
Abhorreth 1	Chastity 2	Guiltless 8	Rob 12	Wrong 7
Admonish 2	Commandment 41	Justice 71	Steal 12	Wronged 4
Admonished 3	Commandments	Lie 23	Unworthily 4	Wrongfully 1
Admonishing 1	211	Murder 35	Unworthiness 3	Wrongs 6
Admonition 1	Commands 9	Obedience 1	Unworthy 5	

Evil (137 words)

Abominable 28	Corruptness 1	False 17	Idols 13	Murdereth 2
Abomination 9	Crime 9	Filth 1	Iniquities 92	Murdering 8
Abominations 78	Crimes 11	Filthiness 17	Iniquitous 1	Murderings 2
Accursed 6	Curse 38	Filthy 16	Iniquity 135	Murderous 3
Adulterers 1	Cursed 30	Fornication 3	Lasciviousness 5	Murders 30
Adulterous 1	Curseth 2	Guilt 16	Liar 9	Mysterious 1
Adultery 11	Cursing 9	Guilty 12	Liars 1	Perverse 6
Astray 8	Cursings 1	Harlot 1	Lucifer 1	Perversion 1
Blaspheme 2	Damnation 10	Harlots 8	Lust 2	Pervert 7
Blasphemy 1	Damned 8	Hell 59	Lusts 3	Perverted 2
Brimstone 10	Demons 1	Hypocrisy 2	Magic 1	Perverteth 1
Carnal 15	Depravity 1	Hypocrite 2	Magics 1	Perverting 4
Carnally 1	Devil 99	Hypocrites 6	Mistress 1	Polluted 5
Concubines 9	Devilish 6	Hypocritical 1	Murder 35	Pollutions 2
Corrupt 10	Devils 9	Idolatries 2	Murdered 28	Priestcraft 4
Corrupted 13	Evil 135	Idolatrous 3	Murderer 5	Priestcrafts 4
Corruption 9	Evils 1	Idolatry 6	Murderers 11	Rob 12

Appendix 203

Robbed 7	Sinful 3	Temptations 9	Transgressor 3	Whore 8
Robber 6	Sinned 5	Tempted 2	Transgressors 2	Whoredoms 27
Robbers 55	Sinner 4	Tempting 2	Trespass 1	Wicked 104
Robbery 1	Sinners 4	Thief 1	Trespasses 6	Wickedly 7
Robbing 4	Sins 162	Thieves 4	Ungodliness 2	Wickedness 161
Robbings 2	Soothsayers 2	Transgress 9	Unholy 5	Witchcraft 1
Satan 26	Sorcerers 1	Transgressed 4	Unquenchable 5	Witchcrafts 2
Secret 82	Sorceries 2	Transgresseth 2	Unrighteous 3	Wizards 1
Secretly 3	Spirits 17	Transgressing 1	Unrighteousness 2	
Sensual 2	Tempt 6	Transgression 30	Vilest 1	
Sin 65	Temptation 10	Transgressions 14	Wanton 1	

Extras (34 words)

Blood 149	Murmur 25	Obeyeth 1	Powerful 14	Suffer 119
Bloodthirsty 2	Murmured 4	Obeying 1	Powerfully 1	Suffered 54
Bloody 1	Murmuring 1	Perish 115	Powers 5	Suffereth 12
Bones 9	Murmurings 3	Perished 15	Promise 42	Suffering 24
Knowledge 128	Noah 47	Perisheth 5	Promised 31	Sufferings 19
Land 253	Oath 28	Perishing 2	Promises 21	Suffers 1
Lands 105	Oaths 13	Power 411	Promising 1	

Family (32 words)

Brother 167	Families 21	Husbands 10	Orphans 1	Widow 2
Brother's 2	Family 23	Kindred 19	Parent 3	Widows 7
Brothers 10	Father 551	Kindreds 22	Parents 19	Wife 30
Child 34	Father's 4	Kinsfolks 3	Sisters 1	Wives 51
Children 348	Fathers 180	Mother 31	Son 341	
Daughter 14	Fathers' 3	Mothers 10	Son's 1	
Daughters 77	Husband 6	Nephew 1	Sons 168	

Gathering (12 words)

Gather 60	Gathering 4	Restoration 19	Scattered 60
Gathered 102	Remnant 60	Restoring 5	Scattereth 1
Gathereth 7	Remnants 2	Scatter 8	Scattering 2

God (31 words)

Almighty 13	Ghost 97	Godliness 1	Lord 1568	Visited 16
Created 50	Glorified 6	Gods 2	Lord's 3	Visiting 4
Creating 1	Glorify 7	Heaven 114	Mysteries 19	Voice 164
Creation 14	Glorious 5	Heavenly 7	Omnipotent 6	
Creator 10	Glory 78	Holiness 10	Paradise 5	
Divine 2	God 1671	Holy 297	Sacred 27	
Eternal 89	God's 2	Jehovah 2	Visit 34	

Government (93 words)

Alliance 2	Assembled 7	Council 4	Decrees 6	Elected 4
Appoint 11	Assemblies 1	Countries 8	Decreeth 1	Embassies 1
Appointed 61	Assembling 2	Country 38	Dethrone 4	Embassy 12
Arrest 1	Assembly 2	Crown 1	Dethroned 1	Execute 12
Arrested 1	Authority 48	Decree 3	Dethroning 1	Executed 5
Assemble 18	Confederacy 2	Decreed 2	Dungeons 2	Executeth 3

Exile 1
Govern 4
Governed 4
Government 24
Governments 2
Governor 26
Governors 1
Insurrections 1
King 509
King's 8
Kingdom 151
Kingdoms 9
Kings 35

Monarchy 1
Nation 32
Nations 81
Nobility 3
Nobles 1
Office 9
Overthrew 1
Overthrow 16
Palace 2
Palaces 1
Prince 2
Princes 4
Prison 74

Prisoner 1
Prisoners 66
Prisons 5
Punish 4
Punished 14
Punishment 15
Punishments 2
Queen 22
Queens 3
Rebellion 20
Rebellions 4
Reign 158
Reigned 14

Reigneth 8
Reigns 4
Revive 1
Revolted 1
Ruler 20
Rulers 7
Ruleth 1
Ruling 1
Scepters 1
Statutes 13
Tax 3
Taxation 1
Taxed 1

Taxes 6
Throne 19
Thrones 4
Traitor 1
Traitors 1
Treaty 3
Tribunal 1
Tribute 8
Tyrant 1
Usurp 3
Usurped 2

Judicial (31 words)

Accusation 1
Accuse 5
Accused 3
Accusing 1
Arraigned 1
Injustice 2
Judge 116

Judged 55
Judges 141
Judgeth 3
Judgment 114
Judgments 42
Just 57
Law 185

Lawful 3
Laws 28
Lawyer 1
Lawyers 17
Penalty 1
Testified 45
Testifies 1

Testifieth 4
Testify 26
Testifying 5
Testimony 33
Unjust 1
Witness 41
Witnessed 9

Witnesses 10
Witnesseth 1
Witnessing 1

Military (127 words)

Adversaries 5
Adversary 5
Armed 12
Armies 151
Arming 1
Armor 8
Armors 1
Arms 57
Army 137
Arrow 4
Arrows 22
Attack 13
Attacked 2
Axe 4
Battle 134
Battles 3
Blade 1
Blades 1
Bloodshed 19
Bloodsheds 7
Bodies 31
Bow 24
Bows 13
Breastplate 1
Breastplates 10
Breastwork 3

Bucklers 1
Captain 10
Captains 27
Captive 32
Captives 6
Carnage 5
Cimeter 3
Cimeters 9
Club 1
Clubs 3
Commander 6
Conquer 6
Conquered 4
Conquerors 1
Daggers 1
Dart 1
Darts 1
Defeat 1
Defence 13
Defend 27
Defended 1
Defending 2
Encamp 2
Encircle 5
Encircled 20
Encircles 1

Enemies 83
Enemy 20
Fight 29
Fighteth 4
Fighting 5
Foes 1
Forces 11
Fort 1
Fortifications 10
Fortified 6
Fortify 15
Fortifying 1
Forts 5
Fought 34
Guard 17
Guarded 3
Guards 30
Hilt 3
Hilts 1
Javelin 3
March 58
Marched 15
Marching 9
Officers 4
Overcome 11
Overpower 14

Overpowered 6
Overpowereth 1
Overpowering 1
Overran 1
Overrun 3
Prisoner 1
Prisoners 66
Provisions 37
Repulsed 2
Retreat 13
Retreated 3
Retreats 1
Shield 1
Shields 12
Siege 6
Slain 151
Slaughter 10
Slaughtered 1
Slaughters 1
Slay 110
Slayeth 2
Slaying 6
Slew 27
Sling 5
Slings 8
Soldier 2

Soldiers 5
Spears 2
Spies 10
Spy 3
Stratagem 4
Stronghold 3
Strongholds 10
Surrendered 2
Sword 116
Swords 42
Victorious 1
Victory 12
War 132
Warfare 3
Warred 1
Warrior 1
Warriors 1
Wars 64
Weapon 2
Weapons 55
Wound 3
Wounded 16
Wounds 12

Money (9 words)

Cent 1
Money 14

Onti 2
Onties 2

Seantum 1
Senine 8

Senum 4
Senums 2

Seon 3

Nomadic/Wilderness (36 words)

Camp 24	Journeyed 9	Snare 5	Traveler 1	Wanderers 3
Camped 1	Journeying 7	Snared 1	Traveleth 1	Wandering 4
Camps 4	Journeyings 7	Snares 4	Traveling 3	Wild 54
Game 5	Journeys 1	Tent 20	Travels 3	Wilderness 255
Hunt 4	Pasture 2	Tents 44	Tribe 3	
Hunted 8	Pastures 1	Traps 1	Tribes 20	
Hunter 2	Shepherd 21	Travel 13	Wander 5	
Journey 27	Shepherds 1	Traveled 13	Wandered 5	

Numbers (58 words)

Eight 6	Five 24	Number 91	Sixteen 2	Thousands 42
Eighteenth 6	Fortieth 2	Numbered 44	Sixteenth 4	Three 86
Eighth 18	Four 49	Numbereth 2	Sixth 25	Thrice 2
Eightieth 3	Fourteen 1	Numberless 4	Sixty 31	Twain 10
Eighty 16	Fourteenth 4	Numbers 19	Ten 17	Twelfth 1
Eleven 11	Fourth 26	Second 54	Tens 7	Twelve 32
Eleventh 5	Hundred 67	Secondly 1	Tenth 10	Twentieth 4
Fifteen 1	Hundredth 6	Seven 6	Third 25	Twenty 57
Fifteenth 5	Nine 12	Seventeenth 4	Thirteenth 4	Twice 3
Fifth 27	Nineteenth 9	Seventh 22	Thirtieth 9	Two 103
Fiftieth 2	Ninetieth 2	Seventy 21	Thirty 37	
Fifty 24	Ninth 20	Six 19	Thousand 55	

Poor (19 words)

Alms 5	Begging 3	Hungered 4	Poorer 1	Widow 2
Beggar 2	Charitable 1	Hungry 12	Poorest 1	Widowhood 1
Beggars 1	Fatherless 3	Orphans 1	Poverty 9	Widows 7
Begged 1	Hunger 21	Poor 32	Privation 1	

Prophecy (12 words)

Prophecies 37	Prophesies 1	Prophesying 17	Prophetess 1
Prophecy 35	Prophesieth 3	Prophesyings 2	Prophets 123
Prophesied 27	Prophesy 44	Prophet 66	Watchmen 4

Revelation (29 words)

Angel 90	Dreams 2	Miraculously 1	Seers 1	Visions 3
Angels 55	Enlighten 1	Reveal 4	Sign 42	Warn 2
Appeared 7	Enlightened 3	Revealed 13	Signs 28	Warned 4
Dream 10	Miracle 8	Revelation 17	Veil 7	Warning 2
Dreamed 2	Miracles 46	Revelations 16	Vision 10	Warnings 1
Dreameth 2	Miraculous 4	Seer 10	Visionary 3	

Rich (44 words)

Abundance 13	Boastings 2	Golden 2	Pomp 2	Precious 54
Abundant 1	Costliness 1	Haughtiness 4	Possess 42	Pride 63
Abundantly 8	Costly 8	Haughty 2	Possessed 24	Prosper 58
Arrogancy 1	Creditors 1	Jewels 2	Possessing 1	Prospered 10
Boast 15	Gain 49	Lucre 2	Possession 65	Prospereth 1
Boasting 6	Gold 60	Pearls 2	Possessions 20	Prospering 1

Prosperity 10	Puffed 9	Rings 2	Treasure 7	Treasury 4
Prosperous 3	Rich 21	Sapphires 1	Treasurers 1	Wealthy 2
Proud 13	Riches 46	Silver 52	Treasures 15	

Sacramental (48 words)

Administer 15	Baptizings 1	Confesses 1	Offered 1	Sacrament 1
Administered 11	Baptism 24	Confessing 2	Offereth 2	Sacrifice 15
Administering 3	Bar 12	Consecrate 8	Offering 7	Sacrificed 2
Altar 4	Bless 32	Consecrated 13	Offerings 6	Sacrifices 3
Anoint 3	Blessed 139	Consecrating 1	Ordain 5	Sanctify 5
Anointed 8	Blessing 19	Observance 1	Ordained 19	Uncircumcised 4
Anointing 1	Blessings 15	Observe 26	Ordinance 3	Unclean 19
Baptize 28	Circumcision 1	Observed 6	Ordinances 8	Uncleanness 3
Baptized 85	Confess 15	Observing 1	Rites 2	
Baptizing 6	Confessed 3	Offer 12	Sackcloth 4	

Slavery (23 words)

Bands 28	Chain 1	Freedom 29	Oppression 3	Slaves 6
Bond 6	Chained 1	Freely 6	Oppressions 1	Yoke 12
Bondage 73	Chains 15	Freemen 7	Oppressor 4	Yoketh 1
Bonds 9	Free 38	Oppress 3	Oppressors 2	
Captivity 61	Freed 1	Oppressed 4	Slavery 1	

Society (119 words)

Apparel 14	Chariots 7	Furnace 5	Marry 1	Silk 1
Art 102	Chief 95	Furnaces 1	Merchants 1	Silks 5
Artificer 1	Cities 78	Garment 10	Metals 2	Soap 1
Arts 4	City 311	Garments 36	Oven 2	Society 4
Barges 5	Civil 1	Gate 19	Pillow 1	Steel 5
Bed 5	Civilization 2	Gates 10	Pins 1	Street 1
Beds 1	Cloth 5	Glass 1	Pipe 1	Streets 7
Bordered 2	Clothe 10	Glasses 1	Razor 1	Timbers 10
Bordering 4	Clothed 5	Harp 1	Read 52	Tongs 1
Borders 75	Clothes 1	Highway 4	Reader 1	Tool 2
Bracelets 2	Clothing 9	Highways 4	Readeth 1	Tools 6
Brass 37	Coat 5	Homes 5	Reading 3	Torches 1
Bricks 1	Compass 7	House 215	Road 1	Tower 24
Bride 1	Copper 8	Houses 22	Roads 4	Towers 4
Build 48	Crafts 2	Inherit 25	Robe 5	Towns 2
Buildeth 6	Cup 10	Inheritance 60	Sail 3	Village 1
Building 13	Divorced 1	Inherited 1	Sailed 2	Villages 7
Buildings 13	Divorcement 2	Iron 18	Servant 80	Wheels 1
Candle 1	Door 7	Ladders 2	Servants 74	Windows 3
Candles 1	Doors 1	Linen 9	Ship 22	Wine 40
Candlestick 1	Dwelling 3	Liquors 1	Shipping 2	Winepresses 1
Carriages 1	Dwellings 1	Market 1	Ships 4	Workmanship 10
Cart 1	Dyed 2	Marriage 1	Shoe's 1	Workmen 2
Cement 4	Epistle 41	Married 2	Sickle 1	

Spirituality (63 words)

Belief 14	Believest 20	Charity 27	Faithful 30	Fastest 1
Believe 202	Believeth 21	Disbelieve 5	Faithfulness 10	Fasting 7
Believed 44	Believing 12	Faith 265	Fasted 5	Humble 55

Appendix

Humbled 9	Praised 3	Repent 205	Soul 161	Unbeliever 1
Humbleth 4	Praises 6	Repentance 99	Souls 90	Unbelievers 5
Humbly 2	Praising 4	Repented 35	Spiritual 20	Unbelieving 4
Humility 13	Pray 74	Repenteth 20	Spiritually 8	Unfaithful 1
Lowliness 4	Prayed 34	Repenting 3	Thank 16	Worship 45
Lowly 6	Prayer 29	Reverence 1	Thankful 2	Worshiped 1
Martyrdom 2	Prayers 30	Righteous 107	Thanking 1	Worshipers 1
Meek 15	Prayest 2	Righteous' 4	Thanks 24	Worshiping 1
Meekness 3	Prayeth 2	Righteously 2	Thanksgiving 6	
Praise 23	Praying 7	Righteousness 104	Unbelief 50	

Trouble (15 words)

Afflict 9	Afflictions 80	Anxiety 9	Awfulness 2	Troubles 5
Afflicted 33	Affrighted 2	Anxious 1	Trouble 5	Worried 3
Affliction 11	Afraid 13	Awful 47	Troubled 6	Worry 1

Index

A

Abinadi, and Earth, 63, 72
    and Law/Command, 28
Alma (2), and Church, 48–50,
    154–55, 165, 172
    compared to Amulek, 27
    compared to Mormon,
        9–10, 11, 14, 162–70
    compared to Moroni (2),
        170–77
    compared to Nephi (1),
        11–14, 152–62
    and Earth, 66, 68, 70, 75,
        79, 155–59, 173–76
    and Ethics, 14
    and Evil, 14
    and Israel, 159, 168, 176
    and Land, 115–16, 138,
        159–62, 168, 176–77
    and Law/Command,
        24–25, 153–54,
        163–65, 171–72
    and Slavery, 14
    and Spirituality, 14
Ammon, and Church, 48
    and Earth, 62, 75, 76
    and Land, 114–15, 138
Amulek, compared to
        Alma (2), 27
    and Land, 116–17
    and Law/Command, 25
Ancient Near East,
    and Alma (2), 12
    and Angel of the Lord, 7
    and Benjamin, 7
    and Enos, 7
    and Israel, 83–84
    and Lehi, 6–7
    and Mormon, 5, 8
    and Mosiah, 7
    and Nephi (1), 5, 12

    and Nephi (2), 8, 83–84
Angel of the Lord, and
        Ancient Near East, 7
    and Church, 43–45
    compared to Nephi (1),
        43–45
    and Earth, 64, 79–80
    and Israel, 88
    and Land, 106, 129, 131
Approach. *See* Methodology
Authors, choice of in study,
        2–3
    and Church, 55
    and Earth, 80–81
    and Israel, 101
    and Land, 146–50
    and Law/Command, 37
    uniqueness of, 5–11
    and word clusters,
        11–19

B

Benjamin, and Ancient Near
        East, 7
    compared to Mosiah, 27
    and Earth, 62, 75
    and Land, 114
    and Law/Command,
        25–26

C

Christology, and Mormon,
        15–16
    and Moroni (2), 16
    and Nephi (1), 13
Church, 41–43
    and Alma (2), 154–55, 165,
        172–73
    and Ammon, 48

and Angel of the Lord,
43–45
author individuality in,
55
false church meaning in,
43–45, 53
and Jacob, 46
and Jesus, 45
local meaning in, 46–47,
53–54
and the Lord, 45–46
and Mormon, 50–54,
165, 188–89
and Moroni (1), 48
and Moroni (2), 46–47,
172–73, 179–80
and Nephi (1), 43–45,
154–55, 179–80,
188–89
New World meaning of,
48–50, 50–51
theological meaning in,
55–57
universal meaning in,
45–46, 51–53
Clusters. *See* Word clusters
Creation, and Nephi (1), 13

E

Earth, 59–60
and Abinadi, 63, 72
and Alma (2), 66, 68,
70, 75, 79, 155–59,
165–68, 173–76
and Ammon, 62, 75, 76
and Angel of the Lord,
64, 79–80
author individuality in,
80–81
and Benjamin, 62, 75
Creator meaning in,
61–63
"ends of earth" meaning
in, 68–69
"essence of earth"
meaning in, 76–77

"face of earth" meaning
in, 65–68
and the Father, 72
globe meaning in, 64–65
God as ruler meaning
in, 63–64
ground meaning in,
73–74
inhabitants meaning in,
71
and Isaiah, 64, 68, 70,
72, 76–77
and Jacob, 62, 75
and Jesus, 63, 68, 70
land meaning in, 78–79
and Lehi, 61, 72, 75, 77
and the Lord, 62–63, 66,
70, 76
and the Lord in Isaiah,
62, 68, 70, 75
miscellaneous meanings
in, 70–71
and Mormon, 67, 69, 70,
72, 74, 77–80,
165–68, 189–91
and Moroni (2), 62,
66–67, 68, 70, 73, 75,
76, 173–76, 180–82
and Nephi (1), 63, 67,
69–70, 73, 75, 76, 78,
155–59, 180–82,
189–91
and Nephi (2), 67–68, 72, 76
people and ground meaning in,
75–76
planet meaning in, 69–70
and Samuel, 63, 75, 77, 78
theological implications in, 81
values meaning in, 79–80
and Zenos, 76, 77
Editing, and Nephi (1), 13
Editions, choice of in study,
1–2
Enos, and Ancient Near East,
7
compared to Jacob, 135
and Land, 135–36
Eschatology, and Alma (2), 13

and Mormon, 17
and Moroni (2), 17
Ethics, and Alma (2), 14
Evil, and Alma (2), 14

F

Father, the, and Earth, 72
  and Israel, 88–89
  and Land, 106, 129

G

Gathering, and Mormon, 16
  and Nephi (1), 13
God. *See* Father, the
God, and Nephi (1), 13

H

Helaman, compared to
    Nephi (2), 140–41
  and Land, 118–19,
    140–41
Hilton, John L., 1, 11–12

I

Isaiah, compared to other
    authors, 11
  compared to Zenos,
    91–93, 108–9, 131–32
  and Earth, 64, 68, 72
  and Israel, 91–93
  and Land, 108–9,
    131–32
Israel, and Alma (2), 159, 168, 176
  and Ancient Near East,
    83–85
  and Angel of the Lord,
    88
  author individuality in,
    101
  and the Father, 88–89
  and Isaiah, 91–93
  and Jacob, 94–98
  and Jesus, 85–86, 89–90
  and Lehi, 94–98

and the Lord, 85, 90–91
and the Lord in Isaiah,
  89
and Mormon, 99–100,
  168, 192–93
and Moroni (2), 99–100,
  176, 183
and Nephi (1), 83–84, 94–98,
  159, 183, 192–93
theological implications in,
  101–2
words used with, 85–87
and Zenos, 91–93

J

Jacob, and Church, 46
  compared to Enos, 135
  compared to Lehi and
    Nephi (1), 94–98
  compared to Moroni (2),
    10
  and Earth, 62, 72, 75
  and Israel, 94–98
  and Land, 112, 135–36
  and Law/Command, 29
Jesus, and Church, 45–46
  and Earth, 63
  and Israel, 85–86, 89–90
  and Land, 107–8, 130
  and Law/Command,
    34–36
  See also Lord, the; Lord
    in Isaiah, the

K

King Benjamin. *See* Benjamin

L

Land, 103–5
  and Alma (2), 115–16,
    138, 147, 159–62,
    168, 176–77
  and Ammon, 114–15,
    138, 147
  and Amulek, 116–17

and Angel of the Lord,
  106, 129, 131
author individuality in,
  146–50
and Benjamin, 114, 147
and Enos, 135
and the Father, 106,
  129, 146
and Helaman, 118–19,
  140–41
and Isaiah, 108–9,
  131–32
and Jacob, 112, 135
and Jesus, 107–8, 130,
  146–47
and Lehi, 110–11,
  132–33, 147
and the Lord, 106–7,
  129–30, 146–47
and the Lord in Isaiah,
  108, 130
and Mormon, 121–22,
  124–26, 141, 144–46,
  148–49, 168, 193–94
and Moroni (1), 117–18,
  138–39, 140–41, 148
and Moroni (2), 121–24,
  126–29, 141–44,
  148–49, 176–77,
  184–85
and Mosiah, 114, 137,
  147
and Nephi (1), 110,
  111–12, 133–35, 147,
  159–62, 184–85,
  193–94
and Nephi (2), 119, 120,
  140–41
and Samuel, 119–20
theological implications
  in, 150
and Zeniff, 112–13, 121,
  131, 136–37, 147
and Zenos, 108–9,
  131–32
Larsen, Wayne, 2, 150
Law/Command, 21–22
and Abinadi, 28

and Alma (2), 24–25,
  153–54, 163–65,
  171–72
and Amulek, 25
author individuality in,
  37
and Benjamin, 25–26
editorial meaning in,
  31–33
ethical meaning in,
  23–27
and Jacob, 29
and Jesus, 33, 34–36
and Lehi, 30
and the Lord, 33–34
and Mormon, 31–33,
  163–65, 187
and Moroni (2), 29,
  171–72, 178–79
and Mosiah, 26
and Nephi (1), 26–27,
  153–54, 178–79, 187
significant use of, 22–23
theological implications
  in, 28–30, 37–39
Lehi, and Ancient Near East,
  6–7
compared to Nephi (1),
  110–11
compared to Nephi and
  Jacob, 94–98
and Earth, 61, 72, 75, 77
and Israel, 94–98
and Land, 110–11,
  132–33, 147
and Law/Command, 30
Lord, the, and Church, 45–46
and Earth, 62–63, 66, 70
and Israel, 85, 90–91
and Land, 106–7,
  129–30
and Law/Command,
  33–34
See also Jesus; Lord in
  Isaiah, the
Lord in Isaiah, the, and
  Earth, 62, 68, 72, 75
and Israel, 89

and Land, 108, 130
See also Jesus; Lord, the

M

Methodology, and choice of
  authors, 2–3
  and choice of editions,
    1–2
  example of, 5–8
Mormon, and Ancient Near
    East, 5, 8
  and Christology, 15–16
  and Church, 50–54,
    165–68, 188–89
  compared to Alma (2),
    9–10, 11, 14, 162–70
  compared to Moroni (2),
    15–18, 99–100,
    121–22, 126–29,
    141–46, 148–49
  compared to Nephi (1),
    11, 16, 185–95
  and Earth, 67, 69, 72,
    74, 77–80, 165–68,
    189–91
  and Eschatology, 17
  and Gathering, 16
  as historian, 17
  and Israel, 98–100, 168,
    192–93
  and Land, 121–22,
    124–29, 141, 144–46,
    148–49, 168, 193–95
  and Law/Command,
    31–33, 163–65, 187
  and Sacramental, 17
  and Spirituality, 16
Moroni (1), and Church, 48
  and Land, 117–18,
    138–39
Moroni (2), and Christology,
    16
  and Church, 46–47,
    172–73, 179–80
  compared to Alma (2),
    170–77
  compared to Jacob, 10

compared to Mormon,
    15–18, 98–100,
    121–22, 126–29,
    141–46, 148–49
  compared to Nephi (1),
    178–85
  and Earth, 62, 66–67,
    68, 70, 73, 75, 76,
    173–76, 180–82
  and Eschatology, 17
  and Gathering, 16
  and Israel, 98–100, 176,
    183–84
  and Land, 121–24,
    126–29, 141–44,
    148–49, 176–77,
    184–85
  and Law/Command, 29,
    171–72, 178–79
  and Sacramental, 17
  and Spirituality, 16
Mosiah, compared to
    Benjamin, 27
  and Land, 114, 137
  and Law/Command, 26

N

Nephi (1), and Ancient Near
    East, 5
  and Christology, 13
  and Church, 43–45,
    154–55, 179–80,
    188–89
  compared to Alma (2),
    11–14, 152–62
  compared to Angel of
    the Lord, 43–45
  compared to Lehi,
    110–11
  compared to Lehi and
    Jacob, 94–98
  compared to Mormon,
    11, 16, 185–95
  compared to Moroni (2),
    178–85
  and Creation, 13

and Earth, 63, 67,
  69–70, 73, 75, 76, 78,
  80, 155–59, 180–82,
  189–91
and Gathering, 13
and God, 13
and Israel, 94–98, 159,
  183–84, 192–93
and Land, 110, 111–12,
  133–35, 147, 159–62,
  184–85, 193–95
and Law/Command,
  26–27, 153–54,
  178–79, 187
and Prophecy, 13
Nephi (2), and Ancient Near
  East, 8, 83–84
  compared to Helaman,
    140–41
  and Earth, 67–68, 72, 76
  and Israel, 83–84
  and Land, 119, 140–41
Normalized number, 5–6
Null-hypothesis, 9–10

P

Prophecy, and Nephi (1), 13

R

Rencher, Alvin, 2, 150

S

Sacramental, and Mormon, 17

and Moroni (2), 17
Samuel, and Earth, 63, 75, 78
  and Land, 119–20
Slavery, and Alma (2), 14
Spirituality, and Alma (2), 14
  and Mormon, 14, 16
  and Moroni (2), 16

T

Theological implications, in
  Church, 55–57
  in Earth, 81
  in Israel, 101–2
  in Land, 150
  in Law/Command,
    37–39

W

Word clusters, 4–5
  and authors, 11–19
  example of use, 5–8
  measurements of
    variations in, 8–11
Wordprints, 2, 11–12

Z

Zeniff, and Land, 112–13,
  136–37
Zenos, compared to Isaiah,
  91–93, 108–9, 131–32
  and Israel, 91–93
  and Land, 108–9,
    131–32